Female Liberation

Edited, with Introductions, by

Roberta Salper   State University of New York, Old Westbury

Alfred A. Knopf   New York

Female
History and
Current Politics

liberation

ISBN: 0-394-31528-6

Library of Congress Catalog Card Number: 74-157188

Manufactured in the United States of America. Composed by Cherry Hill
Composition, Pennsauken, N.J. Printed and bound by Halliday Lithograph Corp.,
West Hanover, Mass.

Design by Karin Gurski Batten

First Edition

987654321

Photo credits: Cover, Peter Hobe; Title page, Bettye Lane; page 5, New York
Public Library; page 11, New York Public Library; page 18, Roberta Salper; page
21, Dagmar; page 23, New York Public Library; page 57, New York Public
Library; page 77, New York Public Library; page 103, Culver; page 122, New
York Public Library; page 135, New York Public Library; page 149, Bettye Lane;
page 161, Eugene Feilen and S. Nickerson, San Diego State College; page 171,
Bettye Lane; page 190, Liberation News Service; page 196, Alan Copeland,
Photon West; page 201, Sid Sattler, Liberation News Service; page 205,
Fredericks of Hollywood; page 215, Robin Forbes; page 223, Bettye Lane; page
242, Michael Abramson, Photon West

To Martha and Gay and to My Other Sisters,
the New Women

Preface

The idea for this anthology came from an experimental course, "The History and Social Role of Women," that three of us worked out in spring 1970 at the University of Pittsburgh. Its content and political position were developed during 1970-1971, when I was teaching "Women in History" and "Contemporary Issues in Women's Liberation" in the ten-course women's studies program that began in fall 1970 at San Diego State College, San Diego, California.

In 1970 women's studies courses or programs developed in hundreds of colleges, universities, and communities throughout the country—"the hottest new wrinkle in higher education," according to *Newsweek*. The goals and perspective of women's studies—education by whom, for whom, and for what—are a current topic of discussion in the women's movement.

Women's studies, like Third World studies, is the academic arm of a broader movement that is challenging time-worn assumptions about North American political and cultural standards—standards determined almost exclusively by Western European culture.

For example, in the conventional Survey of Western Civilization course —the student's introduction to culture—the history of Mexican Americans, Afro-Americans and Puerto Ricans is relegated to footnotes because it is—and this is the crucial point—a history of oppression and colonization by the United States. Academe's relentless devotion to scholarly objectivity and value-free teaching thus become ways of equating political dominance and cultural superiority—because if you win a battle you also win the right to cultural hegemony. Chicanos, Puerto Ricans, black Americans, Asians, and native Americans are without political and economic power in this country, so their cultural contributions become second rate, inferior somehow. Our "Surveys of Western Civilization" mirror this ethic by interpreting history, politics, and culture by and for *victors*, not *victims*.

It is the same with women. A female undergraduate learns little or nothing of her participation in history. (And we all know the suffragists were frustrated, man-hating bitches, so why study them as a legitimate social movement anyway?) Rarely are individual women studied in any course as anything but courtesans, custodians of society's morals, perpetuators of family life and domesticity, or "lady" artists. Why women are notably absent from history, politics, and science is never discussed. Their absence is assumed to be the natural course of events. Simone de Beauvoir stated a problem decades ago and Shulamith Firestone dealt with it recently: "Representation of the world, like the world itself, is the work of men; they describe it from their own point of view, which they confuse with absolute truth."[1] This problem is yet to be faced squarely.

[1] Shulamith Firestone, *The Dialectic of Sex: The Case for Feminist Revolution* (New York: Morrow, 1970), p. 176.

Culture itself is male, and where individual women participate, they do so on male terms and compete as men. No wonder women are judged biologically "unable" to make "great" contributions, if great contributions are de facto male.

The Chronicle of Higher Education[2] recently posed the question "Can Women's Studies be primarily academic or are they sure to become militant and tied to women's liberation?" Setting up this kind of dichotomy between a social movement "out there" and some courses safely nestled within the ivy halls is a very effective way to ensure (1) that the courses do not radically change anyone and (2) that the women's movement does not benefit from the acquisition of skills and other benefits available in the university. It is the old divide-and-conquer principle at work again.

Several years ago McGeorge Bundy, President of the Ford Foundation, said the following about the creation of black studies in the universities: "When you agree that there is a topic, there still follows the question of what you want it for, and how you will pursue it."[3] And referring to a previous speaker, Bundy continued, "it was made clear . . . that his purpose is to establish a balance of power. That seems to me not to be the way to define the interesting topics in Black history. . . . There is a difference, to put it more sharply, between the *political* view of a set of events and a *historical* view of those events."[4] Bundy went on to elaborate on the differences "between [the] picture of the subject in its own right and the picture of the subject as a means for providing a sense of purpose, identity, and direction for young Black men and women, Black students in the university."[5] Finally, Bundy said, "There is nothing *wrong* with providing a sense of direction, identity and purpose; but it is a very dangerous thing to start pushing the subject around for that purpose."[6]

McGeorge Bundy was correct in fearing that the establishment of black studies programs would provide a sense of personal identity and direction and a heightening of political understanding for black men and women. At best, this is exactly what they have done and what they should do. It seems to me that these are precisely the most important reasons for having black and Chicano and women's studies programs. Until an individual who has been oppressed, who has been taught to doubt his personal worth and his capabilities, understands why and how his oppression occurred—which requires an understanding of the political operations of our society—he or she will not be *capable* of carrying out all the admittedly important research on black or female or any branch of history—unless, of course, it is the kind of research that only

[2] The Chronicle of Higher Education (Washington, D.C.), November 30, 1970, Vol. 5, No. 10, p. 1.
[3] McGeorge Bundy, "Some Thoughts on Afro-American Studies," in A. L. Robinson, R. Foster, and D. H. Olgilvi (eds.), Black Studies in the University (New Haven, Conn.: Yale University Press, 1969), p. 172.
[4] Ibid., p. 173.
[5] Ibid., p. 173.
[6] Ibid., p. 173.

reinforces the underlying principles of the present pervading beliefs and social stereotypes.

A women's studies program, then, is desirable and useful if it serves to equip women to struggle for better lives for *many* men and women. This is both a scholarly and a political task, and the curriculum and faculty should be defined and chosen to accomplish both aims: to understand the world and to change it.

Now a few words about the makeup of the book. *Female Liberation* is designed to give an introductory, yet comprehensive, view of the nineteenth-century women's rights movement and the contemporary women's liberation movement. My introduction gives a short history of feminism in the United States and compares the historical and sociological causes for the appearance of the first women's movement, commonly referred to as the suffragist movement, and today's women's liberation movement. The introduction emphasizes a comparison of the past and present movements; Marlene Dixon's "The Rise of Women's Liberation" gives a survey of the tendencies and groups in the current movement. In the Introduction I also talk about the conditions that led me to write this book and about my work today.

Part 1, "History and Background," includes works that shed some light on four social movements that were crucial in the formation of the first woman's rights movement: suffrage, abolition, Marxism, and trade unionism. Because of the limited scope of this book I have necessarily eliminated many, many important voices and documents. Some of these can be found in the six-volume *History of Woman Suffrage,* edited by Elizabeth Cady Stanton, Susan Anthony, Matilda Joslyn Gage and Ida Husted Harper, 1881–1922; Aileen S. Kraditor's *Up From the Pedestal,* 1968; William L. O'Neill's *The Woman Movement: Feminism in the United States and England,* 1969; and the first section of Leslie B. Tanner's *Voices From Women's Liberation,* 1970. I have not included works about the woman's movement outside of the United States, again because of the particular focus of this anthology. Articles on Cuban, Chinese, Vietnamese women, and the women's movements in Canada and in Europe have appeared in many places, for example, Robin Morgan's anthology, *Sisterhood is Powerful* (1970), *Leviathan* (Berkeley, May 1970), *Notes from the Second Year: Women's Liberation* (New York, 1970), and *Women: A Journal of Liberation* (Baltimore, Summer 1970).

Part 2, "The New Feminism," is an overall view of the content and development of the American woman's liberation movement since 1968. Because of the limitations of space, I eliminated many of the well-known studies such as those by Juliet Mitchell and Margaret Benston, as well as important organizational position papers and manifestos. My article in this part is an attempt to summarize what has been left.

Hundreds of good articles have been written in the last several years by, for, and about women. Someday soon I hope we will have a second voluminous *History of Women* in which they all appear, but for the present I have had to select only a few articles, and while I have consulted with other women about the choice, the possible shortcomings reflect my own limitations and experiences most closely.

The bibliography emphasizes key books and journals from today's woman's movement and recent works of general interest for history and background.

I would like to thank my classes in the women's studies program at San Diego State for providing constant feedback, criticism, and stimulation during the preparation of this book. I am also grateful to Rosalyn Baxandall of New York City for her incisive suggestions, to Belvie Rooks and Monica Jardine for being "different models," and to Sheila Kaplan and James B. Smith of Random House for their help and patience.

Contents

Introduction

The woman's movement has the distinction of being the only social movement in the history of the United States that is regarded by its opponents as a joke. And it is not because many of us consider ourselves radicals, socialists, or Marxists that we are ridiculed (the Wobblies had bitter enemies just as the Black Panthers have today, but no one would have dared mock them); it is because we are women. When all is said and done, people do not think very much of women. The majority of our society finds it hard to take seriously anything women do except for the condoned roles of domestic and helpmate. Thus in part our struggle is concerned with the demand for dignity. Securing the kind of dignity we mean involves abolishing institutions (*Playboy*, for example) that humiliate women by reducing them to mere objects of sexual fantasy and pleasure in order to preserve a distorted concept of masculinity, which enables a few men to make a lot of money by packaging these tasty "dishes" for consumers whose appetites have been carefully stimulated. In addition, we must change the stereotype of the female as a scatterbrained, helpless consumer—a stereotype the media project in a hundred ways every day.

But the cry for personal dignity is only a part of our struggle. We also want the freedom not only to function as serious and responsible human beings, but also to effect major social changes that involve women and men.

What is the women's liberation movement (WLM)? When did it begin? How? And why?

In 1964 and 1965 women who were active in the civil rights movement (particularly those in SNCC, the Student Non-Violent Coordinating Committee) wrote criticisms of the subordinate role of women in the radical movement. Their efforts were largely ignored until 1968 when at the Students for a Democratic Society (SDS) convention women demanded that the organization take a strong, affirmative stand on women's liberation. The SDS women lost the convention battle, but by that time a nationwide independent women's movement as well as women's caucuses in male-dominated "Left" organizations was under way.[1]

The politics of women's liberation falls roughly into three categories: One consists of feminists who tend to seek women's equality with men in the present system, typified by the National Organization of Women (NOW). Founded in 1966 by Betty Friedan, authoress of *The Feminine Mystique*, NOW has members in all fifty states and over fifty active chapters throughout the country. It is primarily concerned with reforming legislation that bars women from economic and political leadership and is comprised chiefly of white middle class professional women.

[1] See my article "The Development of the American Women's Liberation Movement, 1967–71" in Part 2 of this book for details of the beginning of the WLM.

The second category is composed of female radicals who work with the women's liberation movement but whose primary loyalties are to the politics of the New or Old Left. This group generally views women's issues as a new means for drawing women into preexisting politics, such as those of the Youth Socialist Alliance (YSA), Workers Socialist Party (WSP), and SDS, as the articles in Part 2 of this book show.[2]

The third category comprises the radical feminists, who see feminist issues not only as women's first priority, but as issues central to any larger revolutionary analysis. In the words of Shulamith Firestone, this feminist movement

is the first to combine effectively the "personal" with the "political" . . . the dichotomy between emotions and intellect has kept the established movement from developing a mass base: on the one hand, there are the orthodox leftists, either abstract university intellectuals out of touch with concrete reality, or, in their activist guise, militantly into *machismo*, self-indulgent in their action with little concern for political effectiveness. On the other, there is Woodstock Nation, the Youth Revolt, the Flower and Drug generation of Hippies . . . who, though they understand that the old leafletting and pamphletting and Marxist analysis are no longer where it's at . . . yet have no solid historical analysis of their own with which to replace it; indeed, who are apolitical. . . . The feminist movement is the urgently needed solder.[3]

Many radical feminists are seeking to redefine socialism for themselves and to work out a new politics that neither defines women's oppression simply as a "secondary contradiction" that will be eliminated when capitalism and imperialism are overthrown nor is anti-intellectual and apolitical, as so many of the responses to classic Marxist analyses have been in this country. (See my article in Part 2 for a more detailed survey of the politics of the contemporary movement.) Anne Farrar observes:

At the present time, what we called the New Left or "the Movement" is disappearing. Thousands of us who were in the New Left are no longer "active" (in the old sense of that word). Thousands more who would have entered the New Left three years ago find no satisfactory organization to join. In this vacuum some people have joined sects with conceptions of socialism (orthodox Marxism) and forms of organization (democratic centralism) much older than the New Left. The Revolutionary Union, Progressive Labor, and even the Communist Party and the Young Socialist Alliance have experienced temporary growth in membership. But many people are groping for a new direction. Some people want to be part of a new socialist movement, but don't know yet what that will mean. . . . Socialists can learn something . . . from the politics developing in the Women's Liberation Movement.[4]

The WLM has used the small rap group, with "consciousness-raising" as its chief form of organization. This is a technique the Chinese use and refer to as "Speaking Pain to Recall Pain."[5] The small group has

---

[2] Anne Farrar analyzes the relationship of women's liberation to the Seattle Liberation Front, "one of the last New Left organizations," in "The Seattle Liberation Front, Women's Liberation, and a New Socialist Politics," *Socialist Revolution* (San Francisco) I (September–October 1970) 124–136.
[3] Shulamith Firestone, *The Dialectic of Sex: The Case for Feminist Revolution* (New York: Morrow, 1970), pp. 43–44.
[4] Farrar, *op. cit.*, pp. 124, 126.
[5] The best description of this is found in William Hinton's *Fanshen: A Documentary of Revolution in a Chinese Village* (New York: Random House, 1966).

4

Lucretia Mott

many positive aspects, such as allowing each woman to develop a political consciousness from an articulation of her own life experience. However, it has also contributed to an isolation and fragmentation in the women's movement and to a reluctance to undertake any type of organizational structure that extends beyond small autonomous groups. In the last year (1970) partial attempts to overcome this isolation and fragmentation have come about in the proliferation of women's centers around the country, which provide space for women to get together, often child-care facilities, abortion counseling, and literature; newspapers, such as *Off Our Backs,* in Washington, D.C., *RAT,* in New York, and *It Ain't Me Babe,* in California; journals, such as *Up From Under,* in New York, *Women: A Journal of Liberation,* in Baltimore, and *Aphra,* in Pennsylvania; and various kinds of mass meetings.[6]

Women's liberation *actions* began several years ago with demonstrations at the Miss America Pageant and the Bridal Fair in New York City.[7] More recently they have concentrated on demands for client-controlled child care, abortion on demand, and the debate about the Equal Rights Amendment. Women in different situations throughout the country have been involved in a plethora of activities: over one hundred colleges and universities are now teaching courses on women, and many academically respectable surveys are "proving" that women form a second class labor and pleasure supply. In one year alone (1970) female workers led strikes at the New York Bell Telephone Company, General Electric, and Bendix; women in the United States armed forces demanded equal promotions and benefits; professional women formed caucuses and became an influential force in the Modern Language Association, American Political Science Association, American Historical Association, and American Sociological Association; welfare mothers angrily protested their living conditions; high school women organized and printed newspapers and journals; women throughout the publishing

[6] For a discussion of the pros and cons of the August 26, 1970, mass demonstration to commemorate suffrage, see *International Socialist Review,* March 1971, pp. 18–19, and the September and October 1970 issues of *Off Our Backs, passim.*

[7] For discussion of this action, see references in "The Development of the American Women's Liberation Movement," *op. cit.*

industry began demanding an end to sexist literature and discriminatory hiring and assignment practices.

Establishing new sexual relations, new living situations, child care, abortion reform, and programs centered both in the university and in the community that allow for development of skills are important steps, but they are not enough. The task that now awaits us is to develop a long-term strategy for liberation that incorporates and goes beyond these initial demands.

Our women's liberation movement is one of the most vital and important social movements of twentieth-century America. It is up to each of us to help determine the next steps. And to do this we should look at the achievements and failures of the first woman's rights movement.

Then and Now

Today's women's movement is the second major American struggle by, for, and about women; the first started well over a hundred years ago. This initial movement is generally referred to as the struggle for suffrage. While it is certainly true that the fight to win the vote was the key issue, American women also participated in the struggle to free women and men from slavery and from oppressive working conditions.

Most early leaders of the nineteenth-century struggle for women's suffrage—Lucretia Mott, Elizabeth Cady Stanton, Susan B. Anthony, Sarah and Angelina Grimké—participated in the antislavery movement before they ignited the struggle for women's rights. Abolitionist activities were a catalyst for the women's movement for a very simple reason: women who started out to speak and act on behalf of the slave found they were ridiculed and attacked as public speakers and barred as delegates to antislavery conventions.

Lucretia Mott's experiences typify the prevailing attitude. She was a Quaker minister and attended a meeting in Philadelphia in 1833 where the American Anti-Slavery Society was formed. When she found that women were barred from access to decision-making positions in that society, she organized the Women's Anti-Slavery Society. However, during the ensuing seven years, the American Anti-Slavery Society itself split over the role of women, and most particularly over the election of a woman, Abby Kelly, to a central committee. The antifemale faction of the society formed a new organization, which sent separate delegates to an international world-wide antislavery convention held in London in 1840. The profemale American Anti-Slavery Society elected Lucretia Mott and two other women to their executive committee. It also selected Lucretia Mott and a black man, Charles Remond, as delegates to the London convention. (Lucretia Mott also headed the delegation from the Women's Anti-Slavery Society.) The antifemale and profemale abolitionists confronted each other in London over the seating of delegates; the misogynists won and the women were relegated to the gallery. Two men, William Lloyd Garrison, who was scheduled to be

6

the main speaker, and Charles Remond, refused their seats in the main hall and went to sit in the gallery with the women.[8] Lucretia Mott met Elizabeth Cady Stanton at this London convention and from their conversations came the idea that was to culminate in the first women's rights convention, the Seneca Falls Convention of 1848.

The Seneca Falls Convention was attended by men and women—in fact, James Mott, Lucretia's husband, chaired the meeting because no woman had any knowledge of parliamentary procedure—and the body adopted a Declaration of Sentiments, modeled on the Declaration of Independence. It was signed by sixty-eight women and thirty-two men and the resolutions concerned legal equity in marriage, property, wages, and the vote, which was the most controversial issue. Lucretia Mott originally believed the demand for suffrage was too radical and would hurt their chances of securing other gains. Elizabeth Cady Stanton persisted, however, and when Stanton introduced the suffrage resolution at the convention, none other than Frederick Douglass seconded the motion and gave a moving speech on the right of the female to total equality.

That was in 1848. National conventions as well as numerous state conventions were held yearly from 1848 to the outset of the Civil War. However, twenty years of agitation did not produce a permanent women's rights organization, only a loosely structured national steering committee consisting of representatives from any state where there was feminist activity. The feminists continued working within antislavery organizations and did not develop an organization of their own because many of the male abolitionists supported them, especially the group centered in Boston and led by William Lloyd Garrison. Thus, the women did not develop a separate national organization which meant that when they had important differences with the antislavery organizations, they had no structure for independent political action.

During the Civil War women's rights leaders temporarily placed their own demands aside and fought for the emancipation of the Negro. The American Equal Rights Association (AERA) was formed at the close of the war to further interests of both Negroes and women. However, when in the summer of 1866 Elizabeth Cady Stanton, Susan B. Anthony, and Lucy Stone read the proposed wording of the Fourteenth Amendment,[9]

---

[8] This dramatic show of unity between black men and white women was not the norm, however. In fact, as many of the articles in Part 1 show, one of history's tragedies is that the struggle of white females was often pitted against black Americans' struggles.
[9] The proposed wording to the second section of the Fourteenth Amendment read as follows: "Representatives shall be apportioned among the several states according to their respective numbers, counting the whole number of persons in each state, excluding Indians not taxed. But when the right to vote at any election for the choice of electors of President and Vice-President of the United States, Representatives in Congress, the Executive and Judicial Officers of a state or the members of the Legislature thereof, is denied to any of the *male* inhabitants of such state, being twenty-one years of age and citizens of the United States, or in any way abridged except for participation in rebellion or any other crime, the basis of proportion therein shall be reduced, in the proportion which the number of such *male* citizens shall bear to the whole number of *male* citizens twenty-one years of age in such state." Italics mine [Ed.].

supported by the AERA, they were stunned. The abolitionists, their allies of twenty years, had deserted them to further "the Negro's hour." Nor were less radical Republican politicians willing to bother about the sensitive issue of female suffrage; they were too eager to capture a potential male Negro vote of several million.

In spite of Stanton and Anthony's work to secure petitions against the Fourteenth Amendment, it was ratified in July 1868. The final blow for the feminists in AERA, however, occurred six months later when the white male leadership among the radical Republicans, seeking further guarantees for the Negro freedman's right to vote, introduced the Fifteenth Amendment: "The right of citizens of the United States to vote shall not be denied or abridged by the United States or any State, on account of race, color, or previous condition of servitude." The word "sex" had been omitted.

The split that developed between the abolitionists and the radical feminists reached the breaking point at a meeting of the AERA in January 1869, when the association rejected the feminists' appeal to endorse a call for a woman suffrage amendment. Stanton and Anthony and their supporters left the AERA, and in May 1869 organized the National Woman Suffrage Association (NWSA), with membership open to any woman (and not to men) who believed in female suffrage. The new organization's political position was immediately announced by its journal, *Revolution:* Women's rights is a multiissue cause. Although the vote is currently of primary importance, other matters are also crucial.

In November 1869, a second, more conservative, feminist organization was created, which admitted men. Under the leadership of Lucy Stone and Henry Ward Beecher (who became its first president), the American Woman Suffrage Association (AWSA) worked out its politics in the *Woman's Journal:* Women can win the vote only by avoiding issues that are "irrelevant" and will alienate the support of influential sectors of the community. The AWSA never attempted to organize working women, nor did they attack the Church or marriage laws and customs.

The first women's rights movement falls into two periods: it took one form before the 1890s and another after that decade. 1890 is a landmark in the women's struggle for several reasons. First of all, in that year, two organizations founded in 1869—the National Woman Suffrage Association (NWSA), led by Susan B. Anthony and Elizabeth Cady Stanton, and the more conservative American Woman Suffrage Association (AWSA), under the direction of Lucy Stone and Henry Ward Beecher— merged into the National American Woman Suffrage Association (NAWSA) with Elizabeth Cady Stanton as the first president. During the years preceding the merger, workers had become disillusioned with the two major parties and conservative unionization policies and had increasingly turned to socialism, anarchism, and communism. As a result, the middle class in general grew to oppose any kind of labor agitation. Individual, sporadic contacts between working class women and feminists (who were largely white middle class) became impossible; circumstances demanded that suffragists take a stand. Unfortunately, the suffrage movement had grown socially more respectable and politically more conservative. This was the time when, in the words of G. William Domhoff, "upper-class women were very important . . . in bringing into existence a more humane and paternalistic social system."[10] As a result, therefore, the more militant stance of NWSA was largely diffused and lost in the merger. The result was a more conservative, large-membership organization whose only membership requirement was that a woman want to vote.

Secondly, by 1890 the term "women's activities" had become legitimate (that is, it meant more than pregnancy, prostitution, and menstruation). In 1832 Oberlin College became the first college to admit women, the first institution of many that were to help educate a token and privileged number of white American women. By the 1870s a considerable group of women, located for the most part in the Northeast, had received the "best" education available to women in the world. Like children who, after they learn how to read, want books to read, women who had been to college did not want to return to the economic, intellectual, and social subjugation their mothers had known. So they looked around the country that was "conceived in liberty and dedicated to the proposition that all men are created equal" for ways to use their talents and to develop potential capacities. A doctor? No, women were not fit for medical school. A lawyer? Well, that's not so ladylike, either. A business*man*? No man would do business with her, so that was out. A scholar? Women's biological destiny prohibits her from thinking rationally and creatively, so why bother? A politician? A *woman* in Washington? What will happen to our families and children?

In response, *new* fields were created for women—jobs that "fit" the female character. These jobs generally involved providing services for children and helping others; women became grade school teachers, librarians, and social workers. Mary McDowell, Lillian Wald, and Jane Addams virtually created the field of social work in Chicago; Emma Willard founded a school for young women in New York that taught biology as well as literature; and so on. The point is though that women who made outstanding contributions to female education and social work really had no choice about entering these fields. They were channeled— or tracked—into these areas because of their gender.

Thirdly, in addition to firmly establishing "female" and "subordinate" as synonyms in the paid labor as well as domestic arenas, the 1890s saw another important (and related) development in the history of American women: the growth of women's clubs and volunteer work.

The growth of women's organizations was impressive. In 1888 the National Council of Women was formed. Two years later the General Federation of Women's Clubs began its fantastic period of expansion. The Woman's Christian Temperance Union was already near the peak of its effectiveness. The first durable settlement house was established in 1889, and by the decade's end the experiment was a clear success with some dozens of settlements in being and

---

[10] G. W. Domhoff, *The Higher Circle: The Governing Class in America* (New York: Random House, 1970), p. 33.

9

hundreds more on the way. In 1899 the several Consumers' Leagues were united into a national organization. Nor was patriotism neglected as women rushed to meet the country's varying needs. In 1890 the Daughters of the American Revolution came into being. Seven years later scattered groups coalesced into the National Congress of Parents and Teachers, bringing some order to the burgeoning PTA movement.

It would be easy to expand this list, but suffice it to say that by 1900 about half of the important American women's organizations had been established, most of them in the 1890's.[11]

Most of the membership of these clubs, at least of the ones of national prominence, consisted of educated and/or socially prominent women who wanted something to do. What did a woman do if she wasn't a superwoman like Jane Addams, Anna Howard Shaw or Frances Kelley? What happened if she were an average person, like the thousands of average men working as doctors, lawyers, professors, politicians? Since most of these women felt intellectual and social urgencies rather than economic and political needs, they tended to look for activities that were (above all) individually satisfying and that would not threaten their social status. Thus, many women flocked to help the Woman's Christian Temperance Union, National Consumers' League, Women's Trade Union League, and the NAWSA. Many of the unique institutions used to socialize women of the upper class—elite girls' schools and colleges, the debut, the Junior League, certain sports, civic and charity work[12]—came into existence in this period. And it was this sector of the female population—some born to privilege, most socialized to want it—that assumed leadership of the suffrage movement in the 1890s. They replaced the old abolitionist fighters who had been involved with social concerns other than the vote, broader concerns that crossed class lines in a way charity and welfare work never could.

From 1890 to 1920, then, the suffrage movement was almost exclusively a single-issue struggle, dominated by the interests of middle class, professional women and directed by either middle class or upper class women.

And finally, another factor that contributed to the more conservative nature of the suffrage struggle in the 1890s was the rise of a woman's movement in the southern states. This movement was composed chiefly of women who believed in white supremacy. Southern leaders also rose to national leadership in the NAWSA and many, like Kate M. Gordon of Louisiana, vice-president of NAWSA in 1910, were elected on overtly racist platforms.[13]

Let us look now at other vital aspects of the struggle for suffrage, a struggle dominated by several basic issues.

The Bible and Church fathers had defined woman's role as one of obeyer and moral custodian. Thus, a frequent argument against female

[11] William L. O'Neill, *Everyone Was Brave* (Chicago: Quadrangle Books, 1969), p. 149.
[12] See Domhoff, "The Feminine Half of the Upper Class," *op. cit.*, pp. 33–56.
[13] See Aileen Kraditor, "The Southern Question," in *The Ideas of the Woman Suffrage Movement, 1890–1920* (New York: Columbia University Press, 1965), for details on this point.

10

emancipation maintained that woman's virtue would be compromised if she obtained the vote and thus stepped out of her condoned role as "obeyer" and gained some control over her life. Thus with the exception of the Quakers, organized religion opposed female suffrage. Their arguments were couched in terms of protecting motherhood, goodness, and charity in the name of obedience to God and Church, and they weighed heavily on a Puritan population imbued with a sense of sin and guilt.

Elizabeth Cady Stanton led one fight to refute these arguments when she organized the writing of *The Woman's Bible*. Victoria Woodhull, an advocate of free love and in 1872 the first female candidate for U.S. President, became a symbol of sexual radicalism and a prime target of attacks from Anthony Comstock, the secretary of the New York Society for the Suppression of Vice, and his followers. Nevertheless, the questions of religion and morality seriously divided the woman's suffrage movement. Only a vocal minority was militantly anticlerical and antireligious. Emma Goldman was one of the most outspoken. As an anarchist, she thought all structured systems of political power were equally absurd. And she thus had little use for the suffragists' fight to secure the vote. As an atheist, she could not support the women's rights movement on religious grounds. She believed that the emancipation sought by the American suffragists would not free women, but would only restrict men to the narrow puritanical ethic advocated by most of the suffragists. Many women, however, were deeply religious and followed the examples of Lucy Stone and Anna Howard Shaw, who worked to reconcile the Church and suffrage.

Another political interest that opposed women's suffrage was the liquor industry. Fearing that women would vote for prohibition if granted suffrage, the Brewers and Wholesale Liquor Dealers Association spent millions of dollars in campaigns against female suffrage that were often successful. In Portland, Oregon, in 1900, for example, the pressure of liquor interests was clearly responsible for the defeat of a proposal to grant suffrage to women.

By 1910, however, a new generation of women had joined the feminist ranks. These new recruits became impatient with NAWSA's theory and practice, and in 1914 a group split from NAWSA and formed the Con-

Susan B. Anthony

gressional Union for Woman Suffrage (CU) under the leadership of Alice Paul. This group functioned as a small, disciplined cadre and used semi-militant tactics (hunger strikes, sit-ins, pickets) learned, in large part, from Alice Paul's experiences in England with Emmeline and Christabel Pankhurst and the British Women's Social and Political Union (WSPU). In 1917 the CU, which was based in the East and South, and a sister organization, the Woman's Party (WP), which was based in the West, merged and formed the National Woman's Party (NWP). The militant strategies of the NWP played the crucial role in hastening (after seventy years!) the passage of the Nineteenth Amendment,[14] notwithstanding frequent opposition from NAWSA and its president, Carrie Chapman Catt.

The white middle class orientation of most of the suffragists clearly made impossible the formation of an ideological framework that would have enabled the women's rights movement to relate in any but a patronizing and ultimately rather useless way to the miserable wages and job conditions of working women. But in order to understand the history of women in America, one must delve into the history of the American labor movement and study women's role in it.[15]

In order to understand the history of women in trade unionism one has to look both at the unions organized by, for, and of women—female labor organizations such as the National Women's Trade Union League (WTUL), founded in 1903—and at the women labor organizers who worked in male-female organizations. (Ella Reeve Bloor [see Part I] is an example of the latter, a woman who considered herself more a female fighter than a feminist.)

The creation of the Women's Trade Union League was the most singular highlight in the development of female labor organizations in the United States,[16] because, among other reasons, it was an attempt to build a large national organization. Tenuous links existed between the WTUL and the suffrage movement—links that consisted primarily in "token" participation by the suffragists: in general they raised money for strike funds, helped arrange for meeting halls, etc., but did not identify with the working woman's condition in such a way as to become an integral part of the labor movement.

In 1909, years after the founding of the WTUL, women from the International Ladies Garment Workers Union (ILGWU) organized mass strikes in New York and Philadelphia. Almost forty thousand women united over the 1909 ILGWU strikes which served as catalysts for the rapid growth of this union in the following years.

Throughout American history—and it is still true today—many fewer female workers have been unionized than males. This is because women

[14] Inez Irwin gives the details in *The Story of the Woman's Party* (New York: Harcourt Brace Jovanovich, 1921).
[15] Meredith Tax of Boston (see Part 2 of this anthology) is working on a book dealing with women's role in the American Labor Movement between 1890 and World War I.
[16] See Helen Marot, *American Labor Unions* (New York: Arno Press, 1914) for chapter on WTUL. Marot was secretary of the New York Women's Trade Union League for several years.

workers usually do "unskilled" labor such as domestic service and waitressing, and the powerful American trade unions, such as the American Federation of Labor (AFL), are concerned only with unionizing the more highly paid "skilled" workers (construction, steel industry, etc.). Most unions have denied membership to women just as consistently as they have—and still try to—deny access to the highly paid jobs to black men. With the notable exception of the International Workers of the World (IWW),[17] the trade unions have been as guilty of male supremacy as they are of racism. And typically, when women *have* been granted membership in unions, they are denied access to leadership positions; in fact, even the top bureaucracy of many all-female unions has been male.

Today's women's liberation movement differs from the nineteenth-century struggle primarily in that in 1971 militant women who can only envision the liberation of women within a revolutionary context are the norm rather than the exception. The dominant ideology of the past movement was one that sought legal reforms to ameliorate the existing social structure for women. Today most of us are asking what *kind* of social revolution we want, not *if* we need one. Serious debates about Marxism are no longer typical only of "leftist dissidents"; rather, they have created the basis for commonality of perspective among many women.

Another marked difference between the two movements is the importance we place today on developing new organizational structures and new definitions for human relationships, sexually and socially.

In the first woman's movement the personal and political were not merged. The fight to get the vote included nothing that resembled the small "consciousness-raising" groups that have sprung up across the nation in the past few years. Organizational structures and hierarchies were not scrutinized as they are today and most of the early feminists separated their personal relationships from the political struggle.

An elemental aspect of the two movements is identical, however. In both, parallel protest movements were present in the black community and among parts of the working class. The fight for the right to vote was intricately wound up with two other major social movements: abolition and trade unionism; and to understand the history of women in the United States one must study abolition and labor struggles as well as the struggle for enfranchisement. Women such as Mother Jones, Emma Goldman, and Ella Reeve Bloor were primarily concerned with working class organizing, not with the struggle for suffrage; Sojourner Truth and Harriet Tubman were abolitionists first, feminists second. Other women fought for abolition and workers' rights through feminist organizations. Minority and Third-World Americans, workers, and women are still the centers of protest today. An understanding of the relationship among these three movements in the nineteenth century—what

---

[17] See Philip Foner, *The Industrial Workers of the World* (New York: International Publishers, 1964) for history of the IWW or "Wobblies."

united them, what kept them apart—is important for solving the problems the woman's movement faces today.

PERSONAL NOTES

The Early Years: Unarticulated Anger and Blind Ambition

I have been an unconscious feminist all my life and a conscious, vocal one for several years. When I was six or seven I remember telling some of my relatives that I didn't want just to have babies when I grew up because any animal could do that. They smiled at me with amused tolerance. A couple of months later my father asked me what I wanted to do when I grew up. I answered I didn't care as long as I was famous. He smiled, too, but with pride and encouragement. I knew at that moment I had said the right thing. In this way the first fires of a driving ambition to succeed, to be good, to be outstanding in everything I undertook, an ambition that was to be characteristic of a large part of my life, were fanned.

My father died suddenly of a coronary thrombosis seven years later when I was thirteen and a freshman in high school in a small town in northern New Jersey. I was living in a modest six-room house with my mother, Louise, and two younger sisters, Gay, nine, and Martha, four.

My mother is the daughter of Russian Jews (as was my father) who immigrated to Boston at the turn of the century. Of eight children, she and her oldest brother and sister were the only three to go to college. It must have required perseverance to go to college during the depression. I remember her saying, "I had to sell stockings at Filenes' to pay the tuition." But like many other women who are victims of unawareness, she tucked the hard-won B.A. in her purse, got married, and gave birth to me before her first wedding anniversary.

I didn't understand this when I was a little girl, but my earliest memories are of not wanting to be like my mother. However, I didn't know anyone else I wanted to be like either. I thought my female school teachers were dull, as were the librarian, the secretaries, and the waitresses who constituted the only women I knew who were anything other than full-time mothers.

Then one day my parents took me to see the Sadlers Wells Ballet in New York (funny, I only remember my father, although my mother must have been there too because they always went out together), and I saw a beautiful woman who did something difficult well and was showered with thundering applause afterward. I asked what she was and immediately announced that I too would become a prima ballerina. I think I was about six or seven then, and I plunged headlong into a program to implement my goal. For the next six years I took tap, ballet, and acrobatic lessons three or four times a week. I out-danced everyone in my hometown classes and the teacher suggested that I go to the American

School of Ballet in New York City and also take private lessons with a certain Russian lady whose name I've forgotten.

I don't remember discussions about financing all this instruction, but they must have taken place, judging by the relieved expression on my mother's face when I announced I was giving up ballet at age thirteen. What I do remember is that my father devoted every Sunday for years to driving me into New York for my lessons. I also remember, somewhat hazily, long discussions about "life" that we had during the drives in the old blue and white Pontiac. I think somewhere out of those talks I must have learned that life was a serious business. Anyway, about that time, people began to tell me that I never smiled. They said that I was such a "serious child," and they frequently asked me if anything was the matter.

High school was a disaster. My father died at the end of my freshman year; my mother alternated between emotional collapse and unpredictable spurts of strength, and I lost most of my earlier convictions about being able to do something "great." I was overpowered by the all-American ethic: most of all I wanted to be popular and especially to be liked by boys. I was crushed when I was not elected to the cheerleading squad my freshman year. Something must be wrong with me: was it because my legs were too heavy, because I still wore braces, or could it be because I was Jewish?

Being Jewish in the small northern New Jersey town I grew up in was an important and painful factor in my life. My parents were political liberals, anxious to be "good neighbors" with everybody, and defensive about their Jewishness. At an early age I felt their insecurity about their own dignity and worth and no amount of "rational" explanation about the superiority of the Jews ("Jesus was a Jew, you know. Jewish people never get drunk. Jewish men make the best husbands. Jews always send their children to college. Intellectual life is of prime importance to Jews. A *Jewish* army general? Roberta, don't be silly.") ever convinced me that I was not in some way inferior. All my life I have automatically accepted negative criticisms as true and positive ones as lies or attempts to flatter or manipulate me.

In my high school yearbook I wrote that my ambition was to be a bilingual secretary. Quite a step down from prima ballerina, or my subsequent, short-lived desire to be a journalist. I had been socialized well throughout four years of high school and had accepted almost completely that the main reason for going to college was to find the right husband. However, I guess I hadn't totally given in to public school socialization because the fact that I had placed "bilingual" before "secretary" represented a consuming desire to travel. I had read *The New York Sunday Times* want ads religiously for four years and the most exciting job under the "Female" column was Spanish-English secretary to an executive in Latin America, Mexico, Argentina, Peru! far away from New Jersey, my family, being Jewish. Freedom, unpredictable experiences and dark, gentle, sensitive men. I don't remember where I first saw pictures of Latin men (probably in *The New York Sunday Times* travel section), but the fascination with Latin males—exotic, romantic, undemanding in their superficial, unreflective commitments—lasted for years.

Although I had given up glorious ambitions at seventeen, I still had the American-Jewish drive "to achieve," so I applied to Radcliffe. I was rejected and instead went to the University of Michigan. I hated Ann Arbor and dorm life, and I felt insecure and inferior among the rich, more confident Jews from Detroit and Chicago suburbs. I felt rejected, inferior, not right somehow. I didn't get "brilliant" grades; I wasn't a leader in any way; and I wasn't "popular" with the boys. The few props that in high school had supported my constantly wavering sense of worth were swept away and I lived in a state of perpetual anguish, insecurity, and semidesperation.

From an early age—probably when my father died—I learned that if you wanted something you fought for it yourself and. counted on no one else. Learning that lesson and having it continually reinforced was a lonely and painful experience, but it gave me a kind of strength before I understood that the American ideal of the "rugged individual" was a political creation and not the measure of a magic moral fortitude. I knew that if my unhappiness at Michigan were to change, I would have to do it myself, so I applied to The Experiment in International Living to spend the summer in Madrid with a Spanish family. I also arranged to transfer to Boston University, primarily because it was near Harvard and I still had hopes of meeting "interesting men."

In Spain, I learned three important things. First, it was acceptable, even desirable, to be Jewish. Spaniards made fun of the WASP American with a grace and humor that allowed me to see the American Anglo-Saxon as a hamburger-loving, insensitive, unsophisticated clod. Spaniards valued my vituperative tongue, "lack of self-control," facility for speaking foreign languages, and appreciation of good food. They thought of Jews in America as "French intellectuals" (the highest compliment from a university-educated Spaniard) and the Anglo-Saxons as bumbling dullards who, by some freaky accident, were in power.

Second, I learned I was a woman whom men found attractive. American men had always made me feel dirty. I went through high school thinking that if I was "sexy" (as on occasion I was told I was), it meant I was in grave danger of becoming a "bad woman." Spaniards made me feel that anything I did was fine and desirable. It took me years to learn that to be placed on a pedestal and unquestionably adored is only another form of not-too-subtle male domination. I marvel at how long I was able to accept the sticky, stereotyped flattery meant to perpetuate the doll-like status of most Spanish women. It was so pleasant to hear nice words that I refused to examine their validity.

Third, I saw real poverty for the first time. It was 1957. Watts had not yet burned and although my hometown was forty-five minutes away from Harlem, like the majority of white Americans, I knew nothing about it and it hadn't occurred to me to care. As I travelled through poverty-stricken southern Spain (Granada, Malaga and Seville), I knew the remarks made by other student members of the group ("Why are they so poor? Why don't they have a democracy like ours? I guess some people just like to be poor.") were wrong. I was beginning to feel the anger that was to develop into deep rage against social inequities.

Spurred by an undefinable urgency, I graduated from Boston University a year early and was accepted to do graduate work in Spanish at Harvard. I still hadn't met the "right man." Maybe being on the other side of the Charles would do it. Being accepted to Harvard was a momentous event in my life. I had crossed the threshold into that wonderful world of "interesting people." Now my life would be full of dynamic, handsome intellectuals, stimulating discussions, theatre, ballet, French restaurants!

But Harvard turned out to be hard work, and the challenge to succeed intellectually absorbed most of my time the first year. I never saw a female professor at Harvard, but two male professors were instrumental in my life that year. I was immediately infatuated with one of my Spanish professors, Steven Gilman (I had never met a gentle Protestant intellectual before) and when he said, somewhat casually as I remember, "Are you here to find a husband or are you going to take all this seriously?" I plunged into my work with a vengeance. I was determined to be a success (and thus get his approval) *no matter what.*

Raimundo Lida was another "important man" to take me seriously. He is a soft-spoken Argentine and a highly respected scholar and teacher in the world of Hispanic letters. From the first day I met him in Widener Library he *assumed* I was a serious scholar who was simply coming to him for aid and guidance. I was astounded. ME? An ex-cheerleader (I had finally been elected to the silly thing) who got to Harvard by accident, a real scholar? It took a year of A's at Harvard and praise by both Gilman and Lida to convince me I could become an "intellectual."

By the end of my second year in Cambridge the newness and glory of belonging to Harvard Square had worn off and I was discontented again. I had met some of the highly prized "interesting people," but I hadn't found the "right man" yet, and studying Spanish literature was beginning not to make much sense. I felt that something must still be wrong with me. As a result, in May 1961 I decided to go back to Spain, and accepted a teaching fellowship at the International Institute in Madrid. I also arranged to work as a governess in Florence for the summer to learn Italian.

Back to Europe. Marriage, Divorce, and Commitment to Feminism

My marriage was chaotic and turbulent, and absurdly romantic from the beginning. Gabriel comes from the wealthy, educated, cultured Madrid bourgeoisie. He has princely tastes, Marxist intellectual leanings, and continental charm. I was especially attracted by the fact that he belonged so solidly to a group that I had designated as 'interesting.' These were the Spanish intellectuals and technocrats who read Marx and Lenin, never took off their spotless dark suits and ties, and had impeccably groomed wives who supervised households with two or three servants. We were married in a civil ceremony in Gibraltar in October 1962 (his family, although atheists, were upset we didn't marry in the Catholic Church for "social reasons") and spent the first year in my father-in-law's summer house on the outskirts of Madrid.

Gabriel and I never confronted any serious problems. He believed love would conquer all, and I was sure I could get my way. I didn't want to live in Spain; I wanted a career as a university professor in the United States. His parents were horrified to think that I would abduct the family jewel to the wilds of America, and Gabriel tried to keep us all happy by never making his desires and plans clear to anyone.

As soon as we were married I urged Gabriel to apply for a Fulbright to study in America. (I had arranged for a year's leave from Harvard. Since I was petrified about taking my PhD. Generals, sure that I didn't have what it took to get a doctorate from H-A-R-V-A-R-D, at first I welcomed the year's respite.) For six months I was an exemplary wife: I made a fetish of cooking gourmet meals, did the dishes, entertained family and friends, and tried to forget how much I hated my father-in-law's constant intervention in my life. My father-in-law was a frustrated intellectual (the civil war had ended a promising university career) and a dictatorial Latin patriarch who smilingly tyrannized his wife and children economically, psychologically, and intellectually. I never had the courage to stand up to him—probably because I didn't fully understand my situation—but I spent long hours contemplating how pleasant my life would be if he were to die.

After six months of marriage I suddenly lost my appetite, got very thin, and was constantly depressed. I hated my life in Madrid, had numerous fits of hysteria, and could only think of returning to America. Apparently my subconscious instinct for survival was telling me that if I didn't get back to the States soon and finish my degree, life would be over for me. Occasionally I would contemplate what it would be like to live this "wonderful life" as the wife of a wealthy Madrid technocrat, a life everyone was pressuring me to accept. *Gabriel* would have an interesting job; *Gabriel* would travel; *Gabriel* would have an entry to decision-making positions. But what about me? All I could see in the future was a comfortable apartment, a maid or two, vacations on the Mediterranean, and boredom and isolation. No, I couldn't do it.

Roberta Salper

Gabriel finally received a Fulbright to study at the University of Wisconsin. Madison was a long way from Cambridge, but I didn't care. I would commute; I would sprout wings; I would do anything to be free of Madrid and his family. Without his father and other family pressures I thought everything would be perfect. I didn't know then that the real problem was not my father-in-law.

We lived as graduate students for three years in Madison. During that time I passed my doctoral exams, finished my thesis, and published an article. During those years I was responsible for the cooking, cleaning, shopping, and every administrative problem in our lives. I also worked fifteen to twenty hours as a project assistant in the Spanish department at the university. I was harassed, nervous, emaciated, and had severe headaches and insomnia, but I thought of myself as happy—at least Gabriel's family was an ocean away.

Since Gabriel had come to the States on a student's visa, he had to return to Spain for two years before he could apply for status as a "resident alien" in America. The question of where we would live permanently was never settled between us. Gabriel simply would not face the problem. He didn't realize the issue went beyond saying "Darling, you're right. You absolutely must have your own career too." During our last year in Madison I taught Spanish literature at a small, nonaccredited college near Madison. I resented the fact that I had to take that job and did not have the freedom to choose another place and city (Gabriel was still working on his degree). But I accepted it as my fate. However, I guess I really didn't resign myself because my unarticulated frustrations came out in a thousand ways: screaming, hysteria, petty fights. These are the "inherently feminine" weapons that, in truth, are tools any human being uses when she or he feels suffocated, trapped, and helpless.

In September 1966, we went back to Spain for a two-year stay. Gabriel had a fellowship to write his thesis, and I had a postdoctoral research grant from Radcliffe to investigate something I thought was totally unimportant. I wanted to stay in the States, teach, and continue an incipient involvement in radical politics.

A turning point came in my life in April 1967, when the Spanish Association of University Women asked me to talk on "some aspect of the American university." Without hesitation, and somewhat to my own surprise, I replied I would talk on the role of women in the university. I knew nothing about the question, and my immediate gut response sprung forth from an unconscious part of me.

I wrote to Dean Kerby-Miller at Radcliffe and she sent me Jessie Barnard's *Academic Women* and Betty Friedan's *Feminine Mystique.* As I read the two books—and I remember it as a painful, laborious task— I knew I had hit on something important. Then I read *The Second Sex* (I had tried to read it before, but somehow never managed to read more than twenty pages. It made me too uncomfortable.) and I began to perceive that my condition as a woman was a social problem and not just a matter of "silly, personal neuroses." I gave the speech, which was subsequently published in a Spanish journal, but I did not as yet have the courage to examine what implications feminism had for me personally. I muddled around for another year in Madrid, miserable, lonely, anguished, still not sure what to do or where to go.

Sometime during the early spring of 1968 I read an article by Marlene Dixon about the creation of a women's caucus in a recently formed organization called the New University Conference. She spelled out the aims of the caucus—to achieve social, economic, and psychological equality for women—and related feminism to radical politics. I was elated and wrote to her at once.

Several months later I returned to the States alone. Gabriel and I both had jobs teaching at the University of Pittsburgh for the fall, but his two-year stay in Spain was not up until September. I invented, and half-believed at the time, a need to return to the States to finish research on a book. The truth was my relationship with him was tense, semihysterical—and I couldn't stand it any longer.

During the summer I went to Chicago to talk to Marlene Dixon. Marlene and her friend Naomi Weisstein were the first feminists I met and it was exciting and encouraging to be with them. We talked about the condition of women and about the state of the women's liberation movement. I didn't know it yet, but the days I spent in Chicago in 1968 were to play a decisive role in my future.

A Token Success

Gabriel and I spent most of our first year at the University of Pittsburgh talking about whether or not to separate. We finally did in April. During the year I had become active in the New University Conference and done some reading on feminism. In March I gave two public lectures at the university on the new feminism.

I had had a relatively successful year teaching. I was the only female —and the only American—in the Spanish department, but since I "played the game" I had no problems. In other words, I smiled a lot, flattered my male colleagues, and was always "so grateful" for their advice. How they loved to help me! But I felt isolated from the department, was never consulted on any important decisions and frequently had the feeling of being liked because they thought I was pretty and charming. Occasionally I wondered if any of my male colleagues received as many compliments about "big blue eyes" as I did. . . .

Two weeks after Gabriel and I separated, a friend of mine was appointed dean of the College of Arts and Sciences and I accepted his offer to be assistant dean. I knew nothing about the job, but I saw it as an opportunity to pursue feminist activities.

During my first weeks as assistant dean the local chapter of the National Organization for Women (NOW) asked me to speak. The local papers took pictures at the meeting and wrote articles about me. I was billed as "the new look in Pitt administrators." For the next six months I was besieged by invitations to speak on radio, television, and at colleges, clubs, and all sorts of other places. I accepted as many invitations as I possibly could and reveled in all the attention. Part of being *the radical feminist* at the university involved instituting and teaching a course on the history of women and helping to organize Pittsburgh Women's Liberation. What gave me the unending stamina to talk, teach, organize, and administrate was all the personal attention and glory I received. I finally felt like I was that prima ballerina I had seen showered with applause over twenty years ago, and I couldn't get enough of it.

Although I had visited Cuba the summer before and was—and am— an enthusiastic supporter of the Revolution, I wasn't ready to distinguish between leadership that comes as a result of understanding and having lived with the political and human needs of a people and leadership imposed from above by dint of a strong will. This was normal since I had been imbued with the "compete-and-win-at-whatever-cost" ethic from an early age. The only thing that separated me from a lot of other people was that I was a woman and relatively good at "winning." It took me a long time to realize that "winning" in the conventional sense was really a terrible loss. It was hard to begin to "get off the ego trip" and learn that people were more than the objects of a conquer-or-be-conquered ethic. I had to learn that, while stepping on someone allowed you to silence him or her, it also meant that you erased his potential to function as a human being. Therefore, surrounded by fawning admirers, liberals who thought my success in the system "admirable" ("She is bright and we all know the women's rights thing is so important."), it was months before I confronted the isolation of being a token radical in an institution run, in large part, by liberal (at best) males.

Aside from honest moments in classes with undergraduates (I found my graduate students by and large uninterested in much beyond getting the best marks, the quickest degree, and the most prestigious letters

of recommendation. Maybe Abbie Hoffman is right and something does happen to our chromosomes as graduate students.), I played the role of the "charming exception" in my academic and public life. I knew that as soon as I stopped smiling, flirting a little, playing all those games designated by our society as "inherently female," my daily life would be a real hassle. In other words, the judgment by my male colleagues of my worth as a *professor* was heavily contingent on being sweet and charming.

I didn't want to continue as assistant dean; being an administrator hindered my relationships with students and activists in the women's movement, which was my primary interest. I had spent several years learning a crucial lesson: a token woman can do little by herself. Often she is used by her employers to show that they are socially conscious, and she is thus resented by those very groups she seeks to help. So when Marlene Dixon called me in Spring 1970, to ask me if I would be interested in working with the newly created women's studies program at San Diego State College, I accepted almost at once, not knowing what would await me in San Diego but feeling that it would be important.

Epilogue: Spring 1971

These personal notes were written a year ago, in June 1970. Rereading them now I am struck by two things: the urgent need I felt "to get it all out" and my inability to generalize from my own experiences and relate them to other women's lives. Friends have correctly pointed out this shortcoming. But rather than try to rewrite these pages, I leave them as they are; perhaps they could be subtitled "self-absorption as a stage of consciousness-raising."

1970 at San Diego has been marked by a deeper understanding of the woman's movement, and consequently, a more profound, more conscious commitment to the struggle for women's liberation. Part of this awareness has come from my classes in the women's studies program, from working with women here in San Diego, and from the slow, painful realization of the destructive nature of seemingly "liberated" male-female relationships. But this is another chapter in an autobiography that still has to be lived.

History and Background

As a moral being I feel I owe it to the slave and the master, to my countrymen and to the world, to do all that I can to overturn a system of complicated crimes built upon the broken hearts and prostrate bodies of my countrymen in chains and cemented by the blood, sweat and tears of my sisters in bond

Angelina Grimké to a Massachusetts legislative

committee in 1832

Certain issues have been constants in the history of women's struggle for liberation. The settings, participants and vocabulary change, but the debate about whether women are biologically capable of equality and whether they have a moral and legal right to it continues. So does the day-to-day political struggle to build a society that not only endorses the total equality of women, but also is structured so that it cannot exist without it.

Mary Wollstonecraft and Harriet Taylor Mill were members of England's intellectual aristocracy in the late 18th and mid-19th centuries, respectively. They were feminists who were theoretical innovators, but who never participated in any active feminist social movement. In 1792 Wollstonecraft published *A Vindication of the Rights of Woman* and challenged the prevailing ideology that woman's concerns in the world are domestic, not political, that she is *naturally* subject to man, as decreed by nature, God and law. The work had a major impact on American feminists. In 1851 Harriet Taylor Mill wrote "On the Enfranchisement of Women": the first political analysis of the significance of the incipient American women's struggle for enfranchisement.

The writings of these two women were products of a society that allowed a few women a certain freedom. In early nineteenth-century London it was economically and politically possible to educate and maintain a select circle of people (mostly men, but even a few women were cultivated) to write novels, publish journals for small audiences, discuss and formulate innovative social theories. This was the world of George Eliot, Herbert Spencer, John Stuart Mill.

However, it was in the United States—less rigid, more socially malleable than "Mother England"—that many of these new ideas, such as the fight for the vote for women, were first practically applied.

But to understand the American woman's rights movement studying the struggle for suffrage is not enough. The history of women in America is intricately linked to the history of abolition and trade unionism and, in a slightly different way, to the rise of Marxism in Europe. Women such as Ella Reeve Bloor, Elizabeth Gurley Flynn, Emma Goldman, Victoria Woodhull were advocates of Marxist ideas. All rejected capitalism in some way, in favor of socialism or communism, although each had different political interpretations and practice. Since these women had an important impact on American political life and all expressed ideas on the role of women, it is important to study the Marxist theory on feminism in order to understand their political positions. Furthermore, Marxist theory is in many ways the foundation of today's movement. For these reasons, I have included a summary of Marx' and Engels' ideas on women's liberation and works by women and men who were involved in the abolition and trade union movements as well as the suffrage struggle: Sojourner Truth, Frederick Douglass, Emma Goldman, Ella Reeve Bloor.

One of the suffrage movement's major shortcomings was the ultimate inability to broaden concerns beyond those defined by its white middle-class constituency. Thus, women like Sojourner Truth, Emma Goldman, and Ella Reeve Bloor, who were primarily concerned with abolition or working class conditions (Mother Jones, Victoria Woodhull, Elizabeth Gurley Flynn are other examples) could relate only tangentially to the suffrage movement even though they also fought for women's rights. They were extraordinary women and outstanding female leaders. Yet they weren't leading feminists, and the reasons for that shed further light on the limitations of the past movement and in certain cases, on these women's political positions. I have included two articles by Frederick Douglass because the relationship among the abolition movement, Douglass, and nineteenth-century feminism parallels and illuminates many of the problems women's liberation and black liberation forces confront today when they attempt to unite. (See my introduction to the articles by Frederick Douglass.)

Marx and Engels evolved a political theory for building a society in which the equality of women is a central issue. The actual condition of women in China, Cuba, the Soviet Union, and the extent to which women's liberation is linked to economic structure and the nuclear family—arguments at the heart of Marx' and Engels' theory—are debated today in every organization that is serious about feminism, as the articles in Part 2 show.

Elizabeth Cady Stanton appears in this section because she was at the very center of the woman's rights movement, participating in the day-to-day struggles for decades. Activist, organizer, writer, she, together with Susan B. Anthony, shaped the course of the suffrage struggle. Like Wollstonecraft, Mill, and Charlotte Perkins Gilman, Stanton also attacked the pillars of her Victorian society—State, Church, and Family, most notably in her forthright rejection of the *Bible's* definition of women.

Charlotte Perkins Gilman was a leading feminist theoretician in America. Although she was not directly involved in the women's rights movement, her works had an important impact on it. In *Woman and Economics* (1898) Gilman argued that the basis of women's independence is economic, and marriage and motherhood should not be synonymous with economic dependence. *The Home: Its Work and Influence* (1913) rejects the notion of the happy housewife, of domesticity as the essence of female bliss, and maintains that child care, cooking, cleaning, as currently executed—by many different women all in separate homes—is a waste of energy, talent and time. Some of her arguments for socialized households are similar to those Margaret Benston makes in her article of 1969, "The Political Economy of Women's Liberation."

To understand the nature of any political struggle it is crucial to see its demands in their historical context. For example, the political significance of arguing for legislative reform and against organized religion has changed in the last hundred years and it is important to articulate how and why. Today legalistic reform within the existing political system is not the same issue it was in 1851. Likewise, the influence of the Church has declined and been altered so that a frontal attack on organized religion is not part of the actual struggle. By comparing and contrasting the following introductions to the issues and ideologies of nineteenth-century feminism with selections in Part 2 that do the same for the current movement, the form and content of both struggles should be clearer.

THE RIGHTS OF WOMAN

Mary Wollstonecraft

Mary Wollstonecraft (1759–1797) belonged to the radical wing of the intellectual elite of late eighteenth-century England—the supporters of the American and French Revolutions, the friends of Tom Paine, the intellectuals who were in sympathy with the most advanced ideas in Europe and America. Her two works, *A Vindication of the Rights of Man* (1790) and *A Vindication of the Rights of Woman* (1791) were originally published as part of a debate among intellectuals concerning the correct interpretation of the French Revolution. Wollstonecraft supported the radical side in direct answer to Edmund Burke's statement of the conservative position, *Reflections on the Revolution in France.* In *A Vindication of the Rights of Woman,* she attacked Rousseau's widely accepted idea that woman was, by nature, the second sex. Human rights, she said, have no sex. Education and social conditions determine one's nature; anatomy is *not* destiny.

Underlying Wollstonecraft's analysis are the basic principles of the Enlightenment: the beliefs in the human capacity to reason and in the concepts of freedom and equality that preceded and accompanied the American and French Revolutions. Like the *philosophes*,[1] she recognized reason as the only authority and argued that unless women were encouraged to develop their rational potential and to rely on their own judgment, the progress of all humanity would be retarded. However, although Wollstonecraft lamented the obvious inequities between "the endless tribe of idle princes and princesses" and "hard-working mechanics, who pay for the support of royalty when they can scarcely stop their children's mouths with bread," her feminism did not cross class lines easily: ". . . though I consider that women in the common walks of life are called to fulfill the duties of wives and mothers, by religion and reason, I cannot help lamenting that women of a superior cast have not a road open by which they can pursue more extensive plans of usefulness and independence." In the following selection she expresses her belief that "the most respectable women are the most oppressed."

The Prevailing Opinion of a Sexual Character Discussed

To account for, and excuse the tyranny of man, many ingenious arguments have been brought forward to prove, that the two sexes, in the acquirement of virtue, ought to aim at attaining a very different character; or, to speak explicitly, women are not allowed to have sufficient strength of mind to acquire what really deserves the name of virtue. . . .

Mary Wollstonecraft, "The Rights of Woman," *The Rights of Woman and The Subjection of Woman* by Mary Wollstonecraft and John Stuart Mill, respectively (New York: Everyman's Library, 1965), Chapter 2, pp. 23, 25–26, 30–32; Chapter 9, pp. 158–164. The heads in the text were chapter titles in the original.

[1] The name given to men and women, particularly in the eighteenth century, who studied philosophy in order to question, and often reject, accepted ideas and concepts.

. . . Women are told from their infancy, and taught by the example of their mothers, that a little knowledge of human weakness, justly termed cunning, softness of temper, *outward* obedience, and a scrupulous attention to a puerile kind of propriety, will obtain for them the protection of man; and should they be beautiful, everything else is needless, for at least twenty years of their lives.

• • •

. . . Men and women must be educated, in a great degree, by the opinions and manners of the society they live in. In every age there has been a stream of popular opinion that has carried all before it, and given a family character, as it were, to the century. It may then fairly be inferred, that, till society be differently constituted, much cannot be expected from education. . . .

Consequently, the most perfect education, in my opinion, is such an exercise of the understanding as is best calculated to strengthen the body and form the heart. Or, in other words, to enable the individual to attain such habits of virtue as will render it independent. In fact, it is a farce to call any being virtuous whose virtues do not result from the exercise of its own reason. This was Rousseau's opinion respecting men; I extend it to women, and confidently assert that they have been drawn out of their sphere by false refinement, and not by an endeavour to acquire masculine qualities. Still the regal homage which they receive is so intoxicating, that until the manners of the times are changed, and formed on more reasonable principles, it may be impossible to convince them that the illegitimate power which they obtain by degrading themselves is a curse, and that they must return to nature and equality if they wish to secure the placid satisfaction that unsophisticated affections impart. But for this epoch we must wait—wait perhaps till kings and nobles, enlightened by reason, and, preferring the real dignity of man to childish state, throw off their gaudy hereditary trappings; and if then women do not resign the arbitrary power of beauty—they will prove that they have *less* mind than man.

I may be accused of arrogance; still I must declare what I firmly believe, that all the writers who have written on the subject of female education and manners, from Rousseau to Dr. Gregory, have contributed to render women more artificial, weak characters, than they would otherwise have been; and consequently, more useless members of society.

• • •

Women are therefore to be considered either as moral beings, or so weak that they must be entirely subjected to the superior faculties of men.

Let us examine this question. Rousseau declares that a woman should never for a moment feel herself independent, that she should be governed by fear to exercise her *natural* cunning, and made a coquettish slave in order to render her a more alluring object of desire, a *sweeter* companion to man, whenever he chooses to relax himself. He carries the arguments, which he pretends to draw from the indications of nature, still further, and insinuates that truth and fortitude, the corner-stones of all human virtue, should be cultivated with certain restrictions, because, with respect to the female character, obedience is the grand lesson which ought to be impressed with unrelenting rigour.

What nonsense! When will a great man arise with sufficient strength of mind to puff away the fumes which pride and sensuality have thus spread over the subject? If women are by nature inferior to men, their virtues must be the same in quality, if not in degree, or virtue is a relative idea; consequently their conduct should be founded on the same principles, and have the same aim.

• • •

Probably the prevailing opinion that woman was created for man, may have taken its rise from Moses' poetical story; yet as very few, it is presumed, who have bestowed any serious thought on the subject ever supposed that Eve was, literally speaking, one of Adam's ribs, the deduction must be allowed to fall to the ground, or only be so far admitted as it proves that man, from the remotest antiquity, found it convenient to exert his strength to subjugate his companion, and his invention to show that she ought to have her neck bent under the yoke, because the whole creation was only created for his convenience or pleasure.

• • •

Youth is the season for love in both sexes; but in those days of thoughtless enjoyment provision should be made for the more important years of life, when reflection takes place of sensation. But Rousseau, and most of the male writers who have followed his steps, have warmly inculcated that the whole tendency of female education ought to be directed to one point—to render them pleasing.

Let me reason with the supporters of this opinion who have any knowledge of human nature. Do they imagine that marriage can eradi-cate the habitude of life? The woman who has only been taught to please will soon find that her charms are oblique sunbeams, and that they cannot have much effect on her husband's heart when they are seen every day, when the summer is passed and gone. Will she then have sufficient native energy to look into herself for comfort, and cultivate her dormant faculties? or is it not more rational to expect that she will try to please other men, and, in the emotions raised by the expectation of new conquests, endeavour to forget the mortification her love or pride has received? When the husband ceases to be a lover, and the time will inevitably come, her desire of pleasing will then grow languid, or become a spring of bitterness; and love, perhaps, the most evanes-cent of all passions, gives place to jealousy or vanity.

I now speak of women who are restrained by principle or prejudice. Such women, though they would shrink from an intrigue with real abhorrence, yet, nevertheless, wish to be convinced by the homage of gallantry that they are cruelly neglected by their husbands; or, days and weeks are spent in dreaming of the happiness enjoyed by congenial souls, till their health is undermined and their spirits broken by discontent. How then can the great art of pleasing be such a necessary study? it is only useful to a mistress. The chaste wife and serious mother should only consider her power to please as the polish of her virtues, and the affection of her husband as one of the comforts that render her task less difficult, and her life happier. But, whether she be loved or neglected, her first wish should be to make herself respectable, and not to rely for all her happiness on a being subject to like infirmities with herself.

• • •

Of the Pernicious Effects Which Arise from the Unnatural Distinctions Established in Society

• • •

Women are, in common with men, rendered weak and luxurious by the relaxing pleasures which wealth procures; but added to this they are made slaves to their persons, and must render them alluring that man may lend them his reason to guide their tottering steps aright. Or should they be ambitious, they must govern their tyrants by sinister tricks, for without rights there cannot be any incumbent duties. The laws respecting woman . . . make an absurd unit of a man and his wife; and then, by the easy transition of only considering him as responsible, she is reduced to a mere cipher.

The being who discharges the duties of its station is independent; and, speaking of women at large, their first duty is to themselves as rational creatures, and the next, in point of importance, as citizens, is that, which includes so many, of a mother. The rank in life which dispenses with their fulfilling this duty, necessarily degrades them by making them mere dolls. Or should they turn to something more important than merely fitting drapery upon a smooth block, their minds are only occupied by some soft platonic attachment; or the actual management of an intrigue may keep their thoughts in motion; for when they neglect domestic duties, they have it not in their power to take the field and march and counter-march like soldiers, or wrangle in the senate to keep their faculties from rusting.

• • •

. . . Still to avoid misconstruction, though I consider that women in the common walks of life are called to fulfil the duties of wives and mothers, by religion and reason, I cannot help lamenting that women of a superior cast have not a road open by which they can pursue more extensive plans of usefulness and independence. I may excite laughter, by dropping an hint, which I mean to pursue, some future time, for I really think that women ought to have representatives, instead of being arbitrarily governed without having any direct share allowed them in the deliberations of government.

But, as the whole system of representation is now, in this country, only a convenient handle for despotism, they need not complain, for they are as well represented as a numerous class of hard-working mechanics, who pay for the support of royalty when they can scarcely stop their children's mouths with bread. How are they represented whose very sweat supports the splendid stud of an heir-apparent, or varnishes the chariot of some female favourite who looks down on shame? Taxes on the very necessaries of life, enable an endless tribe of idle princes and princesses to pass with stupid pomp before a gaping crowd, who almost worship the very parade which costs them so dear. This is mere gothic grandeur, something like the barbarous useless parade of having sentinels on horseback at Whitehall, which I could never view without a mixture of contempt and indignation.

• • •

But what have women to do in society? I may be asked, but to loiter with easy grace; surely you would not condemn them all to suckle fools and chronicle small beer! No. Women might certainly study the art of healing, and be physicians as well as nurses. And midwifery, decency seems to allot to them, though I am afraid, the word midwife, in our dictionaries, will soon give place to *accoucheur,* and one proof of the former delicacy of the sex be effaced from the language.

They might also study politics, . . .

• • •

Business of various kinds, they might likewise pursue, if they were educated in a more orderly manner, which might save many from common and legal prostitution. Women would not then marry for a support, as men accept of places under Government, and neglect the implied duties; nor would an attempt to earn their own subsistence, a most laudable one! sink them almost to the level of those poor abandoned creatures who live by prostitution. For are not milliners and mantua-makers reckoned the next class? The few employments open to women, so far, from being liberal, are menial; and when a superior education enables them to take charge of the education of children as governesses, they are not treated like the tutors of sons, though even clerical tutors are not always treated in a manner calculated to render them respectable in the eyes of their pupils, to say nothing of the private comfort of the individual. But as women educated like gentlewomen, are never designed for the humiliating situation which necessity sometimes forces them to fill; these situations are considered in the light of a degradation; and they know little of the human heart, who need to be told, that nothing so painfully sharpens sensibility as such a fall in life.

Some of these women might be restrained from marrying by a proper spirit of delicacy, and others may not have had it in their power to escape in this pitiful way from servitude; is not that Government then very defective, and very unmindful of the happiness of one-half of its members, that does not provide for honest, independent women, by encouraging them to fill respectable stations? But in order to render their private virtue a public benefit, they must have a civil existence in the State, married or single; else we shall continually see some worthy woman, whose sensibility has been rendered painfully acute by undeserved contempt, droop like "the lily broken down by a plowshare."

It is a melancholy truth; yet such is the blessed effect of civilisation! the most respectable women are the most oppressed; and, unless they have understandings far superior to the common run of understandings, taking in both sexes, they must, from being treated like contemptible beings, become contemptible. How many women thus waste life away the prey of discontent, who might have practised as physicians, regulated a farm, managed a shop, and stood erect, supported by their own industry, instead of hanging their heads surcharged with the dew of sensibility, that consumes the beauty to which it at first gave lustre; nay, I doubt whether pity and love are so near akin as poets feign, for I have seldom seen much compassion excited by the helplessness of females, unless they were fair; then, perhaps, pity was the soft handmaid of love, or the harbinger of lust.

How much more respectable is the woman who earns her own bread by fulfilling any duty, than the most accomplished beauty!—beauty did I say!—so sensible am I of the beauty of moral loveliness, or the harmonious propriety that attunes the passions of a well-regulated mind, that I blush at making the comparison; yet I sigh to think how few women aim at attaining this respectability by withdrawing from the giddy whirl of pleasure, or the indolent calm that stupefies the good sort of women it sucks in.

Proud of their weakness, however, they must always be protected, guarded from care, and all the rough toils that dignify the mind. If this be that fiat of fate, if they will make themselves insignificant and contemptible, sweetly to waste "life away," let them not expect to be valued when their beauty fades, for it is the fate of the fairest flowers to be admired and pulled to pieces by the careless hand that plucked them. In how many ways do I wish, from the purest benevolence, to impress this truth on my sex; yet I fear that they will not listen to a truth that dear bought experience has brought home to many an agitated bosom, nor willingly resign the privileges of rank and sex for the privileges of humanity, to which those have no claim who do not discharge its duties.

• • •

Would men but generously snap our chains, and be content with rational fellowship instead of slavish obedience, they would find us more observant daughters, more affectionate sisters, more faithful wives, more reasonable mothers—in a word, better citizens. We should then love them with true affection, because we should learn to respect ourselves; and the peace of mind of a worthy man would not be interrupted by the idle vanity of his wife, nor the babes sent to nestle in a strange bosom, having never found a home in their mother's.

ON THE ENFRANCHISEMENT OF WOMEN

Harriet Taylor Mill

In 1869 John Stuart Mill published "On the Subjection of Women," one of the most influential of the early feminist texts. With the demise of the first feminist movement, however, Mill's essay was shelved as no longer relevant and "tangential" to the main body of his thought. In the early days of the current women's liberation movement this essay was "rediscovered" and inexpensive editions became available. Several years passed, however, before the role of Harriet Taylor (who married Mill in 1851, seven years before her death) in the development of Mill's feminism and the authorship of her own contributions were satisfactorily explained.[1]

Like Mary Wollstonecraft in the eighteenth century, Harriet Taylor enjoyed the privileged life of England's intellectual aristocracy. She associated with a group of nineteenth-century social innovators who dissented from the prevailing Victorian ethic. These Unitarian Radicals appealed to Harriet Taylor because they advocated socialist reforms on both the domestic and personal level and on the institutional level.

Harriet Taylor's essay, "On the Enfranchisement of Women,"[2] reflects this dual concern. Published in 1851, it was unique in recognizing the political dimensions of the recent demand for suffrage in the United States. Harriet Taylor understood that the demand for the vote marked the beginning of a larger political movement, "practical in its objects . . . a movement not merely *for* women, but *by* them." Furthermore, the essay shows that Harriet Taylor understood the personal consequences of women's legal and social inferiority. Taylor suggested—as Roxanne Dunbar was to do in 1969—that humanity is divided into two castes, one of which rules over the other. She argued against this, that

Harriet Taylor Mill, "On the Enfranchisement of Women," *Westminster Review* (England: July 1851), pp. 93–121. As reprinted in Alice Rossi, *John Stuart Mill and Harriet Taylor Mill, Essays on Sex Equality* (Chicago: University of Chicago Press, 1971), pp. 93–121.

[1] Alice Rossi gives an account of Taylor and Mill's twenty-year friendship and collaboration in her introduction to *Essays on Sex Equality* by John Stuart Mill and Harriet Taylor Mill (Chicago: University of Chicago Press, 1970).

[2] I accept Rossi's contention that Harriet Taylor is the primary author of "On the Enfranchisement of Women." *Ibid.*, p. 41.

is, for the right of women to determine and control their own lives. She also rejected the idea that an entire sex should be coerced to be "either mothers or nothing."

Harriet Taylor's thought was less abstract and philosophical and more radical politically than that of Mary Wollstonecraft. Her few writings are more calls for action than fully developed theories. For example, in her 1851 essay she made one of the first direct attacks on the distribution of power in domestic arrangements: "The real question is, whether it is right and expedient that one-half of the human race should pass through life in a state of forced subordination to the other half . . . for the purpose of bringing up *his* children, and making *his* home pleasant to him." This was almost thirty years before Marx and Engels elaborated their theory of the division of labor and power between the sexes in *The Origins of the Family.* (See Hal Draper's article, "Marx and Engels on Women's Liberation," in Part 1 of this book.)

One wonders what Harriet Taylor might have written had she lived longer and helped John Stuart Mill less.

. . . Most of our readers will probably learn from these pages for the first time, that there has arisen in the United States, and in the most civilized and enlightened portion of them, an organized agitation on a new question—new, not to thinkers, nor to any one by whom the principles of free and popular government are felt as well as acknowledged, but new, and even unheard-of, as a subject for public meetings and practical political action. This question is, the enfranchisement of women; their admission, in law and in fact, to equality in all rights, political, civil, and social, with the male citizens of the community.

It will add to the surprise with which many will receive this intelligence, that the agitation which has commenced is not a pleading by male writers and orators for women, those who are professedly to be benefited remaining either indifferent or ostensibly hostile. It is a political movement, practical in its objects, carried on in a form which denotes an intention to persevere. And it is a movement not merely *for* women, but *by* them. Its first public manifestation appears to have been a Convention of Women, held in the State of Ohio, in the spring of 1850. Of this meeting we have seen no report. On the 23rd and 24th of October last, a succession of public meetings was held at Worcester in Massachusetts, under the name of a "Women's Rights Convention," of which the president was a woman, and nearly all the chief speakers women: numerously reinforced, however, by men, among whom were some of the most distinguished leaders in the kindred cause of negro emancipation. A general and four special committees were nominated, for the purpose of carrying on the undertaking until the next annual meeting.

According to the report in the *New York Tribune,* above a thousand persons were present throughout, and "if a larger place could have been had, many thousands more would have attended." The place was described as "crowded from the beginning with attentive and interested listeners." In regard to the quality of the speaking, the proceedings bear an advantageous comparison with those of any popular movement with which we are acquainted, either in this country or in America. Very rarely in the oratory of public meetings is the part of verbiage and declamation so small, that of calm good sense and reason so considerable. The result of the Convention was in every respect encouraging to those by whom it was summoned: and it is probably destined to inaugurate one of the most important of the movements towards political and social reform, which are the best characteristics of the present age.

That the promoters of this new agitation take their stand on principles, and do not fear to declare these in their widest extent, without time-serving or compromise, will be seen from the resolutions adopted by the Convention, part of which we transcribe.

Resolved That every human being, of full age, and resident for a proper length of time on the soil of the nation, who is required to obey the law, is entitled to a voice in its enactment; that every such person, whose property or labour is taxed for the support of the government, is entitled to a direct share in such government; therefore,

Resolved That women are entitled to the right of suffrage, and to be considered eligible to office, . . . and that every party which claims to represent the humanity, the civilization, and the progress of the age, is bound to inscribe on its banners equality before the law, without distinction of sex or colour.

Resolved That civil and political rights acknowledge no sex, and therefore the word "male" should be struck from every State Constitution.

Resolved That, since the prospect of honourable and useful employment in after-life is the best stimulus to the use of educational advantages, and since the best education is that we give ourselves, in the struggles, employments, and discipline of life; therefore it is impossible that women should make full use of the instruction already accorded to them, or that their career should do justice to their faculties, until the avenues to the various civil and professional employments are thrown open to them.

Resolved That every effort to educate women, without according to them their rights, and arousing their conscience by the weight of their responsibilities, is futile, and a waste of labour.

Resolved That the laws of property, as affecting married persons, demand a thorough revisal, so that all rights be equal between them; that the wife have, during life, an equal control over the property gained by their mutual toil and sacrifices, and be heir to her husband precisely to that extent that he is heir to her, and entitled at her death to dispose by will of the same share of the joint property as he is.

The following is a brief summary of the principal demands.

1. *Education* in primary and high schools, universities, medical, legal, and theological institutions.
2. *Partnership* in the labours and gains, risks and remunerations, of productive industry.
3. *A coequal share* in the formation and administration of laws—municipal, state, and national—through legislative assemblies, courts, and executive offices.

It would be difficult to put so much true, just, and reasonable meaning into a style so little calculated to recommend it as that of some of
the resolutions. But whatever objection may be made to some of the
expressions, none, in our opinion, can be made to the demands themselves. As a question of justice, the case seems to us too clear for
dispute. As one of expediency, the more thoroughly it is examined the
stronger it will appear.

That women have as good a claim as men have, in point of personal
right, to the suffrage, or to a place in the jury-box, it would be difficult
for any one to deny. It cannot certainly be denied by the United States
of America, as a people or as a community. Their democratic institutions
rest avowedly on the inherent right of every one to a voice in the
government. Their Declaration of Independence, framed by the men who
are still their great constitutional authorities—that document which has
been from the first, and is now, the acknowledged basis of their polity,
commences with this express statement:

We hold these truths to be self-evident: that all men are created equal; that
they are endowed by their Creator with certain inalienable rights; that among
these are life, liberty, and the pursuit of happiness; that to secure these rights,
governments are instituted among men, deriving their just powers from the
consent of the governed.

We do not imagine that any American democrat will evade the force
of these expressions by the dishonest or ignorant subterfuge, that
"men," in this memorable document, does not stand for human beings,
but for one sex only; that "life, liberty, and the pursuit of happiness"
are "inalienable rights" of only one moiety of the human species; and
that "the governed," whose consent is affirmed to be the only source
of just power, are meant for that half of mankind only, who, in relation
to the other, have hitherto assumed the character of governors. The
contradiction between principle and practice cannot be explained away.
A like dereliction of the fundamental maxims of their political creed has
been committed by the Americans in the flagrant instance of the
negroes; of this they are learning to recognise the turpitude. After a
struggle which, by many of its incidents, deserves the name of heroic,
the abolitionists are now so strong in numbers and in influence that
they hold the balance of parties in the United States. It was fitting that
the men whose names will remain associated with the extirpation, from
the democratic soil of America, of the aristocracy of colour, should be
among the originators, for America and for the rest of the world, of the
first collective protest against the aristocracy of sex; a distinction as
accidental as that of colour, and fully as irrelevant to all questions of
government.

Not only to the democracy of America, the claim of women to civil
and political equality makes an irresistible appeal, but also to those
Radicals and Chartists in the British islands, and democrats on the
Continent, who claim what is called universal suffrage as an inherent
right, unjustly and oppressively withheld from them. For with what truth

or rationality could the suffrage be termed universal, while half the human species remained excluded from it? To declare that a voice in the government is the right of all, and demand it only for a part—the part, namely, to which the claimant himself belongs—is to renounce even the appearance of principle. The Chartist who denies the suffrage to women, is a Chartist only because he is not a lord: he is one of those levellers who would level only down to themselves.

Even those who do not look upon a voice in the government as a matter of personal right, nor profess principles which require that it should be extended to all, have usually traditional maxims of political justice with which it is impossible to reconcile the exclusion of all women from the common rights of citizenship. It is an axiom of English freedom that taxation and representation should be co-extensive. Even under the laws which give the wife's property to the husband, there are many unmarried women who pay taxes. It is one of the fundamental doctrines of the British Constitution, that all persons should be tried by their peers: yet women, whenever tried, are tried by male judges and a male jury. To foreigners the law accords the privilege of claiming that half the jury should be composed of themselves; not so to women. Apart from maxims of detail, which represent local and national rather than universal ideas; it is an acknowledged dictate of justice to make no degrading distinctions without necessity. In all things the presumption ought to be on the side of equality. A reason must be given why anything should be permitted to one person and interdicted to another. But when that which is interdicted includes nearly everything which those to whom it is permitted most prize, and to be deprived of which they feel to be most insulting; when not only political liberty but personal freedom of action is the prerogative of a caste; when even in the exercise of industry, almost all employments which task the higher faculties in an important field, which lead to distinction, riches, or even pecuniary independence, are fenced round as the exclusive domain of the predominant section, scarcely any doors being left open to the dependent class, except such as all who can enter elsewhere disdainfully pass by; the miserable expediencies which are advanced as excuses for so grossly partial a dispensation, would not be sufficient, even if they were real, to render it other than a flagrant injustice. While, far from being expedient, we are firmly convinced that the division of mankind into two castes, one born to rule over the other, is in this case, as in all cases, an unqualified mischief; a source of perversion and demoralization, both to the favoured class and to those at whose expense they are favoured; producing none of the good which it is the custom to ascribe to it, and forming a bar, almost insuperable while it lasts, to any really vital improvement, either in the character or in the social condition of the human race.

These propositions it is now our purpose to maintain. But before entering on them, we would endeavour to dispel the preliminary objections which, in the minds of persons to whom the subject is new, are apt to prevent a real and conscientious examination of it. The chief of these obstacles is that most formidable one, custom. Women never have had equal rights with men. The claim in their behalf, of the common rights of mankind, is looked upon as barred by universal practice. This strongest of prejudices, the prejudice against what is new and unknown, has, indeed, in an age of changes like the present, lost much of its force; if it had not, there would be little hope of prevailing against it. Over three-fourths of the habitable world, even at this day, the answer, "it has always been so," closes all discussion. But it is the boast of modern Europeans, and of their American kindred, that they know and do many things which their forefathers neither knew nor did; and it is perhaps the most unquestionable point of superiority in the present above former ages, that habit is not now the tyrant it formerly was over opinions and modes of action, and that the worship of custom is a declining idolatry. An uncustomary thought, on a subject which touches the greater interests of life, still startles when first presented; but if it can be kept before the mind until the impression of strangeness wears off, it obtains a hearing, and as rational a consideration as the intellect of the hearer is accustomed to bestow on any other subject.

In the present case, the prejudice of custom is doubtless on the unjust side. Great thinkers, indeed, at different times, from Plato to Condorcet, besides some of the most eminent names of the present age, have made emphatic protests in favour of the equality of women. And there have been voluntary societies, religious or secular, of which the Society of Friends is the most known, by whom that principle was recognised. But there has been no political community or nation in which, by law and usage, women have not been in a state of political and civil inferiority. In the ancient world the same fact was alleged, with equal truth, in behalf of slavery. It might have been alleged in favour of the mitigated form of slavery, serfdom, all through the middle ages. It was urged against freedom of industry, freedom of conscience, freedom of the press; none of these liberties were thought compatible with a well-ordered state, until they had proved their possibility by actually existing as facts. That an institution or a practice is customary is no presumption of its goodness, when any other sufficient cause can be assigned for its existence. There is no difficulty in understanding why the subjection of women has been a custom. No other explanation is needed than physical force.

That those who were physically weaker should have been made legally inferior, is quite conformable to the mode in which the world has been governed. Until very lately, the rule of physical strength was the general law of human affairs. Throughout history, the nations, races, classes, which found themselves the strongest, either in muscles, in riches, or in military discipline, have conquered and held in subjection the rest. If, even in the most improved nations, the law of the sword is at last discountenanced as unworthy, it is only since the calumniated eighteenth century. Wars of conquest have only ceased since democratic revolutions began. The world is very young, and has but just begun to cast off injustice. It is only now getting rid of negro slavery. It is only now getting rid of monarchical despotism. It is only now getting rid of hereditary feudal nobility. It is only now getting rid of disabilities on the ground of religion. It is only beginning to treat any *men* as citizens, except the rich and a favoured portion of the middle class. Can we wonder that it has not yet done as much for women? As society was constituted until the last few generations, inequality was its very basis; association grounded on equal rights scarcely existed; to be equals was to be enemies; two persons could hardly co-operate in anything, or meet in any amicable relation, without the law's appointing that one of them should be the superior of the other. Mankind have outgrown this state, and all things now tend to substitute, as the general principle of human relations, a just equality, instead of the dominion of the strongest. But of all relations, that between men and women being the nearest and most intimate, and connected with the greatest number of strong emotions, was sure to be the last to throw off the old rule and receive the new: for in proportion to the strength of a feeling, is the tenacity with which it clings to the forms and circumstances with which it has even accidentally become associated.

When a prejudice, which has any hold on the feelings, finds itself reduced to the unpleasant necessity of assigning reasons, it thinks it has done enough when it has re-asserted the very point in dispute, in phrases which appeal to the pre-existing feeling. Thus, many persons think they have sufficiently justified the restrictions on women's field of action, when they have said that the pursuits from which women are excluded are *unfeminine,* and that the *proper sphere* of women is not politics or publicity, but private and domestic life.

We deny the right of any portion of the species to decide for another portion, or any individual for another individual, what is and what is not their "proper sphere." The proper sphere for all human beings is the largest and highest which they are able to attain to. What this is, cannot be ascertained, without complete liberty of choice. The speakers at the Convention in America have therefore done wisely and right, in refusing to entertain the question of the peculiar aptitudes either of women or of men, or the limits within this or that occupation may be supposed to be more adapted to the one or to the other. They justly maintain, that these questions can only be satisfactorily answered by perfect freedom. Let every occupation be open to all, without favour or discouragement to any, and employments will fall into the hands of those men or women who are found by experience to be most capable of worthily exercising them. There need be no fear that women will take out of the hands of men any occupation which men perform better than they. Each individual will prove his or her capacities, in the only way in which capacities can be proved—by trial; and the world will have the benefit of the best faculties of all its inhabitants. But to interfere beforehand by an arbitrary limit, and declare that whatever be the genius, talent, energy, or force of mind of an individual of a certain sex or class, those faculties shall not be exerted, or shall be exerted only in some few of the many modes in which others are permitted to use theirs, is not only an injustice to the individual, and a detriment to society, which loses what it can ill spare, but is also the most effectual mode of providing that, in the sex or class so fettered, the qualities which are not permitted to be exercised shall not exist.

We shall follow the very proper example of the Convention, in not entering into the question of the alleged differences in physical or mental qualities between the sexes; not because we have nothing to say, but because we have too much; to discuss this one point tolerably would need all the space we have to bestow on the entire subject.[1] But if those who assert that the "proper sphere" for women is the domestic, mean by this that they have not shown themselves qualified for any other, the assertion evinces great ignorance of life and of history. Women have shown fitness for the highest social functions, exactly in proportion as they have been admitted to them. By a curious anomaly, though ineligible to even the lowest offices of State, they are in some countries admitted to the highest of all, the regal; and if there is any one function for which they have shown a decided vocation, it is that of reigning. Not to go back to ancient history, we look in vain for abler or firmer rulers than Elizabeth; than Isabella of Castile; than Maria Teresa; than Catherine of Russia; than Blanche, mother of Louis IX of France; than Jeanne d'Albret, mother of Henri Quatre. There are few kings on record who contended with more difficult circumstances, or overcame them more triumphantly, than these. Even in semi-barbarous Asia, princesses who have never been seen by men, other than those of their own family, or even spoken with them unless from behind a curtain, have as regents, during the minority of their sons, exhibited many of the most brilliant examples of just and vigorous administration. In the middle ages, when the distance between the upper and lower ranks was greater than even between women and men, and the women of the privileged class, however subject to tyranny from the men of the same class, were at a less distance below them than any one else was, and often in their absence represented them in their functions and authority —numbers of heroic châtelaines, like Jeanne de Montfort, or the great Countess of Derby as late even as the time of Charles I, distinguished

[1] An excellent passage on this part of the subject, from one of Sydney Smith's contributions to the Edinburgh Review, we will not refrain from quoting: "A great deal has been said of the original difference of capacity between men and women, as if women were more quick and men more judicious—as if women were more remarkable for delicacy of association, and men for stronger powers of attention. All this, we confess, appears to us very fanciful. That there is a difference in the understandings of the men and the women we every day meet with, everybody, we suppose, must perceive; but there is none surely which may not be accounted for by the difference of circumstances in which they have been placed, without referring to any conjectural difference of original conformation of mind. As long as boys and girls run about in the dirt, and trundle hoops together, they are both precisely alike. If you catch up one-half of these creatures, and train them to a particular set of actions and opinions, and the other half to a perfectly opposite set, of course their understandings will differ, as one or the other sort of occupations has called this or that talent into action. There is surely no occasion to go into any deeper or more abstruse reasoning, in order to explain so very simple a phenomenon." *(Sydney Smith's Works,* vol. i. p. 200.)

themselves not only by their political but their military capacity. In the centuries immediately before and after the Reformation, ladies of royal houses, as diplomatists, as governors of provinces, or as the confidential advisers of kings, equalled the first statesmen of their time: and the treaty of Cambray, which gave peace to Europe, was negotiated in conferences where no other person was present, by the aunt of the Emperor Charles the Fifth, and the mother of Francis the First.

Concerning the fitness, then, of women for politics, there can be no question: but the dispute is more likely to turn upon the fitness of politics for women. When the reasons alleged for excluding women from active life in all its higher departments are stripped of their garb of declamatory phrases, and reduced to the simple expression of a meaning, they seem to be mainly three: first, the incompatibility of active life with maternity, and with the cares of a household; secondly, its alleged hardening effect on the character; and thirdly, the inexpediency of making an addition to the already excessive pressure of competition in every kind of professional or lucrative employment.

The first, the maternity argument, is usually laid most stress upon: although (it needs hardly be said) this reason, if it be one, can apply only to mothers. It is neither necessary nor just to make imperative on women that they shall be either mothers or nothing; or that if they have been mothers once, they shall be nothing else during the whole remainder of their lives. Neither women nor men need any law to exclude them from an occupation, if they have undertaken another which is incompatible with it. No one proposes to exclude the male sex from Parliament because a man may be a soldier or sailor in active service, or a merchant whose business requires all his time and energies. Nine-tenths of the occupations of men exclude them *de facto* from public life, as effectually as if they were excluded by law; but that is no reason for making laws to exclude even the nine-tenths, much less the remaining tenth. The reason of the case is the same for women as for men. There is no need to make provision by law that a woman shall not carry on the active details of a household, or of the education of children, and at the same time practise a profession, or be elected to parliament. Where incompatibility is real, it will take care of itself: but there is gross injustice in making the incompatibility a pretence for the exclusion of those in whose case it does not exist. And these, if they were free to choose, would be a very large proportion. The maternity argument deserts its supporters in the case of single women, a large and increasing class of the population; a fact which, it is not irrelevant to remark, by tending to diminish the excessive competition of numbers, is calculated to assist greatly the prosperity of all. There is no inherent reason or necessity that all women should voluntarily choose to devote their lives to one animal function and its consequences. Numbers of women are wives and mothers only because there is no other career open to them, no other occupation for their feelings or their activities. Every improvement in their education, and enlargement of their faculties, everything which renders them more qualified for any other mode of life, increases the number of those to whom it is an injury and an oppression to be denied the choice. To say that women must be excluded from active life because maternity disqualifies them for it, is in fact to say, that every other career should be forbidden them in order that maternity may be their only resource.

But secondly, it is urged, that to give the same freedom of occupation to women as to men, would be an injurious addition to the crowd of competitors, by whom the avenues to almost all kinds of employment are choked up, and its remuneration depressed. This argument, it is to be observed, does not reach the political question. It gives no excuse for withholding from women the rights of citizenship. The suffrage, the jury-box, admission to the legislature and to office, it does not touch. It bears only on the industrial branch of the subject. Allowing it, then, in an economical point of view, its full force; assuming that to lay open to women the employments now monopolized by men, would tend, like the breaking down of other monopolies, to lower the rate of remuneration in those employments; let us consider what is the amount of this evil consequence, and what the compensation for it. The worst ever asserted, much worse than is at all likely to be realized, is that if women competed with men, a man and a woman could not together earn more than is now earned by the man alone. Let us make this supposition, the most unfavourable supposition possible: the joint income of the two would be the same as before, while the woman would be raised from the position of a servant to that of a partner. Even if every woman, as matters now stand, had a claim on some man for support, how infinitely preferable is it that part of the income should be of the woman's earning, even if the aggregate sum were but little increased by it, rather than that she should be compelled to stand aside in order that men may be the sole earners, and the sole dispensers of what is earned. Even under the present laws respecting the property of women, a woman who contributes materially to the support of the family, cannot be treated in the same contemptuously tyrannical manner as one who, however she may toil as a domestic drudge, is a dependent on the man for subsistence.[2] As for the depression of wages by increase of competition, remedies will be found for it in time. Palliatives might be applied immediately; for instance, a more rigid exclusion of children from industrial employment, during the years in which they ought to be working only to strengthen their bodies and minds for after-life. Children are necessarily dependent, and under the power of others; and their labour, being not for themselves but for the gain of their parents, is a proper subject for legislative regulation. With respect to the future, we neither believe that improvident multiplication, and the consequent excessive

---

[2] The truly horrible effects of the present state of the law among the lowest of the working population, is exhibited in those cases of hideous maltreatment of their wives by working men, with which every newspaper, every police report, teems. Wretches unfit to have the smallest authority over any living thing, have a helpless woman for their household slave. These excesses could not exist if women both earned, and had the right to possess, a part of the income of the family.

42

difficulty of gaining a subsistence, will always continue, nor that the division of mankind into capitalists and hired labourers, and the regulation of the reward of labourers mainly by demand and supply, will be for ever, or even much longer, the rule of the world. But so long as competition is the general law of human life, it is tyranny to shut out one-half of the competitors. All who have attained the age of self-government have an equal claim to be permitted to sell whatever kind of useful labour they are capable of, for the price which it will bring.

The third objection to the admission of women to political or professional life, its alleged hardening tendency, belongs to an age now past, and is scarcely to be comprehended by people of the present time. There are still, however, persons who say that the world and its avocations render men selfish and unfeeling; that the struggles, rivalries, and collisions of business and of politics make them harsh and unamiable; that if half the species must unavoidably be given up to these things, it is the more necessary that the other half should be kept free from them; that to preserve women from the bad influences of the world, is the only chance of preventing men from being wholly given up to them.

There would have been plausibility in this argument when the world was still in the age of violence; when life was full of physical conflict, and every man had to redress his injuries or those of others, by the sword or by the strength of his arm. Women, like priests, by being exempted from such responsibilities, and from some part of the accompanying dangers, may have been enabled to exercise a beneficial influence. But in the present condition of human life, we do not know where those hardening influences are to be found, to which men are subject and from which women are at present exempt. Individuals now-a-days are seldom called upon to fight hand to hand, even with peaceful weapons; personal enmities and rivalities count for little in worldly transactions; the general pressure of circumstances, not the adverse will of individuals, is the obstacle men now have to make head against. That pressure, when excessive, breaks the spirit, and cramps and sours the feelings, but not less of women than of men, since they suffer certainly not less from its evils. There are still quarrels and dislikes, but the sources of them are changed. The feudal chief once found his bitterest enemy in his powerful neighbour, the minister or courtier in his rival for place: but opposition of interest in active life, as a cause of personal animosity, is out of date; the enmities of the present day arise not from great things but small, from what people say of one another, more than from what they do; and if there are hatred, malice, and all uncharitableness, they are to be found among women fully as much as among men. In the present state of civilization, the notion of guarding women from the hardening influences of the world, could only be realized by secluding them from society altogether. The common duties of common life, as at present constituted, are incompatible with any other softness in women than weakness. Surely weak minds in weak bodies must ere long cease to be even supposed to be either attractive or amiable.

But, in truth, none of these arguments and considerations touch the foundations of the subject. The real question is, whether it is right and expedient that one-half of the human race should pass through life in a state of forced subordination to the other half. If the best state of human society is that of being divided into two parts, one consisting of persons with a will and a substantive existence, the other of humble companions to these persons, attached, each of them to one, for the purpose of bringing up *his* children, and making *his* home pleasant to him; if this is the place assigned to women, it is but kindness to educate them for this; to make them believe that the greatest good fortune which can befall them, is to be chosen by some man for this purpose; and that every other career which the world deems happy or honourable, is closed to them by the law, not of social institutions, but of nature and destiny.

When, however, we ask why the existence of one-half the species should be merely ancillary to that of the other—why each woman should be a mere appendage to a man, allowed to have no interests of her own, that there may be nothing to compete in her mind with his interests and his pleasure; the only reason which can be given is, that men like it. It is agreeable to them that men should live for their own sake, women for the sake of men: and the qualities and conduct in subjects which are agreeable to rulers, they succeed for a long time in making the subjects themselves consider as their appropriate virtues. Helvetius [French thinker of the Enlightenment, born in Paris in 1715] has met with much obloquy for asserting, that persons usually mean by virtues the qualities which are useful or convenient to themselves. How truly this is said of mankind in general, and how wonderfully the ideas of virtue set afloat by the powerful, are caught and imbibed by those under their dominion, is exemplified by the manner in which the world were once persuaded that the supreme virtue of subjects was loyalty to kings, and are still persuaded that the paramount virtue of womanhood is loyalty to men. Under a nominal recognition of a moral code common to both, in practice self-will and self-assertion form the type of what are designated as manly virtues, while abnegation of self, patience, resignation, and submission to power, unless when resistance is commanded by other interests than their own, have been stamped by general consent as pre-eminently the duties and graces required of women. The meaning being merely, that power makes itself the centre of moral obligation, and that a man likes to have his own will, but does not like that his domestic companion should have a will different from his.

We are far from pretending that in modern and civilized times, no reciprocity of obligation is acknowledged on the part of the stronger. Such an assertion would be very wide of the truth. But even this reciprocity, which has disarmed tyranny, at least in the higher and middle classes, of its most revolting feaures, yet when combined with the original evil of the dependent condition of women, has introduced in its turn serious evils.

In the beginning, and among tribes which are still in a primitive condition, women were and are the slaves of men for purposes of toil. All
the hard bodily labour devolves on them. The Australian savage is idle,
while women painfully dig up the roots on which he lives. An American
Indian, when he has killed a deer, leaves it, and sends a woman to carry
it home. In a state somewhat more advanced, as in Asia, women were
and are the slaves of men for purposes of sensuality. In Europe there
early succeeded a third and milder dominion, secured not by blows, nor
by locks and bars, but by sedulous inculcation on the mind; feelings also
of kindness, and ideas of duty, such as a superior owes to inferiors
under his protection, became more and more involved in the relation.
But it did not, for many ages, become a relation of companionship, even
between unequals. The lives of the two persons were apart. The wife
was part of the furniture of home—of the resting-place to which the
man returned from business or pleasure. His occupations were, as they
still are, among men; his pleasures and excitements also were, for the
most part, among men—among his equals. He was a patriarch and a
despot within four walls, and irresponsible power had its effect, greater
or less according to his disposition, in rendering him domineering,
exacting, self-worshipping, when not capriciously or brutally tyrannical.
But if the moral part of his nature suffered, it was not necessarily so,
in the same degree, with the intellectual or the active portion. He might
have as much vigour of mind and energy of character as his nature
enabled him, and as the circumstances of his times allowed. He might
write the *Paradise Lost,* or win the battle of Marengo. This was the
condition of the Greeks and Romans, and of the moderns until a recent
date. Their relations with their domestic subordinates occupied a mere
corner, though a cherished one, of their lives. Their education as men,
the formation of their character and faculties, depended mainly on a
different class of influences.

It is otherwise now. The progress of improvement has imposed on all
possessors of power, and of domestic power among the rest, an
increased and increasing sense of correlative obligation. No man now
thinks that his wife has no claim upon his actions but such as he may
accord to her. All men of any conscience believe that their duty to their
wives is one of the most binding of their obligations. Nor is it supposed
to consist solely in protection, which, in the present state of civilization,
women have almost ceased to need: it involves care for their happiness
and consideration of their wishes, with a not unfrequent sacrifice of
their own to them. The power of husbands has reached the stage which
the power of kings had arrived at, when opinion did not yet question
the rightfulness of arbitrary power, but in theory, and to a certain
extent in practice, condemned the selfish use of it. This improvement in
the moral sentiments of mankind, and increased sense of the consideration due by every man to those who have no one but himself to look to,
has tended to make home more and more the centre of interest, and
domestic circumstances and society a larger and larger part of life, and
of its pursuits and pleasures. The tendency has been strengthened by

the changes of tastes and manners which have so remarkably distinguished the last two or three generations. In days not far distant, men found their excitement and filled up their time in violent bodily exercises, noisy merriment, and intemperance. They have now, in all but the very poorest classes, lost their inclination for these things, and for the coarser pleasures generally; they have now scarcely any tastes but those which they have in common with women, and, for the first time in the world, men and women are really companions. A most beneficial change, if the companionship were between equals; but being between unequals, it produces, what good observers have noticed, though without perceiving its cause, a progressive deterioration among men in what had hitherto been considered the masculine excellences. Those who are so careful that women should not become men, do not see that men are becoming, what they have decided that women should be—are falling into the feebleness which they have so long cultivated in their companions. Those who are associated in their lives, tend to become assimilated in character. In the present closeness of association between the sexes, men cannot retain manliness unless women acquire it.

There is hardly any situation more unfavourable to the maintenance of elevation of character or force of intellect, than to live in the society, and seek by preference the sympathy, of inferiors in mental endowments. Why is it that we constantly see in life so much of intellectual and moral promise followed by such inadequate performance, but because the aspirant has compared himself only with those below himself, and has not sought improvement or stimulus from measuring himself with his equals or superiors. In the present state of social life, this is becoming the general condition of men. They care less and less for any sympathies, and are less and less under any personal influences, but those of the domestic roof. Not to be misunderstood, it is necessary that we should distinctly disclaim the belief, that women are even now inferior in intellect to men. There are women who are the equals in intellect of any men who ever lived; and comparing ordinary women with ordinary men, the varied though petty details which compose the occupation of most women, call forth probably as much of mental ability, as the uniform routine of the pursuits which are the habitual occupation of a large majority of men. It is from nothing in the faculties themselves, but from the petty subjects and interests on which alone they are exercised, that the companionship of women, such as their present circumstances make them, so often exercises a dissolvent influence on high faculties and aspirations in men. If one of the two has no knowledge and no care about the great ideas and purposes which dignify life, or about any of its practical concerns save personal interests and personal vanities, her conscious, and still more her unconscious influence, will, except in rare cases, reduce to a secondary place in his mind, if not entirely extinguish, those interests which she cannot or does not share.

Our argument here brings us into collision with what may be termed the moderate reformers of the education of women; a sort of persons who cross the path of improvement on all great questions; those who would maintain the old bad principles, mitigating their consequences. These say, that women should be, not slaves, nor servants, but companions; and educated for that office (they do not say that men should be educated to be the companions of women). But since uncultivated women are not suitable companions for cultivated men, and a man who feels interest in things above and beyond the family circle wishes that his companion should sympathize with him in that interest; they therefore say, let women improve their understanding and taste, acquire general knowledge, cultivate poetry, art, even coquet with science, and some stretch their liberality so far as to say, inform themselves on politics; not as pursuits, but sufficiently to feel an interest in the subjects, and to be capable of holding a conversation on them with the husband, or at least of understanding and imbibing his wisdom. Very agreeable to him, no doubt, but unfortunately the reverse of improving. It is from having intellectual communion only with those to whom they can lay down the law, that so few men continue to advance in wisdom beyond the first stages. The most eminent men cease to improve, if they associate only with disciples. When they have overtopped those who immediately surround them, if they wish for further growth, they must seek for others of their own stature to consort with. The mental companionship which is improving, is communion between active minds, not mere contact between an active mind and a passive. This inestimable advantage is even now enjoyed, when a strong-minded man and a strong-minded woman are, by a rare chance, united: and would be had far oftener, if education took the same pains to form strong-minded women which it takes to prevent them from being formed. The modern, and what are regarded as the improved and enlightened modes of education of women, abjure, as far as words go, an education of mere show, and profess to aim at solid instruction, but mean by that expression, superficial information on solid subjects. Except accomplishments, which are now generally regarded as to be taught well if taught at all, nothing is taught to women thoroughly. Small portions only of what it is attempted to teach thoroughly to boys, are the whole of what it is intended or desired to teach to women. What makes intelligent beings is the power of thought: the stimuli which call forth that power are the interest and dignity of thought itself, and a field for its practical application. Both motives are cut off from those who are told from infancy that thought, and all its greater applications, are other people's business, while theirs is to make themselves agreeable to other people. High mental powers in women will be but an exceptional accident, until every career is open to them, and until they, as well as men, are educated for themselves and for the world—not one sex for the other.

In what we have said on the effect of the inferior position of women, combined with the present constitution of married life, we have thus far had in view only the most favourable cases, those in which there is some real approach to that union and blending of characters and of lives, which the theory of the relation contemplates as its ideal standard. But if we look to the great majority of cases, the effect of women's legal inferiority, on the character both of women and of men, must be painted in far darker colours. We do not speak here of the grosser brutalities, nor of the man's power to seize on the woman's earnings, or compel her to live with him against her will. We do not address ourselves to any one who requires to have it proved that these things should be remedied. We suppose average cases, in which there is neither complete union nor complete disunion of feelings and character; and we affirm that in such cases the influence of the dependence on the woman's side, is demoralizing to the character of both.

The common opinion is, that whatever may be the case with the intellectual, the moral influence of women over men is almost salutary. It is, we are often told, the great counteractive of selfishness. However the case may be as to personal influence, the influence of the position tends eminently to promote selfishness. The most insignificant of men, the man who can obtain influence or consideration nowhere else, finds one place where he is chief and head. There is one person, often greatly his superior in understanding, who is obliged to consult him, and whom he is not obliged to consult. He is judge, magistrate, ruler, over their joint concerns; arbiter of all differences between them. The justice or conscience to which her appeal must be made, is his justice and conscience: it is his to hold the balance and adjust the scales between his own claims or wishes and those of another. His is now the only tribunal, in civilized life, in which the same person is judge and party. A generous mind, in such a situation, makes the balance incline against its own side, and gives the other not less, but more, than a fair equality; and thus the weaker side may be enabled to turn the very fact of dependence into an instrument of power, and in default of justice, take an ungenerous advantage of generosity; rendering the unjust power, to those who make an unselfish use of it, a torment and a burthen. But how is it when average men are invested with this power, without reciprocity and without responsibility? Give such a man the idea that he is first in law and in opinion—that to will is his part, and hers to submit; it is absurd to suppose that this idea merely glides over his mind, without sinking into it, or having any effect on his feelings and practice. The propensity to make himself the first object of consideration, and others at most the second, is not so rare as to be wanting where everything seems purposely arranged for encouraging its indulgence. If there is any self-will in the man, he becomes either the conscious or unconscious despot of his household. The wife, indeed, often succeeds in gaining her objects, but it is by some of the many various forms of indirectness and management.

Thus the position is corrupting equally to both; in the one it produces the vices of power, in the other those of artifice. Women, in their present physical and moral state, having stronger impulses, would naturally be franker and more direct than men; yet all the old saws and traditions represent them as artful and dissembling. Why? Because their only way to their objects is by indirect paths. In all countries where women have strong wishes and active minds, this consequence is inevitable: and if it is less conspicuous in England than in some other places, it is because Englishwomen, saving occasional exceptions, have ceased to have either strong wishes or active minds.

We are not now speaking of cases in which there is anything deserving the name of strong affection on both sides. That, where it exists, is too powerful a principle not to modify greatly the bad influences of the situation; it seldom, however, destroys them entirely. Much oftener the bad influences are too strong for the affection, and destroy it. The highest order of durable and happy attachments would be a hundred times more frequent than they are, if the affection which the two sexes sought from one another were that genuine friendship, which only exists between equals in privileges as in faculties. But with regard to what is commonly called affection in married life—the habitual and almost mechanical feeling of kindliness, and pleasure in each other's society, which generally grows up between persons who constantly live together, unless there is actual dislike—there is nothing in this to contradict or qualify the mischievous influence of the unequal relation. Such feelings often exist between a sultan and his favourites, between a master and his servants; they are merely examples of the pliability of human nature, which accommodates itself in some degree even to the worst circumstances, and the commonest natures always the most easily.

With respect to the influence personally exercised by women over men, it, no doubt, renders them less harsh and brutal; in ruder times, it was often the only softening influence to which they were accessible. But the assertion, that the wife's influence renders the man less selfish, contains, as things now are, fully as much error as truth. Selfishness towards the wife herself, and towards those in whom she is interested, the children, though favoured by her dependence, the wife's influence, no doubt, tends to counteract. But the general effect on him of her character, so long as her interests are concentrated in the family, tends but to substitute for individual selfishness a family selfishness, wearing an amiable guise, and putting on the mask of duty. How rarely is the wife's influence on the side of public virtue; how rarely does it do otherwise than discourage any effort of principle by which the private interests or worldly vanities of the family can be expected to suffer. Public spirit, sense of duty towards the public good, is of all virtues, as women are now educated and situated, the most rarely to be found among them; they have seldom even, what in men is often a partial substitute for public spirit, a sense of personal honour connected with any public duty. Many a man, whom no money or personal flattery would have bought, has bartered his political opinions against a title or invitations for his wife; and a still greater number are made mere hunters after the puerile vanities of society, because their wives value them. As for opinions; in Catholic countries, the wife's influence is another name for that of the priest; he gives her, in the hopes and emotions connected with a future life, a consolation for the sufferings and disappointments which are her ordinary lot in this. Elsewhere, her weight is thrown into the scale either of the most commonplace, or of the most outwardly prosperous opinions: either those by which censure will be escaped, or by which worldly advancement is likeliest to be procured. In England, the wife's influence is usually on the illiberal and anti-popular side: this is generally the gaining side for personal interest and vanity; and what to her is the democracy or liberalism in which she has no part—which leaves her the Pariah it found her? The man himself, when he marries, usually declines into Conservatism; begins to sympathize with the holders of power, more than with its victims, and thinks it his part to be on the side of authority. As to mental progress, except those vulgar attainments by which vanity or ambition are promoted, there is generally an end to it in a man who marries a woman mentally his inferior; unless, indeed, he is unhappy in marriage, or becomes indifferent. From a man of twenty-five or thirty, after he is married, an experienced observer seldom expects any further progress in mind or feelings. It is rare that the progress already made is maintained. Any spark of the *mens divinior* which might otherwise have spread and become a flame, seldom survives for any length of time unextinguished. For a mind which learns to be satisfied with what it already is—which does not incessantly look forward to a degree of improvement not yet reached—becomes relaxed, self-indulgent, and loses the spring and the tension which maintain it even at the point already attained. And there is no fact in human nature to which experience bears more invariable testimony than to this—that all social or sympathetic influences which do not raise up, pull down; if they do not tend to stimulate and exalt the mind, they tend to vulgarize it.

For the interest, therefore, not only of women but of men, and of human improvement in the widest sense, the emancipation of women, which the modern world often boasts of having effected, and for which credit is sometimes given to civilization, and sometimes to Christianity, cannot stop where it is. If it were either necessary or just that one portion of mankind should remain mentally and spiritually only half developed, the development of the other portion ought to have been made, as far as possible, independent of their influence. Instead of this, they have become the most intimate, and it may now be said, the only intimate associates of those to whom yet they are sedulously kept inferior; and have been raised just high enough to drag the others down to themselves.

We have left behind a host of vulgar objections, either as not worthy of an answer, or as answered by the general course of our remarks. A few words, however, must be said on one plea, which in England is made much use of for giving an unselfish air to the upholding of selfish privileges, and which, with unobserving, unreflecting people, passes for much more than it is worth. Women, it is said, do not desire—do not seek, what is called their emancipation. On the contrary, they generally disown such claims when made in their behalf, and fall with *acharnement* upon any one of themselves who identifies herself with their common cause.

Supposing the fact to be true in the fullest extent ever asserted, if it proves that European women ought to remain as they are, it proves exactly the same with respect to Asiatic women; for they too, instead of murmuring at their seclusion, and at the restraint imposed upon them, pride themselves on it, and are astonished at the effrontery of women who receive visits from male acquaintances, and are seen in the streets unveiled. Habits of submission make men as well as women servile-minded. The vast population of Asia do not desire or value, probably would not accept, political liberty, nor the savages of the forest, civilization; which does not prove that either of those things is undesirable for them, or that they will not, at some future time, enjoy it. Custom hardens human beings to any kind of degradation, by deadening the part of their nature which would resist it. And the case of women is, in this respect, even a peculiar one, for no other inferior caste that we have heard of have been taught to regard their degrada-tion as their honour. The argument, however, implies a secret con-sciousness that the alleged preference of women for their dependent state is merely apparent, and arises from their being allowed no choice; for if the preference be natural, there can be no necessity for enforcing it by law. To make laws compelling people to follow their inclination, has not hitherto been thought necessary by any legislator. The plea that women do not desire any change, is the same that has been urged, times out of mind, against the proposal of abolishing any social evil— "there is no complaint"; which is generally not true, and when true, only so because there is not that hope of success, without which com-plaint seldom makes itself audible to unwilling ears. How does the objector know that women do not desire equality and freedom? He never knew a woman who did not, or would not, desire it for herself individually. It would be very simple to suppose, that if they do desire it they will say so. Their position is like that of the tenants or labourers who vote against their own political interests to please their landlords or employers; with the unique addition, that submission is inculcated on them from childhood, as the peculiar attraction and grace of their char-acter. They are taught to think, that to repel actively even an admitted injustice done to themselves, is somewhat unfeminine, and had better be left to some male friend or protector. To be accused of rebelling against anything which admits of being called an ordinance of society, they are taught to regard as an imputation of a serious offence, to say the least, against the proprieties of their sex. It requires unusual moral courage as well as disinterestedness in a woman, to express opinions favourable to women's enfranchisement, until, at least, there is some prospect of obtaining it. The comfort of her individual life, and her social consideration, usually depend on the good-will of those who hold the undue power; and to possessors of power any complaint, however bitter, of the misuse of it, is a less flagrant act of insubordination than to protest against the power itself. The professions of women in this matter remind us of the State offenders of old, who, on the point of execution, used to protest their love and devotion to the sovereign by whose unjust mandate they suffered. Griselda herself might be matched from the speeches put by Shakespeare into the mouths of male victims of kingly caprice and tyranny: the Duke of Buckingham, for example, in *Henry the Eighth,* and even Wolsey. The literary class of women, especially in England, are ostentatious in disclaiming the desire for equality or citizenship, and proclaiming their complete satisfaction with the place which society assigns to them; exercising in this, as in many other respects, a most noxious influence over the feelings and opinions of men, who unsuspectingly accept the servilities of toadyism as concessions to the force of truth, not considering that it is the personal interest of these women to profess whatever opinions they expect will be agreeable to men. It is not among men of talent, sprung from the people, and patronized and flattered by the aristocracy, that we look for the leaders of a democratic movement. Successful literary women are just as unlikely to prefer the cause of women to their own social consideration. They depend on men's opinion for their literary as well as for their feminine successes; and such is their bad opinion of men, that they believe there is not more than one in ten thousand who does not dislike and fear strength, sincerity, or high spirit in a woman. They are therefore anxious to earn pardon and toleration for whatever of these qualities their writings may exhibit on other subjects, by a studied display of submission on this: that they may give no occasion for vulgar men to say (what nothing will prevent vulgar men from saying), that learning makes women unfeminine, and that literary ladies are likely to be bad wives.

But enough of this: especially as the fact which affords the occasion for this notice, makes it impossible any longer to assert the universal acquiescence of women (saving individual exceptions) in their dependent condition. In the United States, at least, there are women, seemingly numerous, and now organized for action on the public mind, who demand equality in the fullest acceptation of the word, and demand it by a straightforward appeal to men's sense of justice, not plead for it with a timid deprecation of their displeasure.

Like other popular movements, however, this may be seriously retarded by the blunders of its adherents. Tried by the ordinary standard of public meetings, the speeches at the Convention are remarkable for the preponderance of the rational over the declamatory element; but there are some exceptions; and things to which it is impossible to attach any rational meaning, have found their way into the resolutions. Thus, the resolution which sets forth the claims made in behalf of women, after claiming equality in education, in industrial pursuits, and in political rights, enumerates as a fourth head of demand something under the name of "social and spiritual union," and "a medium of expressing the highest moral and spiritual views of justice," with other similar verbiage, serving only to mar the simplicity and rationality of the other demands; resembling those who would weakly attempt to combine nominal equality between men and women, with enforced distinctions in their privileges and functions. What is wanted for women is equal rights, equal admission to all social privileges; not a position apart, a sort of sentimental priesthood. To this, the only just and rational principle, both the resolutions and the speeches, for the most part, adhere. They contain so little which is akin to the nonsensical paragraph in question, that we suspect it not to be the work of the same hands as most of the other resolutions. The strength of the cause lies in the support of those who are influenced by reason and principle; and to attempt to recommend it by sentimentalities, absurd in reason, and inconsistent with the principle on which the movement is founded, is to place a good cause on a level with a bad one.

There are indications that the example of America will be followed on this side of the Atlantic; and the first step has been taken in that part of England where every serious movement in the direction of political progress has its commencement—the manufacturing districts of the North. On the 13th of February 1851, a petition of women, agreed to by a public meeting at Sheffield, and claiming the elective franchise, was presented to the House of Lords by the Earl of Carlisle.

THE WOMAN'S BIBLE

Elizabeth Cady Stanton, et al.

Mary Wollstonecraft's and Harriet Taylor Mill's treatises on feminism were products of astute observations and reasoning alone; the writings of Elizabeth Cady Stanton[1] (1815–1902) result from her daily struggle to build a women's movement in America—a struggle she participated in for over fifty years. She was the archetype of the radical feminist who believes that all women are oppressed:

When the majority of women are seemingly happy, it is natural to suppose that the discontent of the minority is the result of their unfortunate individual idiosyncrasies, and not of adverse influences in established conditions. But the history of the world shows that the vast majority, in every generation, passively accept the conditions into which they are born, while those who demand larger

Elizabeth Cady Stanton, *et al., The Woman's Bible* (New York: European Publishing Company, 1895), Preface, pp. 5–6; Introduction, pp. 7, 9, 10; Chapter 1, pp. 14–19; Chapter 7, pp. 45–50; Chapter 2, pp. 73–74, 82–83. The heads in the text were part and chapter titles in the original reading.

[1] In 1880, Elizabeth Cady Stanton, Susan B. Anthony, and Matilda Joslyn Gage began to edit the *History of Woman Suffrage.* All six volumes were not completed until 1922. Stanton also coedited (with Anthony) the journal *Revolution* in 1869–1870; organized the writing of *The Woman's Bible* in the 1890s, and wrote her autobiography *Eighty Years and More.*

liberties are ever a small, ostracized minority, whose claims are ridiculed and ignored. From our standpoint we would honor any Chinese woman who claimed the right to her feet and powers of locomotion; the Hindoo widows who refused to ascend the funeral pyre of their husbands; the Turkish women who threw off their veils and left the harem . . . Why not equally honor the intelligent minority of American women who protest against the artificial disabilities by which their freedom is limited and their development arrested? That only a few, under any circumstances, protest against the injustice of long-established laws and customs, does not disprove the fact of the oppressions, while the satisfaction of the many, if real, only proves their apathy and deeper degradation.[2]

Unwilling to place female liberation second to other demands for social equality, she opposed the ratification of the Fourteenth Amendment:

It is all very well for the privileged order to look down and complacently tell us, 'This is the negro's hour; do not clog his way; do not embarrass the Republican party with any new issue; be generous and magnanimous; the negro once safe, the woman comes next.' Now, if our prayer involved a new set of measures, or a new train of thought, it would be cruel to tax 'white male citizens' with even two simple questions at a time; but the disenfranchised all make the same demand, and the same logic and justice that secures suffrage to one class gives it to all.[3]

She also advocated female sexual liberation and attacked the marriage institution: "How can [woman] calmly contemplate the barbarous code of laws which govern her civil and political existence? How can she devoutly subscribe to a theology which makes her the conscientious victim of another's will, forever subject to the triple bondage of the man, the priest, and the law?"[4]

Elizabeth Cady Stanton was born in New York State; her father was a prosperous judge and a Congressman. In 1840 she married abolitionist leader Henry B. Stanton and the same year accompanied him to an antislavery convention in London. There she met Lucretia Mott, president of the Boston-based Female Anti-Slavery Association, and together they planned the first woman's rights convention, the Seneca Falls Convention of 1848.

Elizabeth Cady Stanton supported unpopular causes such as the candidacy of socialist and free-love advocate Victoria Woodhull for President of the United States in 1872, organized a group of women to systematically refute the Church's derogatory attitude toward women, and consistently supported women who chose not to marry because she understood that female liberation involved changing established systems of human relationships, not simply winning the right to vote.

Although Stanton eventually became the first president of the conservative NAWSA (the result of a merger between NWSA and AWSA) she remained adamant on her views of marriage and religion. Between 1895 and 1898 she

[2] *Eighty Years and More*, E. C. Stanton's autobiography edited by Theodore Stanton and Harriet Stanton Blatch (New York: 1922), Vol. 1, pp. 269–270.

[3] *History of Woman Suffrage*, Vol. 2, pp. 94–95. (From a letter dated December 26, 1865, New York).

[4] From a letter to Lucy Stone, 1856. As reprinted in *History of Woman Suffrage, op. cit.,* Vol. 1.

published the feminist critique of the Bible, *The Woman's Bible* (the NAWSA convention of 1896 passed a resolution explicitly disavowing any responsibility for it).

Stanton, together with Susan Anthony, stand as models of courageous and dedicated feminism to many women today. When, in December, 1969, Diana Crowthers, Shulamith Firestone, Ann Koedt and Cellestine Ware set up the New York Radical Feminists (NYRF), an organization of many small brigades or cells that believes "the eradication of women's oppression requires a single-minded concentration on the issues that determine the lives of women"[5] and "feminism is the only truly radical political cause now in existence,"[6] they, the original founding unit, chose to call themselves the Stanton-Anthony Brigade.

Preface

So many letters are daily received asking questions about the Woman's Bible,—as to the extent of the revision, and the standpoint from which it will be conducted—that it seems best, though every detail is not as yet matured, to state the plan, as concisely as possible, upon which those who have been in consultation during the summer, propose to do the work.

I. The object is to revise only those texts and chapters directly referring to women, and those also in which women are made prominent by exclusion. As all such passages combined form but one-tenth of the Scriptures, the undertaking will not be so laborious as, at the first thought, one would imagine. These texts, with the commentaries, can easily be compressed into a duodecimo volume of about four hundred pages.

II. The commentaries will be of a threefold character, the writers in the different branches being selected according to their special aptitude for the work:

1. Two or three Greek and Hebrew scholars will devote themselves to the translation and the meaning of particular words and texts in the original.

2. Others will devote themselves to Biblical history, old manuscripts, to the new version, and to the latest theories as to the occult meaning of certain texts and parables.

3. For the commentaries on the plain English version a committee of some thirty members has been formed. These are women of earnestness and liberal ideas, quick to see the real purport of the Bible as regards their sex. Among them the various books of the Old and New Testament will be distributed for comment.

III. There will be two or more editors to bring the work of the various committees into one consistent whole.

IV. The completed work will be submitted to an advisory committee

---

[5] Cellestine Ware, *Woman Power: The Movement for Women's Liberation* (New York: Tower Books, 1970).

[6] *Ibid.*, p. 107.

assembled at some central point, as London, New York, or Chicago, to sit in final judgment on "The Woman's Bible."

As to the manner of doing the practical work:

Those who have been engaged this summer have adopted the following plan, which may be suggestive to new members of the committee. Each person purchased two Bibles, ran through them from Genesis to Revelations, marking all the texts that concerned women. The passages were cut out, and pasted in a blank book, and the commentaries then written underneath.

Those not having time to read all the books can confine their labors to the particular ones they propose to review.

It is thought best to publish the different parts as soon as prepared so that the Committee may have all in print in a compact form before the final revision.

August 1st, 1895.   E.C.S.
[Elizabeth Cady Stanton]

Introduction

From the inauguration of the movement for woman's emancipation the Bible has been used to hold her in the "divinely ordained sphere," prescribed in the Old and New Testaments.

The canon and civil law; church and state; priests and legislators; all political parties and religious denominations have alike taught that woman was made after man, of man, and for man, an inferior being, subject to man. Creeds, codes, Scriptures and statutes, are all based on this idea. The fashions, forms, ceremonies and customs of society, church ordinances and discipline all grow out of this idea.

Of the old English common law, responsible for woman's civil and political status, Lord Brougham said, "it is a disgrace to the civilization and Christianity of the Nineteenth Century." Of the canon law, which is responsible for woman's status in the church, Charles Kingsley said, "this will never be a good world for women until the last remnant of the canon law is swept from the face of the earth."

The Bible teaches that woman brought sin and death into the world, that she precipitated the fall of the race, that she was arraigned before the judgment seat of Heaven, tried, condemned and sentenced. Marriage for her was to be a condition of bondage, maternity a period of suffering and anguish, and in silence and subjection, she was to play the role of a dependent on man's bounty for all her material wants, and for all the information she might desire on the vital questions of the hour, she was commanded to ask her husband at home. Here is the Bible position of woman briefly summed up.

• • •

Listening to the varied opinions of women, I have long thought it would be interesting and profitable to get them clearly stated in book form.

56

Elizabeth Cady Stanton

To this end six years ago I proposed to a committee of women to issue a Woman's Bible, that we might have women's commentaries on women's position in the Old and New Testaments. It was agreed on by several leading women in England and America and the work was begun, but from various causes it has been delayed, until now the idea is received with renewed enthusiasm, and a large committee has been formed, and we hope to complete the work within a year.

Those who have undertaken the labor are desirous to have some Hebrew and Greek scholars, versed in Biblical criticism, to gild our pages with their learning. Several distinguished women have been urged to do so, but they are afraid that their high reputation and scholarly attainments might be compromised by taking part in an enterprise that for a time may prove very unpopular. Hence we may not be able to get help from that class.

Others fear that they might compromise their evangelical faith by affiliating with those of more liberal views, who do not regard the Bible as the "Word of God," but like any other book, to be judged by its merits. If the Bible teaches the equality of Woman, why does the church refuse to ordain women to preach the gospel, to fill the offices of deacons and elders, and to administer the Sacraments, or to admit them as delegates to the Synods, General Assemblies and Conferences of the different denominations? They have never yet invited a woman to join one of their Revising Committees, nor tried to mitigate the sentence pronounced on her by changing one count in the indictment served on her in Paradise.

The large number of letters received, highly appreciative of the undertaking, is very encouraging to those who have inaugurated the movement, and indicate a growing self-respect and self-assertion in the women of this generation. But we have the usual array of objections to meet and answer. One correspondent conjures us to suspend the work, as it is "ridiculous" for "women to attempt the revision of the Scriptures." I wonder if any man wrote to the late revising committee of Divines to stop their work on the ground that it was ridiculous for men to revise the Bible. Why is it more ridiculous for women to protest against her present status in the Old and New Testament, in the ordinances and discipline of the church, than in the statutes and constitution of the state? Why is it more ridiculous to arraign ecclesiastics for their false teaching and acts of injustice to women, than members of Congress and the House of Commons? Why is it more audacious to review Moses than Blackstone, the Jewish code of laws, than the English system of jurisprudence? Women have compelled their legislators in every state in this Union to so modify their statutes for women that the old common law is now almost a dead letter. Why not compel Bishops and Revising Committees to modify their creeds and dogmas? Forty years ago it seemed as ridiculous to timid, time-serving and retrograde folk for women to demand an expurgated edition of the laws, as it now does to demand an expurgated edition of the Liturgies and the Scriptures. Come, come, my conservative friend, wipe the dew off your spectacles, and see that the world is moving. Whatever your views may be as to the importance of the proposed work, your political and social degradation are but an outgrowth of your status in the Bible. When you express your aversion, based on a blind feeling of reverence in which reason has no control, to the revision of the Scriptures, you do but echo Cowper, who, when asked to read Paine's "Rights of Man," exclaimed, "No man shall convince me that I am improperly governed while I *feel* the contrary."

· · ·

E.C.S.

The Book of Genesis

Chapter I

Genesis i: 26, 27, 28.
  26 And God said, Let us make man in our image, after our likeness: and let them have dominion over the fish of the sea, and over the fowl of the air, and over the cattle, and over all the earth, and over every creeping thing that creepeth upon the earth.
  27 So God created man in his *own* image, in the image of God created he him; male and female created he them.
  28 And God blessed them, and God said unto them, Be fruitful, and multiply, and replenish the earth, and subdue it; and have dominion over the fish of the sea, and over the fowl of the air, and over every living thing that moveth upon the earth.

Here is the sacred historian's first account of the advent of woman; a simultaneous creation of both sexes, in the image of God. It is evident from the language that there was consultation in the Godhead, and that the masculine and feminine elements were equally represented. Scott in his commentaries says, "this consultation of the Gods is the origin of the doctrine of the trinity." But instead of three male personages, as generally represented, a Heavenly Father, Mother, and Son would seem more rational.

58

The first step in the elevation of woman to her true position, as an equal factor in human progress, is the cultivation of the religious sentiment in regard to her dignity and equality, the recognition by the rising generation of an ideal Heavenly Mother, to whom their prayers should be addressed, as well as to a Father.

If language has any meaning, we have in these texts a plain declaration of the existence of the feminine element in the Godhead, equal in power and glory with the masculine. The Heavenly Mother and Father! "God created man in his *own image, male and female.*" Thus Scripture, as well as science and philosophy, declares the eternity and equality of sex—the philosophical fact, without which there could have been no perpetuation of creation, no growth or development in the animal, vegetable, or mineral kingdoms, no awakening nor progressing in the world of thought. The masculine and feminine elements, exactly equal and balancing each other, are as essential to the maintenance of the equilibrium of the universe as positive and negative electricity, the centripetal forces, the laws of attraction which bind together all we know of this planet whereon we dwell and of the system in which we revolve.

In the great work of creation the crowning glory was realized, when man and woman were evolved on the sixth day, the masculine and feminine forces in the image of God, that must have existed eternally, in all forms of matter and mind. All the persons in the Godhead are represented in the Elohim the divine plurality taking counsel in regard to this last and highest form of life. Who were the members of this high council, and were they a duality or a trinity? Verse 27 declares the image of God male and female. How then is it possible to make woman an afterthought? We find in verses 5-16 the pronoun "he" used. Should it not in harmony with verse 26 be "they," a dual pronoun? We may attribute this to the same cause as the use of "his" in verse 11 instead of "it." The fruit tree yielding fruit after "his" kind instead of after "its" kind. The paucity of a language may give rise to many misunderstandings.

The above texts plainly show the simultaneous creation of man and woman, and their equal importance in the development of the race. All those theories based on the assumption that man was prior in the creation, have no foundation in Scripture.

As to woman's subjection, on which both the canon and the civil law delight to dwell, it is important to note that equal dominion is given to woman over every living thing, but not one word is said giving man dominion over woman.

Here is the first title deed to this green earth giving alike to the sons and daughters of God. No lesson of woman's subjection can be fairly drawn from the first chapter of the Old Testament.

E.C.S.

The most important thing for a woman to note, in reading Genesis, is that that portion which is now divided into "the first three chapters" (there was no such division until about five centuries ago), contains two entirely separate, and very contradictory, stories of creation, written by two different, but equally anonymous, authors. No Christian theologian of to-day, with any pretensions to scholarship, claims that Genesis was written by Moses. As was long ago pointed out, the Bible itself declares that all the books the Jews originally possessed were burned in the destruction of Jerusalem, about 588 B. C., at the time the people were taken to Babylonia as slaves to the Assyrians, (see II Esdras, ch. xiv, v. 21, Apocrypha). Not until about 247 B. C. (some theologians say 226 and others 169 B. C.) is there any record of a collection of literature in the re-built Jerusalem, and, then, the anonymous writer of II Maccabees briefly mentions that some Nehemiah "gathered together the acts of the kings and the prophets and those of David" when "founding a library" for use in Jerusalem. But the earliest mention anywhere in the Bible of a book that might have corresponded to Genesis is made by an apocryphal writer, who says that *Ezra* wrote "all that hath been done in the world since the beginning," after the Jews returned from Babylon, under his leadership, about 450 B. C. (see II Esdras, ch. xiv, v. 22, of the Apocrypha).

When it is remembered that the Jewish books were written on rolls of leather, without much attention to vowel points and with no division into verses or chapters, by uncritical copyists, who altered passages greatly, and did not always even pretend to understand what they were copying, then the reader of Genesis begins to put herself in position to understand how it can be contradictory. Great as were the liberties which the Jews took with Genesis, those of the English translators, however, greatly surpassed them.

The first chapter of Genesis, for instance, in Hebrew, tells us, in verses one and two, "As to origin, created the gods (Elohim) these skies (or air or clouds) and this earth . . . And a wind moved upon the face of the waters." Here we have the opening of a polytheistic fable of creation, but, so strongly convinced were the English translators that the ancient Hebrews must have been originally monotheistic that they rendered the above, as follows: "In the beginning God created the heaven and the earth. . . . And the spirit of God (!) moved upon the face of the waters."

It is now generally conceded that some one (nobody pretends to know who) at some time (nobody pretends to know exactly when), copied two creation myths on the same leather roll, one immediately following the other. About one hundred years ago, it was discovered by Dr. Astruc, of France, that from Genesis ch. i, v. 1 to Genesis ch. ii, v. 4, is given one complete account of creation, by an author who always used the term "the gods" (*Elohim*), in speaking of the fashioning of the universe, mentioning it altogether thirty-four times, while, in Genesis ch. ii, v. 4, to the end of chapter iii, we have a totally different narrative, by an author of unmistakably different style, who uses the term "Iahveh of the gods" twenty times, but "Elohim" only three times. The first author, evidently, attributes creation to a council of gods, acting in concert, and seems never to have heard of Iahveh. The second attributes creation to Iahveh, a tribal god of ancient Israel, but represents Iahveh as one of two or more gods, conferring with them (in Genesis ch. xiii, v. 22) as to the danger of man's acquiring immortality.

Modern theologians have, for convenience sake, entitled these two fables, respectively, the Elohistic and the Iahoistic stories. They differ, not only in the point I have mentioned above, but in the order of the "creative acts"; in regard to the mutual attitude of man and woman, and in regard to human freedom from prohibitions imposed by deity. In order to exhibit their striking contradictions, I will place them in parallel columns:

Elohistic.	Iahoistic.
Order of Creation: First—Water. Second—Land. Third—Vegetation. Fourth—Animals. Fifth—Mankind; male and female.	Order of Creation: First—Land. Second—Water. Third—Male Man, only. Fourth—Vegetation. Fifth—Animals. Sixth—Woman.
In this story male and female man are created simultaneously, both alike, in the image of the gods, *after* all animals have been called into existence.	In this story male man is sculptured out of clay, *before* any animals are created, and *before* female man has been constructed.
Here, joint dominion over the earth is given to woman and man, without limit or prohibition.	Here, woman is punished with subjection to man for breaking a prohibitory law.
Everything, without exception, is pronounced "very good."	There is a tree of evil, whose fruit, is said by Iahveh to cause sudden death, but which does not do so, as Adam lived 930 years after eating it.
Man and woman are told that "every plant bearing seed upon the face of the earth and *every tree*. . . . "To you it shall be for meat." They are thus given perfect freedom.	Man is told there is *one tree* of which he must not eat, "for in the day thou eatest thereof, thou shalt surely die."
Man and woman are given special dominion over all the animals— "every creeping thing that creepeth upon the earth."	An animal, a "creeping thing," is given dominion over man and woman, and proves himself more truthful than Iahveh Elohim. (Compare Genesis chapter ii, verse 17, with chapter iii, verses 4 and 22.)

61

Now as it is manifest that both of these stories cannot be true; intelligent women, who feel bound to give the preference to either, may decide according to their own judgment of which is more worthy of an intelligent woman's acceptance. Paul's rule is a good one in this dilemma, "Prove all things: hold fast to that which is good." My own opinion is that the second story was manipulated by some Jew, in an endeavor to give "heavenly authority" for requiring a woman to obey the man she married. In a work which I am now completing, I give some facts concerning ancient Israelitish history, which will be of peculiar interest to those who wish to understand the origin of woman's subjection.

E.B.D.
[Ellen Battelle Dietrick]

Many orientalists and students of theology have maintained that the consultation of the Gods here described is proof that the Hebrews were in early days polytheists—Scott's supposition that this is the origin of the Trinity has no foundation in fact, as the beginning of that conception is to be found in the earliest of all known religious nature worship. The acknowledgment of the dual principle, masculine and feminine, is much more probably the explanation of the expressions here used.

In the detailed description of creation we find a gradually ascending series. Creeping things, "great sea monsters," (chap. I, v. 21, literal translation). "Every bird of wing," cattle and living things of the earth, the fish of the sea and the "birds of the heavens," then man, and last and crowning glory of the whole, woman.

It cannot be maintained that woman was inferior to man even if, as asserted in chapter ii, she was created after him without at once admitting that man is inferior to the creeping things, because created after them.

L. D. B.
[Lillie Devereux Blake]

. . .

Chapter VII

Genesis xxiv.

37 And my master made me swear, saying, Thou shalt not take a wife to my son of the daughters of the Canaanites in whose land I dwell.

38 But thou shalt go unto my father's house, and to my kindred, and take a wife unto my son.

39 And I said unto my master, Peradventure the woman will not follow me.

40 And he said unto me, The Lord, before whom I walk, will send his angel with thee, and prosper thy way; and thou shalt take a wife for my son of my kindred, and of my father's house:

42 And I came this day unto the well, and said, O Lord of my master Abraham, if now thou do prosper my way which I go:

43 Behold, I stand by the well of water; and it shall come to pass, that when the virgin cometh to draw *water,* and I say to her, Give me, I pray thee, a little water of thy pitcher to drink:

44 And she say to me, Both drink thou, and *I* will also draw for thy camels: *let* the same *be* the woman whom the Lord hath appointed out for my master's son.

45 And before I had done speaking in mine heart behold Rebekah came forth with her pitcher on her shoulder; and she went down unto the well, and drew *water*: and I said unto her; Let me drink, I pray thee.

46 And she made haste, and let down her pitcher from her *shoulder,* and said, Drink, and I will give thy camels drink also: so I drank, and she made the camels drink also.

47 And I asked her, and said, Whose daughter *art* thou? And she said, The daughter of Bethuel Nahor's son, whom Malcah bare unto him: and I put the earring upon her face, and the bracelets upon her hands.

49 And now, if ye will deal kindly and truly with my master, tell me: and if not, tell me; that I may turn to the right hand, or to the left.

50 Then Laban and Bethuel answered and said: The thing proceedeth from the Lord: we cannot speak unto thee bad or good.

51 Behold, Rebekah *is* before thee; take *her,* and go, and let her be thy master's son's wife, as the Lord hath spoken.

53 And the servant brought forth jewels of silver, and jewels of gold, and raiment, and gave *them* to Rebekah; he gave also to her brother and to her mother precious things.

56 And he said unto them, Hinder me not, seeing the Lord hath prospered my way; send me away that I may go to my master.

57 And they said, we will call the damsel and inquire at her mouth.

58 And they called Rebekah, and said unto her, Wilt thou go with this man? And she said, I will go.

59 And they sent away Rebekah their sister, and her nurse and Abraham's servant, and his men.

61 And Rebekah arose, and her damsels, and they rode upon the camels, and followed the man: and the servant took Rebekah and went his way.

63 And Isaac went out to meditate in the field at the eventide: and he lifted up his eyes, and saw, and behold, the camels *were* coming.

64 And Rebekah lifted up her eyes, and when she saw Isaac she lighted off the camel.

65 For she *had* said unto the servant, What man *is* this that walketh in the field to meet us? And the servant *had* said, It *is* my master: therefore she took a veil, and covered herself.

66 And the servant told Isaac all things that he had done.

67 And Isaac brought her into his mother Sarah's tent, and took Rebekah, and she became his wife; and he loved her: and Isaac was comforted after his mother's *death.*

Here is the first account we have of a Jewish courtship. The women seem quite as resigned to the custom of "being taken" as the men "to take." Outside parties could no doubt in most cases make more judicious selections of partners, than young folks themselves under the glamour of their ideals. Altogether the marriage of Isaac, though rather prosaic, has a touch of the romantic.

It has furnished the subject for some charming pictures, that decorate the galleries in the old world and the new. "Rebekah at the well," has been immortalized both on canvas and in marble. Women as milk-maids and drawers of water, with pails and pitchers on their heads, are always artistic, and far more attractive to men than those with votes in their hands at the polling booths, or as queens, ruling over the destinies of nations.

In fact, as soon as man left Paradise, he began by degrees to roll off of his own shoulders all he could of his curse, and place it on woman. Why did not Laban and Bethuel draw the water for the household and the cattle. Scott says that Eliezer had attendants with him who might have saved Rebekah the labor of drawing water for ten camels, but he would not interfere, as he wished to see whether she possessed the virtues of industry, affability and cheerfulness in being serviceable and hospitable.

It was certainly a good test of her patience and humility to draw water for an hour, with a dozen men looking on at their ease, and none offering help. The Rebekahs of 1895 would have promptly summoned the spectators to share their labors, even at the risk of sacrificing a desirable matrimonial alliance. The virtue of self-sacrifice has its wise limitations. Though it is most commendable to serve our fellow-beings, yet woman's first duty is to herself, to develop all her own powers and possibilities, that she may better guide and serve the next generation.

It is refreshing to find in the fifty-eighth verse that Rebekah was really supposed to have some personal interest and rights in the betrothal.

The meeting of Isaac and Rebekah in the field at eventide is charming. That sweet restful hour after the sun had gone down, at the end of a long journey from a far-off country. Rebekah must have been in just the mood to appreciate a strong right arm on which to rest, a loving heart to trust, on the threshold of her conjugal life. To see her future lord for the first time, must have been very embarrassing to Rebekah. She no doubt concealed her blushes behind her veil, which Isaac probably raised at the first opportunity, to behold the charms of the bride whom the Lord had chosen for him. As Isaac was forty years old at this time, he probably made a most judicious and affectionate husband.

The 67th verse would be more appropriate to the occasion if the words "took Rebekah" had been omitted, leaving the text to read thus: "And Isaac brought her into his mother's tent, and she became his wife, and he loved her." This verse is remarkable as the first announcement of love on the part of a husband at first sight. We may indulge the hope that he confessed his love to Rebekah, and thus placed their conjugal relations on a more spiritual plane than was usual in those days. The Revising Committees by the infusion of a little sentiment into these ancient manuscripts, might have improved the moral tone of our ancestors' domestic relations, without falsifying the important facts of history. Many ancient writings in both sacred and profane history might be translated into more choice language, to the advantage of the rising generation. What we glean in regard to Rebekah's character in the following chapter shows, she, too, is lacking in a nice sense of honor.

With our ideal of the great first cause, a God of justice, wisdom and truth, the Jewish Lord, guiding and directing that people in all their devious ways, and sanctioning their petty immoralities seems strangely out of place; a very contradictory character, unworthy our love and admiration. The ancient Jewish ideal of Jehovah was not an exalted one.

E. C. S.

This romantic pastoral is most instructive as to the high position which women really held among the people whose religious history is the foundation of our own, and still further substantiates our claim that the Bible does not teach woman's subordination. The fact that Rebekah was drawing water for family use does not indicate lack of dignity in her position, any more than the household tasks performed by Sarah. The wives and daughters of patriarchal families had their maid-servants just as the men of the family had their man-servants, and their position indicates only a division of responsibility. At this period, although queens and princesses were cooks and waiters, kings and princes did not hesitate to reap their own fields and slay their own cattle. We are told that Abraham rushed out to his herd and caught a calf to make a meal for the strangers, and that while he asked Sarah to make the cakes, he turned over the calf to a man servant to prepare for the table. Thus the labor of securing the food fell upon the male sex, while the labor of preparing it was divided between both.

The one supreme virtue among the patriarchs was hospitality, and no matter how many servants a person had it must be the royal service of his own hands that he performed for a guest. In harmony with this spirit Rebekah volunteered to water the thirsty camels of the tired and way-worn travellers. It is not at all likely that, as Mr. Scott suggests, Eliezer waited simply to test Rebekah's amiability. The test which he had asked for was sufficiently answered by her offering the service in the first place, and doubtless it would have been a churlish and ungracious breach of courtesy to have refused the proffered kindness.

That the Jewish women were treated with greater politeness than the daughters of neighboring peoples we may learn from the incident narrated of the daughters of Jethro who, even though their father was high priest of the country were driven away by the shepherds from the wells where they came to water their flocks. Of all outdoor occupations that of watering thirsty animals is, perhaps, the most fascinating, and if the work was harder for Rebekah than for our country maidens who water their animals from the trough well filled by the windmill she had the strength and the will for it, else she would have entrusted the task to some of the damsels of whom we read as her especial servants and who, as such, accompanied her to the land of Canaan.

The whole narrative shows Rebekah's personal freedom and dignity. She was alone at some distance from her family. She was not afraid of the strangers, but greeted them with the self-possession of a queen. The decision whether she would go or stay, was left wholly with herself, and her nurse and servants accompanied her. With grace and modesty she relieved the embarrassment of the situation by getting down from the altitude of the camel when Isaac came to meet her, and by enshrouding herself in a veil she very tactfully gave him an opportunity to do his courting in his own proper person, if he should be pleased to do so after hearing the servant's report.

It has been the judgment of masculine commentators that the veil was a sign of woman's subject condition, but even this may be disputed now that women are looking into history for themselves. The fashion of veiling a prospective bride was common to many nations, but to none where there were brutal ceremonies. The custom was sometimes carried to the extent, as in some parts of Turkey, of keeping the woman wholly covered for eight days previous to marriage, sometimes, as among the Russians, by not only veiling the bride, but putting a curtain between her and the groom at the bridal feast. In all cases the veil seems to have been worn to protect a woman from premature or unwelcome intrusion, and not to indicate her humiliated position. The veil is rather a reflection upon the habits and thoughts of men than a badge of inferiority for women.

How serenely beautiful and chaste appear the marriage customs of the Bible as compared with some that are wholly of man's invention. The Kamchatkan had to find his future wife alone and then fight with her and her female friends until every particle of clothing had been stripped from her and then the ceremony was complete. This may be called the other extreme from the veil. Something akin to this appears among our own kith and kin, so to speak, in modern times. Many instances of marriage *en chemise* are on record in England of quite recent dates, the notion being that if a man married a woman in this garment only he was not liable for any debts which she might previously have contracted. At Whitehaven, England, 1766, a woman stripped herself to her chemise in the church and in that condition stood at the altar and was married.

There is nothing so degrading to the wife in all Oriental customs as our modern common law ruling that the husband owns the wife's clothing. This has been so held times innumerable, and in Connecticut quite recently a husband did not like the gowns his wife bought so he burned them. He was arrested for destruction of property, but his claim was sustained that they were his own so he could not be punished.

As long as woman's condition, outside of the Bible, has been as described by Macaulay when he said: "If there be a word of truth in history, women have been always, and still are over the greater part of the globe, humble companions, playthings, captives, menials, and beasts of burden," it is a comfort to reflect that among the Hebrews, whose records are relied on by the enemies of woman's freedom to teach her subjection, we find women holding the dignified position in the family that was held by Sarah and Rebekah.

C. B. C.
[Clara Bewick Colby]

• • •

The Book of Exodus

Exodus iii.

19 And I am sure that the king of Egypt will not let you go, no, not by a mighty hand.

66

20 And I will stretch out my hand, and smite Egypt with all my wonders which I will do in the midst thereof: and after that he will let you go.

21 And I will give this people favour in the sight of the Egyptians: and it shall come to pass, that, when ye go, ye shall not go empty:

22 But every woman shall borrow of her neighbour, and of her that sojourneth in her house, jewels of silver, and jewels of gold, and raiment: and ye shall put them upon your sons, and upon your daughters; and ye shall spoil the Egyptians.

The role assigned the women, in helping the children of Israel to escape in safety from bondage, is by no means complimentary to their heroism or honesty. To help bear the expenses of the journey, they were instructed to steal all the jewels of silver and gold, and all the rich raiment of the Egyptian ladies. The Lord and Moses no doubt went on the principle that the Israelites had richly earned all in the years of their bondage. This is the position that some of our good abolitionists took, when Africans were escaping from American bondage, that the slaves had the right to seize horses, boats, anything to help them to Canada, to find safety in the shadow of the British lion. Some of our pro-slavery clergymen, who no doubt often read the third chapter of Exodus to their congregations, forgot the advice of Moses, in condemning the abolitionists; as the Americans had stolen the African's body and soul, and kept them in hopeless bondage for generations—they had richly earned whatever they needed to help them to the land of freedom. Stretch the principle of natural rights a little further, and ask the question, why should women, denied all their political rights, obey laws to which they have never given their consent, either by proxy or in person? Our fathers in an inspired moment said, "No just government can be formed without the consent of the governed."

Women have had no voice in the canon law, the catechisms, the church creeds and discipline, and why should they obey the behests of a strictly masculine religion, that places the sex at a disadvantage in all life's emergencies?

Our civil and criminal codes reflect at many points the spirit of the Mosaic. In the criminal code we find no feminine pronouns, as "He," "His," "Him," we are arrested, tried and hung, but singularly enough, we are denied the highest privileges of citizens, because the pronouns "She," "Hers" and "Her," are not found in the constitutions. It is a pertinent question, if women can pay the penalties of their crimes as "He," why may they not enjoy the privileges of citizens as "He"?

E. C. S.

• • •

Exodus xvi.

15 Six days may work be done; but in the seventh *is* the sabbath of rest, holy to the Lord: whosoever doeth *any* work in the sabbath day, he shall surely be put to death.

As the women continued to work and yet seemed to live in the flesh, it may refer to the death of their civil rights, their individuality, as nonentities without souls or personal responsibility.

A critical reading of the ten commandments will show that they are chiefly for men. After purifying themselves by putting aside their wives and soiled clothes, they assembled at the foot of Mount Sinai. We have no hint of the presence of a woman. One commandment speaks of visiting the iniquities of the fathers upon the children. There is an element of justice in this, for to talk of children getting iniquities from their mothers, in a history of males, of fathers and sons, would be as ridiculous as getting them from the clothes they wore.

"Six days shalt thou labor and do all thy work." With the majority of women this is impossible. Men of all classes can make the Sabbath a day of rest, at least a change of employment, but for women the same monotonous duties must be performed. In the homes of the rich and poor alike, most women cook, clean, and take care of children from morning till night. Men must have good dinners Sundays above all other days, as then they have plenty of time in which to eat. If the first born male child lifts up his voice at the midnight hour, the female attendant takes heed to his discontent; if in the early morning at the cock crowing, or the eventide, she is there. They who watch and guard the infancy of men are like faithful sentinels, always on duty.

The fifth commandment will take the reader by surprise. It is rather remarkable that the young Hebrews should have been told to honor their mothers, when the whole drift of the teaching thus far has been to throw contempt on the whole sex. In what way could they show their mothers honor? All the laws and customs forbid it. Why should they make any such manifestations? Scientists claim that the father gives the life, the spirit, the soul, all there is of most value in existence. Why honor the mother, for giving the mere covering of flesh. It was not her idea, but the father's, to start their existence. He thought of them, he conceived them. You might as well pay the price of a sack of wheat to the field, instead of the farmer who sowed it, as to honor the mother for giving life. According to the Jewish code, the father is the great factor in family life, the mother of minor consideration. In the midst of such teachings and examples of the subjection and degradation of all womankind, a mere command to honor the mother has no significance.

E. C. S.

LIFE AND WRITINGS OF FREDERICK DOUGLASS

Frederick Douglass

The history of the role of Frederick Douglass (1817–1895) in the struggle for women's rights provides a striking example of how American ruling class interests can impede unity among various groups seeking equality and pit them against each other in the name of political expediency.

Beginning in 1832 female antislavery societies fought on behalf of the Negro, and no one recognized and valued their efforts more than Frederick Douglass. As soon as the 1848 Seneca Falls Convention was announced, Douglass consistently supported the idea in his paper, *The North Star,* and on the speaker's platform. At the convention itself he seconded Elizabeth Cady Stanton's demand for woman suffrage, and was the only man to play a prominent part in the convention's proceedings.

Douglass was present at the National Woman's Rights Convention held on October 23, 1850, in Worcester (the motto of the convention was "Equality before the law without distinction of sex or color"), and attended almost every woman's rights convention thereafter until the outbreak of the Civil War in 1861.

Feminist activity was generally suspended until after the war. Then, in May 1866, the American Equal Rights Association (AERA) was founded with the goal of winning suffrage for Negro men and for all women. It was at the 1866 Albany convention of the AERA that Douglass first clashed with feminist leaders. He maintained that political realities demanded that women wait until Negro men had won the vote. Linking woman suffrage with Negro suffrage, he said, would lessen the chance of winning the vote for Negroes, who needed it more urgently. He maintained this stand at the 1869 AERA convention. Elizabeth Cady Stanton pleaded eloquently against the idea that there was a hierarchy of oppression, but to no avail. (See Stanton's speech on the "Negro's hour" on page 54.)

Douglass was sincere in his commitment to the struggle for women's suffrage. Several months after Negro men won the vote (March 30, 1870) he issued a call in his journal *The New National Era* for a renewed campaign for female suffrage. (The following articles are from this period.[1]) But by separating the black man's fight from the women's, women waited fifty years more to be enfranchised. More important, political women spent half a century fighting for a single issue, separated and divided from the struggles of black men— struggles that certainly did not cease with the acquisition of the vote.

Frederick Douglass put too much faith in a commitment to justice and democracy on the part of President U. S. Grant and the liberal wing of the Republican Party simply because they had supported Negro suffrage at a moment in history when it was politically expedient to do so. This led Douglass to speak against Cuban independence in 1871, and in favor of acquisition by the United States because he believed that would insure the speedy abolition of slavery in Cuba. Even though he didn't think the Republican Party had yet done enough for the Negro, he supported Grant for reelection in 1872 and urged all Negro men to do so, despite the fact that he had been nominated for Vice-President of the United States by the new, socialist Equal Rights Party (ERP). Victoria Woodhull, an advocate of woman suffrage and leader of section No. 12 of the American

Frederick Douglass, *Life and Writings of Frederick Douglass* ed. by Philip S. Foner, 4 vols. (New York: International Publishers, 1955), vol. 4, pp. 231–233, 235–239. The heads in the text were originally titles of articles.
[1] Douglass made an eloquent speech on "The Woman's Suffrage Movement" before the Woman Suffrage Association in April 1888. Due to lack of space, I have not included it here. (It was reproduced in the *Woman's Journal* on April 14, 1888.)

sections of the International Workingmen's Association (the First International), was the Presidential candidate. The motto of the ERP was "The Woman's, Negro's and Workingman's Ticket—Victoria Woodhull of New York for President; Frederick Douglass of the District of Columbia for Vice-President." Nonetheless, Douglass campaigned for Grant's reelection. One can well imagine Douglass' disappointment when President Grant subsequently ignored pressures from militant Republicans to secure a high government post for a Negro leader and did not deem it necessary to reward Douglass for his support.

Woman Suffrage Movement

The simplest truths often meet the sternest resistance, and are slowest in getting general acceptance. There are none so blind as those who will not see, is an old proverb. Usage and prejudice, like forts built of sand, often defy the power of shot and shell, and play havoc with their besiegers. No simpler proposition, no truth more self-evident or more native to the human soul, was ever presented to human reason or consciousness than was that which formed our late anti-slavery movement. It only affirmed that every man is, and of right ought to be, the owner of his own body; and that no man can rightfully claim another man as his property. And yet what a tempest and whirlwind of human wrath, what clouds of ethical and theological dust, this simple proposition created. Families, churches, societies, parties, and States were riven by it, and at last the sword was called in to decide the questions which it raised. What was true of this simple truth was also true as to the people's right to a voice in their own Government, and the right of each man to form for himself his own religious opinions. All Europe ran blood before humanity and reason won this sacred right from priestcraft, bigotry, and superstition. What to-day seems simple, obvious, and undeniable, men looking through old customs, usages, and prejudices in other days denied altogether. Our friends of the woman's suffrage movement should bear this fact in mind, and share the patience of truth while they advocate the truth. It is painful to encounter stupidity as well as malice; but such is the fate of all who attempt to reform an abuse, to urge on humanity to nobler heights, and illumine the world with a new truth.

Now we know of no truth more easily made appreciable to human thought than the right of woman to vote, or, in other words, to have a voice in the Government under which she lives and to which she owes allegiance. The very admission that woman owes allegiance, implies her right to vote. No man or woman who is not consulted can contract an obligation, or have an obligation created for him or her as the case may be. We can owe nothing by the mere act of another. Woman is not a consenting party to this Government. She has never been consulted. Ours is a Government of men, by men, each agreeing with all and all agreeing with each in respect to certain fundamental propositions, and women are wholly excluded. So far as respects its relation to woman, our Government is in its essence, a simple usurpation, a Government of force, and not of reason. We legislate for woman, and protect her, precisely as we legislate for and protect animals, asking the consent of neither.

It is nothing against this conclusion that our legislation has for the most part been eminently just and humane. A despotism is no less a despotism because the reigning despot may be a wise and good man. The principle is unaffected by the character of the man who for the moment may represent it. He may be kind or cruel, benevolent or selfish, in any case he rules according to his own sovereign will—and precisely such is the theoretical relation of our American Government toward woman. It simply takes her money without asking her consent and spends the same without in any wise consulting her wishes. It tells her that there is a code of laws which men have made, and which she must obey or she must suffer the consequences. She is absolutely in the hands of her political masters: and though these may be kind and tender hearted, (the same was true of individual slave masters, as before stated,) this in nowise mitigates the harshness of the principle —and it is against this principle we understand the woman's suffrage movement to be directed. It is intended to claim for woman a place by the side of man, not to rule over him, not to antagonize him, but to rule with him, as an equal subject to the solemn requirements of reason and law.

To ourselves the great truth underlying this woman's movement is just as simple, obvious, and indisputable as either of the great truths referred to at the beginning of this article. It is a part of the same system of truths. Its sources are individuality, rationality, and sense of accountability.

If woman is admitted to be a moral and intellectual being, possessing a sense of good and evil, and a power of choice between them, her case is already half gained. Our natural powers are the foundation of our natural rights; and it is a consciousness of powers which suggests the exercise of rights. Man can only exercise the powers he possesses, and he can only conceive of rights in presence of powers. The fact that woman has the power to say "I choose *this* rather than *that*" is all-sufficient proof that there is no natural reason against the exercise of that power. The power that makes her a moral and an accountable being gives her a natural right to choose the legislators who are to frame the laws under which she is to live, and the requirements of which she is bound to obey. By every fact and by every argument which man can wield in defence of his natural right to participate in government, the right of woman so to participate is equally defended and rendered unassailable.

Thus far all is clear and entirely consistent. Woman's natural abilities and possibilities, not less than man's, constitute the measure of her rights in all directions and relations, including her right to participate in shaping the policy and controlling the action of the Government under which she lives, and to which she is assumed to owe obedience. Unless it can be shown that woman is morally, physically, and intellectually incapable of performing the act of voting, there can be no natural prohibition of such action on her part. Usage, custom, and deeply rooted prejudices are against woman's freedom. They have been against man's freedom, national freedom, religious freedom, but these will all subside in the case of woman as well as elsewhere. The thought has already been conceived; the word has been spoken; the debate has begun; earnest men and women are choosing sides. Error may be safely tolerated while truth is left free to combat it, and nobody need fear the result. The truth can hurt nothing which ought not to be hurt, and it alone can make men and women free.

The New National Era, October 20, 1870

Woman and the Ballot

In the number [of *The New National Era*] preceding the present the natural right of woman to a voice in the Government under which she lives and to which she is assumed to owe allegiance, and for the support of which she is compelled like male citizens to pay taxes, was briefly discussed. It is proposed now to adduce some reasons resting on other facts why woman should be allowed to exercise her indisputable natural right to participate in government through the same channels and instrumentalities employed by men. That society has a right to employ for its preservation and success all the mental, moral, and physical power it thus possesses and can make available, is a truth requiring no argument to make it clear. Not less clear is it, at least to some minds, that society, through its forms of government, ought to exercise that right. It has many rights and duties; but the right and duty to cripple and maim itself, or to deprive itself of any power it naturally possesses, are not among them. A man may cut off his arms and feet, pluck out his eyes, and society may deprive itself of its natural powers for guidance and well-being, but enlightened reason assents neither to the action of the one nor of the other. In this respect nations and individuals stand upon the same footing. The highest good is the supreme law for both, and each after his kind must bear the penalty attached to transgression. The Chinese woman may cripple her feet in obedience to custom, and the Hindoo woman throw herself in the consuming flame for superstition, but nature's laws exact their full measure of pain from whatever motive or through whatever ignorance her mandates are violated.

The grand idea of American liberty is coupled with that of universal suffrage; and universal suffrage is suggested and asserted by universal intelligence. Without the latter the former falls to the ground; and unless suffrage is made co-extensive with intelligence something of the natural power of society essential to its guidance and well-being is lost. To deny that woman is capable of forming an intelligent judgment concerning public men and public measures, equally with men, does not meet the case; for, even if it were granted, the fact remains the same that woman, equally with men, possesses such intelligence; and that such as it is, and because it is such as it is, woman, in her own proper person, has a right for herself to make it effective. To deprive her of this right is to deprive her of a part of her natural dignity, and the State of a part of its mental power of direction, prosperity, and safety; and thus a double wrong is perpetrated.

Man in his arrogance has hitherto felt himself fully equal to the work of governing the world without the help of woman. He has kept the reins of power securely in his own hands, and the history of nations and the present experience of the world show the woeful work he has made of governing. He has made human history a history of war and blood even until now. The world to-day seems as fierce, savage, and bloody as a thousand years ago, and there is not one of all the civilized nations of the earth which has not mortgaged the energies of unborn generations to pay debts contracted by the crimes and blunders of its Government. Whether the case would have been different had woman's voice been allowed in national affairs, admits of little debate. War is among the greatest calamities incident to the lives of nations. They arrest the progress of civilization, corrupt the sources of morality, destroy all proper sense of sacredness of human life, perpetuate the national hate, and weigh down the necks of after coming generations with the burdens of debt. To nothing more than to war is woman more instinctively opposed. If the voices of wives, sisters, and mothers could be heard, no standing armies would menace the peace of the world to-day, and France and Prussia would not be bathing their hands in each other's warm blood. Napoleon told us the "Empire means peace," and we say that Republics mean peace, but neither Empires, Republics, nor Monarchies can mean peace while men alone control them. The vote of women is essential to the peace of the world. Her hand and voice naturally rises against the shedding of human blood. Against this con-clusion cases may be cited, but they are exceptional and abnormal. Woman as woman, far more than man as man, is for peace. That slavery imparted something of its own blood-thirsty spirit to the women of the South—that superstition and fanaticism have led some women to con-sent to the slaughter of their children and to the destruction of them-selves—cannot be taken against the natural gentleness and forbearance of the sex as a whole. She naturally shudders at the thought of subject-ing her loved ones to the perils and horrors of war, and her vote would be a peace guaranty to the world. While society consents to exclude women from all participation in the guidance of its Government, it must consent to standing armies, preparations for war calculated to bring them on, and smite itself into blood and death.

But whatever may be thought as to the consequences of allowing women to vote, it is plain that women themselves are divested of a large measure of their natural dignity by their exclusion from such participation in Government. Power is the highest object of human respect. Wisdom, virtue, and all great moral qualities command respect only as powers. Knowledge and wealth are nought but powers. Take from money its purchasing power, and it ceases to be the same object of respect. We pity the impotent and respect the powerful everywhere. To deny woman her vote is to abridge her natural and social power, and deprive her of a certain measure of respect. Everybody knows that a woman's opinion of any law-maker would command a larger measure of attention had she the means of making opinion effective at the ballot-box. We despise the weak and respect the strong. Such is human nature. Woman herself loses in her own estimation by her enforced exclusion from the elective franchise just as slaves doubted their own fitness for freedom, from the fact of being looked upon as only fit for slaves. While, of course, woman has not fallen so low as the slave in the scale of being, (her education and her natural relation to the ruling power rendering such degradation impossible,) it is plain that, with the ballot in her hand, she will ascend a higher elevation in her own thoughts, and even in the thoughts of men, than without that symbol of power. She has power now—mental and moral power—but they are fettered. Nobody is afraid of a chained lion or an empty gun.

It may be said that woman does already exercise political power— that she does this through her husband, her father and others related to her, and hence there is no necessity for extending suffrage to her, and allowing her to hold office. This objection to the extension of suffrage, is true in the same sense, that every disfranchised people, especially if intelligent, must exert some influence and compel a certain degree of consideration among governing classes, but it is no conclusive argument. If a man is represented in part by another, there is no reason in that why he may not represent himself as a whole, or if he is represented by another, there is no reason in that why he may not represent himself—and the same is true of woman. The claim is that she is represented by man, and that she does therefore indirectly participate in Government. Suppose she does, and the question at once comes if it be right for woman to participate in government indirectly how can it be wrong for her to do so directly? That which is right in itself, is equally right whether done by the principal or the agent especially if equally well done. So far as ability to perform the mere act of voting is concerned woman is as well qualified to do that as to drop a letter in the post office, or to receive one at the window. Let her represent herself. This is the simplest and surest mode of representation. The old slave-holders used to represent the slaves, the rich landowners of other countries represent the poor, and the men in our country claim to represent woman, but the true doctrine of American liberty plainly is, that each class and each individual of a class should be allowed to represent himself—that taxation and representation should go together. Woman having intelligence, capable of an intelligent preference for the kind of men who shall make the laws under which she is to live, her natural dignity and self-respect coupled with the full enjoyment of all her rights as a citizen, her welfare and happiness equally the objects of solicitude to her as to others, affected as deeply by the errors, blunders, mistakes and crimes committed by the Government, as any part of society, especially suffering from the evils of war, drunkenness and immoralities of every kind, instinctively gentle, tender, peaceful, and orderly. She needs the ballot for her own protection, and men as well as women need its concession to her for the protection of the whole. Long deprived of the ballot, long branded as an inferior race— long reputed as incapable of exercising the elective franchise, and only recently lifted into the privileges of complete American citizenship, we cannot join with those who would refuse the ballot to women or to any others of mature age and proper residence, who bear the burdens of the Government and are obedient to the laws.

The New National Era, October 27, 1870

NARRATIVE OF A LIFE

Sojourner Truth

Sojourner Truth was a great American woman, an ex-slave who never learned to read or write, yet who was probably a more powerful force in the war against slavery than any other woman. She and other black women like Frances E. W. Harper and Sarah Remond actively worked with white feminists in the first decades of the woman's rights movement when abolition and feminism were closely related struggles. Her attitude about women's rights was down to earth: "Ef women want any rights more'n dey's got, why don't dey jes' *take 'em,* an' not be talken' about it? Some on 'em came round me, an' asked why I didn't 'ear bloomers. An' I told 'em I had bloomers enough when I was en bondage." She attended the first National Woman's Rights Convention in Worcester, Massachusetts on October 23, 1850, and a year later at a convention in Akron, Ohio, in her famous "Ain't I a Woman?" speech, defended her sex at a moment when no other woman in the room—white or black—had the courage to do so. Sojourner Truth was also a member of the Rochester, New York, Female Anti-Slavery Society together with Elizabeth Cady Stanton, Susan B. Anthony, and other female leaders.

Sojourner Truth, *Narrative of Sojourner Truth* (New York: Arno Press and New York Times, 1968). Originally published for the author in Battle Creek, Michigan, in 1878. Excerpts include pp. 129–135, 165–166, 217–220, 242–245. The title is supplied by the editor. The first text head was originally a part title; any heads following are taken from the original reading.

Born a slave in New York state around 1797, Sojourner Truth's first name was Isabella; as a slave she was considered property of her master, so she never had a surname and was simply called "Belle." (Her master, John Dumont, is believed to have sired all five of Sojourner Truth's children.) Later in life, responding to what she claimed to be a call from the Lord, Isabella changed her name first to "Sojourner" then added "Truth" and used these names until her death in 1883. The New York state emancipation laws of 1827 freed her when she was thirty—"freed her" to work as a maid in New York City for ten years. In 1843 she began to travel and preach; she was both a revivalist and an active abolitionist. In 1850 the Fugitive Slave Law was passed to placate the South (the North was afraid the southern states were going to secede from the Union). From then on Sojourner Truth devoted herself to aiding its victims. She worked in Washington, D.C. with newly freed Negroes whose children were being kidnapped and sent to Maryland, still a slave state; organized the mothers to issue warrants to get their children back; worked as a nurse in the freedman's hospital; and later agitated for legislation to obtain land in the West for the ex-slaves so they could become self-supporting.

The *Narrative of Sojourner Truth* is divided into two parts. The first consists largely of her recollections of life in servitude. It was written for her by Olive Gilbert, a white friend, and published in 1850 with an introduction by William Lloyd Garrison. The second part is a record of her activities—speeches, encounters, struggles—until the end of her life. She is said to have carried a large book filled with blank pages wherever she went and asked people to write in it. This is presumably the source of much of the material. The second part also includes letters she received, autographs she asked for, and accounts of her published elsewhere.

Book of Life

The preceding narrative has given us a partial history of Sojourner Truth. This biography was published not many years after her freedom had been secured to her. Having but recently emerged from the gloomy night of slavery, ignorant and untaught in all that gives value to human existence, she was still suffering from the burden of acquired and transmitted habits incidental to her past condition of servitude. Yet she was one whose life forces and moral perceptions were so powerful and clear cut that she not only came out from this moral gutter herself, but largely assisted in elevating others of her race from a similar state of degradation. It was the "oil of divine origin" which quickened her soul and fed the vital spark, that her own indomitable courage fanned to an undying flame. *She was one of the first to enlist in the war against slavery, and fought the battles for freedom by the side of its noble leaders.*

A true sentinel, she slumbered not at her post. To hasten the enfranchisement of her own people was the great work to which she consecrated her life; yet, ever responsive to the calls of humanity, she

cheerfully lent her aid to the advancement of other reforms, *especially woman's rights and temperance.*

During the last twenty-five years, she has traveled thousands of miles, lectured in many States of the Union, spoken in Congress, and has received tokens of friendship such as few can produce. The following article was published in a Washington Sunday paper during the administration of President Lincoln:

It was our good fortune to be in the marble room of the senate chamber, a few days ago, when that old land-mark of the past—the representative of the forever-gone age—Sojourner Truth, made her appearance. It was an hour not soon to be forgotten; for it is not often, even in this magnanimous age of progress, that we see reverend senators—even him that holds the second chair in the gift of the Republic—vacate their seats in the hall of State, to extend the hand of welcome, the meed of praise, and substantial blessings, to a poor negro woman, whose poor old form, bending under the burden of nearly four-score and ten years, tells but too plainly that her marvelously strange life is drawing to a close. But it was as refreshing as it was strange to see her who had served in the shackles of slavery in the great State of New York for nearly a quarter of a century before a majority of these senators were born now holding a levee with them in the marble room, where less than a decade ago she would have been spurned from its outer corridor by the lowest menial, much less could she have taken the hand of a senator. Truly, the spirit of progress is abroad in the land, and the leaven of love is working in the hearts of the people, pointing with unerring certainty to the not far distant future, when the ties of affection shall cement all nations, kindreds and tongues into one common brotherhood.

She carries with her a book that she calls the Book of Life, which contains the autographs of many distinguished personages—the good and great of the land. No better idea can be given of the estimation in which she is held than by transcribing these testimonials and giving them to the public. It will be difficult to arrange these accounts in the chronological order of events, but no effort has been spared to furnish correct dates.

In the year 1851 she left her home in Northampton, Mass., for a lecturing tour in Western New York, accompanied by the Hon. George Thompson of England, and other distinguished abolitionists. To advocate the cause of the enslaved at this period was both unpopular and unsafe. Their meetings were frequently disturbed or broken up by the pro-slavery mob, and their lives imperiled. At such times, Sojourner fearlessly maintained her ground, and by her dignified manner and opportune remarks would disperse the rabble and restore order.

She spent several months in Western New York, making Rochester her head-quarters. Leaving this State, she traveled westward, and the next glimpse we get of her is in a Woman's Rights Convention at Akron, Ohio. Mrs. Frances D. Gage, who presided at that meeting, relates the following:

The cause was unpopular then. The leaders of the movement trembled on seeing a tall, gaunt black woman, in a gray dress and white turban, surmounted by an uncouth sun-bonnet, march deliberately into the church, walk with the air of a queen up the aisle, and take her seat upon the pulpit steps. A buzz of disapprobation was heard all over the house, and such words as these fell upon listening ears:

"An abolition affair!" "Woman's rights and niggers!" "We told you so!" "Go it, old darkey!"

I chanced upon that occasion to wear my first laurels in public life as president of the meeting. At my request, order was restored and the business of the hour went on. The morning session was held; the evening exercises came and went. Old Sojourner, quiet and reticent as the "Libyan Statue," sat crouched against the wall on the corner of the pulpit stairs, her sun-bonnet shading her eyes, her elbows on her knees, and her chin resting upon her broad, hard palm. At intermission she was busy, selling *The Life of Sojourner Truth,* a narrative of her own strange and adventurous life. Again and again timorous and trembling ones came to me and said with earnestness, "Don't let her speak, Mrs. Gage, it will ruin us. Every newspaper in the land will have our cause mixed with abolition and niggers, and we shall be utterly denounced." My only answer was, "We shall see when the time comes."

The second day the work waxed warm. Methodist, Baptist, Episcopal, Presbyterian, and Universalist ministers came in to hear and discuss the resolutions presented. One claimed superior rights and privileges for man on the ground of superior intellect; another, because of the manhood of Christ. "If God had desired the equality of woman, he would have given some token of his will through the birth, life, and death of the Saviour." Another gave us a theological view of the sin of our first mother. There were few women in those days that dared to "speak in meeting," and the august teachers of the people were seeming to get the better of us, while the boys in the galleries and the sneerers among the pews were hugely enjoying the discomfiture, as they supposed, of the "strong minded." Some of the tender-skinned friends were on the point of losing dignity, and the atmosphere of the convention betokened a storm.

Slowly from her seat in the corner rose Sojourner Truth, who, till now, had scarcely lifted her head. "Don't let her speak!" gasped half a dozen in my ear. She moved slowly and solemnly to the front, laid her old bonnet at her feet, and turned her great, speaking eyes to me. There was a hissing sound of disapprobation above and below. I rose and announced "Sojourner Truth," and begged the audience to keep silence for a few moments. The tumult subsided at once, and every eye was fixed on this almost Amazon form, which stood nearly six feet high, head erect, and eye piercing the upper air, like one in a dream. At her first word, there was a profound hush. She spoke in deep tones, which, though not loud, reached every ear in the house, and away through the throng at the doors and windows:

"Well, chilern, whar dar is so much racket dar must be something out o' kilter. I tink dat 'twixt de niggers of de Souf and de women at de Norf all a talkin' 'bout rights, de white men will be in a fix pretty soon. But what's all dis here talkin' 'bout? Dat man ober dar say dat women needs to be helped into carriages, and lifted ober ditches, and to have de best place every whar. Nobody eber help me into carriages, or ober mud puddles, or gives me any best place [and raising herself to her full height and her voice to a pitch like rolling thunder, she asked], and ar'n't I a woman? Look at me! Look at my arm! [And she bared her right arm to the shoulder, showing her tremendous muscular power.] I have plowed, and planted, and gathered into barns, and no man could head me—and ar'n't I a woman? I could work as much and eat as much as a man (when I could get it), and bear de lash as well—and ar'n't I a woman? I have borne thirteen chilern and seen 'em mos' all sold off into slavery, and when I cried out with a mother's grief, none but Jesus heard—and ar'n't I a woman? Den dey talks 'bout dis ting in de head—what dis dey call it?" "Intellect," whispered some one near. "Dat's it honey. What's dat got to do with woman's rights or niggers' rights? If my cup won't hold but a pint and yourn holds a quart, wouldn't ye be mean not to let me have my little half-measure full?" And she pointed her significant finger and sent a keen glance at the minister who had made the argument. The cheering was long and loud.

"Den dat little man in black dar, he say women can't have as much rights as man, cause Christ warnt a woman. Whar did your Christ come from?" Rolling thunder could not have stilled that crowd as did those deep, wonderful tones, as she stood there with outstretched arms and eye of fire. Raising her voice still louder, she repeated, "Whar did your Christ come from? From God and a woman. Man had nothing to do with him." Oh! what a rebuke she gave the little man.

Turning again to another objector, she took up the defense of mother Eve. I cannot follow her through it all. It was pointed, and witty, and solemn, eliciting at almost every sentence deafening applause; and she ended by asserting that "if de fust woman God ever made was strong enough to turn the world upside down, all 'lone, dese togedder [and she glanced her eye over us], ought to be able to turn it back and get it right side up again, and now dey is asking to do it, de men better let em." Long-continued cheering. "Bleeged to ye for hearin' on me, and now ole Sojourner ha'n't got nothing more to say."

Amid roars of applause, she turned to her corner, leaving more than one of us with streaming eyes and hearts beating with gratitude. She had taken us up in her strong arms and carried us safely over the slough of difficulty, turning the whole tide in our favor. I have never in my life seen anything like the magical influence that subdued the mobbish spirit of the day and turned the jibes and sneers of an excited crowd into notes of respect and admiration. Hundreds rushed up to shake hands, and congratulate the glorious old mother and bid her God speed on her mission of "testifying again concerning the wickedness of this 'ere people."

• • •

"Sojourner, what do you think of women's Rights?"

"Well, honey, I's ben to der meetins, an' harked a good deal. Dey wanted me fur to speak. So I got up. Says I, 'Sisters, I a'n't clear what you'd be after. Ef women want any rights mor'n dey's got, why don't dey jes' *take 'em,* an' not be talkin' about it?' Some on 'em came round me, an' asked why I did n't wear bloomers. An' I told 'em I had bloomers enough when I was in bondage. You see," she said, "dey used to weave what dey called nigger-cloth, an' each one of us got jes' sech a strip, an' had to wear it width-wise. Them that was short got along pretty well, but as for me"—She gave an indescribably droll glance at her long limbs and then at us, and added, "Tell *you,* I had enough of bloomers in them days."

Sojourner then proceeded to give her views of the relative capacity of the sexes, in her own way.

"S'pose a man's mind holds a quart, an a woman's do n't hold but a pint; ef her pint is *full,* it's as good as his quart."

. . .

WOMAN'S SUFFRAGE ASSOCIATION—This morning's session of the Woman's Right's Convention was opened at ten o'clock. After the transaction of some business, Col. T. W. Higginson, of Newport, was introduced to the audience, mostly composed of ladies, whose number increased as the hour advanced. The main object of the speaker was to rally the women of our State and induce them to come forward in the defense of their own rights. As one result of female eloquence, he said, Mrs. Lucy Stone had succeeded in melting the heart of the chairman of the judiciary committee in our general assembly. At the conclusion of Col. Higginson's address a string of resolutions was introduced bearing on the question of Woman's Suffrage. Sojourner Truth, who was sitting on the platform, was invited to speak, and made one of her characteristic addresses, favoring a grant of land to the freedmen of Washington, and such a provision of educational privileges as will tend to the elevation of this unfortunate class.

The great speech of the morning was made by Mrs. Livermore, of Boston, whose statement of facts was better than any labored argument. Her account of the restricted female suffrage in Kansas was highly interesting and instructive. The women in that State are allowed to vote in matters pertaining to public schools, and they use their privileges for the promotion of good education, and really out-wit the men in carrying their points. In the territory of Wyoming, where female suffrage is secured, the women have joined *en masse* in favor of temperance and morality, defeating the vile demagogues who strove for office, and electing persons whose character and principles are a guaranty of public order and security.

Another journal speaks of Sojourner Truth's presence at this meeting thus:

Mrs. Paulina W. Davis said they had a venerable lady on the platform who commenced her life a slave, was forty years in that condition, and since that time had labored for the emancipation of her race.

Sojourner Truth, who seems to carry her weight of years very heartily, said she was somewhat pleased to come before them to bear testimony, although she had a limited time—only a few minutes—but as many friends wanted to hear Sojourner's voice, she thought she would accept the offer. She spoke when the spirit moved her—not when the people moved her, but when the spirit moved her—for when she was limited to a few minutes, the people moved her. She was in the woman movement, for she was a woman herself. The Friend said that woman ought to have her rights for her own benefit, she ought to have them, not only for her own benefit, but for the benefit of the whole creation, not only the women, but all the men on the face of the earth, for they were the mothers of them. Therefore she ought to have her God-given right, and be the equal of men, for she was the resurrection of them. There was another question which lay near her heart, and that was the condition of the poor colored people around Washington, remnants of the slavery which was ended by the war. Sojourner earnestly urged that land be given to these poor people in order that they might be made self-supporting, and concluded her remarks by saying, in her naive way, that she would stop before she was stopped.

THE AMERICAN SIBYL—Sojourner Truth, whom Mrs. Stowe has honored with the title of "The American Sibyl," is spending a few days in our city, and we hope our citizens will have the pleasure of listening to her graphic descriptions of the condition of the freedmen of the city of Washington, where she spent three years during the war in nursing and teaching the poor soldiers and the emancipated people who followed the army. She has been there again recently, endeavoring in her zeal and goodness of heart to help the aged colored people to find comfortable homes in some rural district. She has spoken in nearly all the cities, and has just come from Fall River, where she spoke in two of the churches to large and enthusiastic audiences, who listened with delight to the words of wit and wisdom which fell from the lips of the ancient colored philosopher. She was, as is well known, a slave in New York the first forty years of her life, and since her emancipation and remarkable conversion to Christianity, she has labored unceasingly for the good of her race and for oppressed humanity everywhere.

PERSONAL—"Sister Sojourner Truth" was in town yesterday and visited the Woman Suffrage Bazaar, where she could not resist the movings of the spirit to say a few words upon her "great mission," which now is to "stir up the United States to give the colored people about Washington, and who are largely supported by charity, a tract of land down South, where they can support themselves." She do n't believe in keeping them paupers, and thinks they have earned land enough for white people in past days to be entitled to a small farm apiece themselves. She says she is going to accomplish her mission in this respect before she dies, and she wants an opportunity to address the people of Boston and to get up petitions to Congress in its favor. She means to "send tons of paper down to Washington for them spouters to chaw on." Sojourner believes in women's voting, and thinks the men are very pretentious in denying them the right. Still she thinks there has been a great change for the better in this respect the last few years. She is rather severe on the sterner sex, and asks, by way of capping her argument in favor of her sex: "Did Jesus ever say anything against women? Not a word. But he did speak awful hard things against the men. You know what they were. And he knew them to be true. But he did n't say nothing 'gainst de women." And solacing herself with this reflection the old heroine retired to admire the beautiful bouquets in the flower department of the Fair.

. . .

SOJOURNER TRUTH'S LECTURE—At Franklin Hall, last evening, was in the main an exhortation to all interested in the elevation of the blacks to petition the authorities at Washington for land out West whereon to locate the surplus freedmen, and let them earn their own living, which she argued would be cheaper and better for the government than to care for them in any other way. Her matter and manner were simply indescribable, often straying far away from the starting point; but each digression was fraught with telling logic, rough humor, or effective sarcasm. She thought she had a work to do, and had considerable faith in what she was accomplishing; but she said to her audience, "With all your opportunities for readin' and writin,' you do n't take hold and do anything. My God, I wonder what you are in the world for!" She had infinite faith in the influence which the majority had with Congress and believed that whatever they demanded, good or bad, Congress would grant; hence she was working to make majorities. She leaves the East soon never to return, and goes to Kansas where the Lord had plainly called her by prompting a man whom she had never seen or heard of to invite her and pay her expenses. Her enthusiasm over the prospect was unbounded, and she said that, like the New

Jerusalem, if she didn't find the West all she had expected, she would have a good time thinking about it. A good deal of sound orthodox theology was mingled with her discourse, as well as a description of her visit to the White House, and the reformation she effected in the Washington horse-car system. The whole was followed by a valedictory song in true plantation style. A large and interested audience was present to get the benefit of her remarks.

Her views on the question of woman's dress and the prevailing fashions are interesting. They are substantially these: "I'm awful hard on dress, you know. Women, you forget that you are the mothers of creation; you forget your sons were cut off like grass by the war, and the land was covered with their blood; you rig yourselves up in panniers and Grecian-bend backs and flummeries; yes, and mothers and gray-haired grandmothers wear high-heeled shoes and humps on their heads, and put them on their babies, and stuff them out so that they keel over when the wind blows. O mothers, I'm ashamed of ye! What will such lives as you live do for humanity? When I saw them women on the stage at the Woman's Suffrage Convention, the other day, I thought, What kind of reformers be you, with goose-wings on your heads, as if you were going to fly, and dressed in such ridiculous fashion, talking about reform and women's rights? 'Pears to me, you had better reform yourselves first. But Sojourner is an old body, and will soon get out of this world into another, and wants to say when she gets there, Lord, I have done my duty, I have told the whole truth and kept nothing back."

In another issue the Tribune[1] says:

Mrs. Sojourner Truth, a venerable colored woman, who has been heard before, gave her testimony the other day, in Providence, against the flummery and folly of "feminine vestments," and specially did she rebuke the "women on the stage at the Woman's Suffrage Convention." Hark to her!
"When I saw them women on the stage at the Woman's Suffrage Convention, the other day, I thought, What kind of reformers be you, with goose wings on your heads, as if you were going to fly, and dresses in such ridiculous fashion, talking about reform and women's rights? 'Pears to me you had better reform yourselves first."
Just before this, Mrs. Sojourner had freed her mind respecting "panniers and Grecian-bend backs, high-heeled shoes, and humps on the head." We should earnestly join in Mrs. Truth's protest against the manifold absurdities of woman's clothing, if we thought reform possible; but we do n't. There has been no simplicity of attire since our grandmother Eve made her first apron of fig-leaves.

THE FASHIONS—Sojourner says that "the women wear two heads on their shoulders with but little if any brains in either." She knew of a young woman who had her hair cut on account of an impotency in her head and eyes. After the hair was cut, she put it into a net and wore it for a waterfall—getting rest for the head only during the night. Her hair grew again but still she continued to wear the extra hair with the addition of several skeins of stocking or other sort of yarn. Her impotencies of course *"grew no better"* very fast. Perhaps there is no truer saying than that "folly is a fund that will never lose ground while fools are so rife in the nation." The trouble of the thing is, or the reason why we have the trouble is, that the priests are dumb dogs and dare not bark or bring out the truths of the gospel against such gigantic evils, as *war, slavery,* and the *prided fashions.* We leave Sojourner Truth with her intuitiveness and

[1] The reference is to the *New York Tribune* [Ed.].

without the letter, to battle almost alone these world-wide evils. May Heaven bless and sustain her in her humanitarian work and "God-like mission."

SELAHOMMAH

. . .

MARX AND ENGELS ON WOMEN'S LIBERATION*

Hal Draper

For the complete emancipation of women and for their real equality with men, it is necessary to establish social economy and the participation of women in general productive labor.

> V. I. Lenin, Speech to the Fourth Non-Party Conference on Working Women, Moscow, September 25, 1919.

The decay . . . of bourgeois marriage with its difficult dissolution, its licence for the husband and bondage for the wife, and its disgustingly false sex morality and relations fill the best and most spiritually active of people with the utmost loathing.

> V. I. Lenin, Interview with Clara Zetkin, 1920.

The role of women, monogamy, and the family in society is an essential part of communist theory. Marx, Engels, Stalin, and Lenin wrote extensively on "the woman question,"[1] and their arguments that a specific economic structure is the prerequisite for women's liberation are the theoretical bases for the thought of today's feminists who also consider themselves socialists. Hal Draper's article traces the evolution of Marxist feminist theory from the presocialist works to *The Origins of the Family* (1884).

Hal Draper, "Marx and Engels on Women's Liberation." Copyright © 1970 by Hal Draper; reprinted by permission of the author and of the Independent Socialist Committee. This is a chapter of a work-in-progress by Hal Draper on *Karl Marx's Theory of Revolution.* References to other chapters have been left standing, indicating points of contact with other material. Footnotes have been renumbered by the editor.

*English translations are cited, wherever possible, from the two-volume Marx-Engels *Selected Works* (Moscow, Foreign Lang. Pub. House, 1955), abbreviated *ME:SW.* Untranslated German texts are cited, wherever possible, from the Marx-Engels *Werke* (Berlin, Dietz, 1961–68), abbreviated *ME:W.* In other cases, full bibliographic data are given on first appearance of a title, and abbreviated afterward. Volume and page number are abbreviated as follows: e.g. 3:207 = Vol. 3, page 207. In all abbreviations, M = Marx, E = Engels, ME = Marx & Engels.

[1] Selections from the writings of these four men are published in *The Woman Question* (New York: International Publishers, 1951).

Lenin's writings about women date mainly from the first decades of the twentieth century.[2] Most interesting from today's point of view is his 1920 interview with Clara Zetkin, a leader of the German socialist and labor movement.

Clara, . . . I have been told that at the evenings arranged for reading and discussion with working women, sex and marriage problems come first. They are said to be the main objects of interest in your political instruction and education work. I could not believe my ears when I heard that. . . . I mistrust those who are always absorbed in the sex problems, the way an Indian saint is absorbed in the contemplation of his navel. It seems to me that this superabundance of sex theories [Lenin refers primarily to Freud], which for the most part are mere hypotheses, and often quite arbitrary ones, stems from a personal need. It springs from the desire to justify one's own abnormal or excessive sex life before bourgeois morality and to plead for tolerance towards oneself.[3]

Lenin thus unjustifiably dismisses the importance of an equivalent of today's small rap group and ignores the need for women to share problems of personal and social oppression in sex and marriage. But he then gives a precise description of the excessive, distorted preoccupation with sex so much a part of American life today. Later he clarifies the Marxist theory of "free love":

No doubt you have heard about the famous theory that in communist society satisfying sexual desire and the craving for love is as simple and trivial as "drinking a glass of water." A section of our youth has gone mad, absolutely mad, over this "glass of water theory." It has been fatal to many a young boy and girl. Its devotees assert that it is a Marxist theory. I want no part of the kind of Marxism which infers all phenomena and all changes in the ideological superstructure of society directly and blandly from its economic basis, for things are not as simple as all that.[4]

Finally, his comments on the sexual behavior of women and men who consider themselves serious political radicals is noteworthy, especially in light of the general confusion about the implications of women's liberation:

You know the young comrade X. He is a splendid lad, and highly gifted. For all that, I am afraid that he will never amount to anything. He has one love affair after another. This is not good for the political struggle and for the revolution. I will not vouch for the reliability or the endurance of women whose love affair in intertwined with politics, or for the men who run after every petticoat and let themselves in with every young female. No, no, that does not go well with revolution.[5]

Not paradoxically, discussion of the revolution in Man begins with woman.

The perspective of eventually abolishing the division of labor in society, and therefore also the distortion of human relations which it imposes, leads back to what Marx and Engels pointed to as the very

[2] See V. I. Lenin, *The Emancipation of Women* (New York: International Publishers, 1966).
[3] *Ibid.*, p. 101.
[4] *Ibid.*, p. 106.
[5] *Ibid.*, p. 107.

starting-point of the social division of labor: the division of labor between the sexes.[1] And this in turn raises all the questions about the past and future of the family, forms of marriage, sexual relations, etc.— the complex of questions relating to what was then called "the woman question."

Once this question is seen within the context, not simply of a social psychology and attitude (like "male chauvinism"), but of the primordial division of labor, then it is clear that for Marx its roots go more deeply into man's past than capitalism, or the state, or the division between town and country, or even private property. By the same token, it should be expected, the social attitudes which result from *this* division of labor will be most resistant to uprooting.

1: Marx's Early Views (1842–1846)

Before Marx became a socialist, let alone a "Marxist," it is clear that he held more or less traditional attitudes on marriage, the family and related issues. This appears from two articles he wrote in 1842, his first years as a left-liberal journalist, both of them for the *Rheinische Zeitung,* the Cologne newspaper of which he became editor in October.

In what was only the third article he had ever published up to then, a criticism of the "historical school of law," the young man attacked Gustav Hugo for taking a relativistic attitude toward the institution of marriage:

But the sanctification of the sex drive through *exclusiveness,* the restraint of the drive through law, the *ethical beauty* which turns nature's command into an ideal moment [aspect] of spiritual union—the *spiritual essence* of marriage— this is what is *suspect* in marriage for Herr Hugo.[2]

To rebut this "frivolous shamelessness" of Hugo's viewpoint, Marx offers a prissy passage from the French liberal Benjamin Constant; and finally he reprovingly quotes Hugo's further opinion that our "animal nature" is opposed to the convention that "outside of marriage the satisfaction of the sex drive is not permissible."[3]

[1] Cf. *ME: German Ideology* (see Ref. n.10), 42–43. In this early manuscript (1845–46) the sexual division of labor is still largely ascribed to the supposed *inherent* physical weakness of women—a notion Engels later rejected; in many societies women worked harder than men. (Cf. Engels' letter to Marx, 8 Dec. 1882, in *ME: Selected Correspondence* (N.Y., 1935), 406; and his *Origin of the Family,* in *ME:SW* 2:209–10, which we quote below.) Bebel, in *Woman and Socialism* (see Ref. n.53), 26–27, devotes over a page to refuting the "weakness" theory. In any case a distinction must be made between ability to work "hard" (involving stamina) and ability to exert bursts of strength (as in combat); also between "weakness" and the child-bearing function, which is relevant to the type of work feasible for women rather than strength.
[2] From "The Philosophical Manifesto of the Historical School of Law," *Rheinische Zeitung,* 9 Aug. 1842; in *Marx: Writings of the Young Marx on Philosophy and Society,* ed. Easton & Guddat (Garden City, Doubleday, 1967), 101–102. But this section, headed "Chapter on Marriage," was not in fact published at the time since it was excised by the censor; first published in 1927 from Marx's ms.
[3] Ibid., 102.

But there is no attempt at analysis here.

The Article on Divorce

Toward the end of that year, an article by Marx "On a Proposed Divorce Law" sheds more light on his pre-socialist ideas. He states he will "develop the concept of marriage and its implications" in accordance with a "philosophy of law," but the short article does not carry that ball very far.[4]

To be sure, his first interest is in arguing for a purely secular approach to the question.[5] Not "spiritual sacredness" but rather "human ethics" is "the essence of marriage"; not "determination from above" but "self-determination." He also makes the point that a human-ethical divorce law will be guaranteed "only when law is the conscious expression of the will of the people, created with and through it." His starting-point is radical democracy.

But his views are still cast in typically Hegelian-idealist terms, about the immanent "will of marriage" and "the ethical substance of this relationship," etc.; he still thinks of marriage, not as a historical social institution, but as the realization of an ethical norm derived by thought from the "nature of man." This leads him to criticize "the numerous and frivolous reasons for divorce" in the existing Prussian code, and to look askance at permissiveness.

The following gives the crux of his approach, as he chides those who "always talk of the misery of spouses bound to each other against their will":

They think only of two individuals and forget the *family*. They forget that nearly every dissolution of a marriage is the dissolution of a family and that the children and what belongs to them should not be dependent on arbitrary whims, even from a purely legal point of view. If marriage were not the basis of the family, it would not be subject to the legislation, just as friendship is not.[6]

And in fact, it is going to be through a historical reappraisal of the family, and not merely of the relation between the "two individuals," that this pre-socialist approach will be abandoned by Marx by 1845. Then the last sentence in the above passage could cease to be conditional.

First Socialist Opinions

But in-between, the first impact on Marx's views made by his reading in socialist and communist literature in 1843–44 concerned precisely the

[4] This article, "On a Proposed Divorce Law," appeared in the *Rhein. Zeit.* 19 Dec. 1842. It is quoted here from *M: Writgs. Yg. Mx.,* 137, 141, 139.
[5] The *Rhein. Zeit.* had earlier, on 15 Nov. 1842, carried an editorial note, written by Marx, appended to another's article on the bill. Here Marx called for a purely secular analysis of the divorce issue, based on "human ethics," &c. and already set down some of the ideas of the 19 Dec. article. For this editorial note, see *ME:W* Erg. Bd. 1, 389–91.
[6] "On a Proposed Divorce Law," 139.

"two individuals," that is, sexual relations and the place of woman in society. (It may also be relevant that he had himself entered the institution of marriage in 1843.)

The influence of Fourier is evident in one of the first lucubrations of this newfledged socialist, his "Paris manuscripts" of 1844. He enthusiastically adopts the view that "man's whole level of development" is, in a basic sense, measured by the man-woman relationship in society. In these notes, his first criticism of "crude communism" is directed against its (alleged) advocacy of "community of women." He attacks it with the following line of thought:

The direct, natural, and necessary relation of person to person is the *relation of man to woman.* In this *natural* relationship of the sexes man's relation to nature is immediately his relation to man. . . In this relationship, therefore, is *sensuously manifested,* reduced to an observable *fact,* the extent to which the human essence has become nature to man. . . From this relationship one can therefore judge man's whole level of development. . . . It therefore reveals the extent to which man's *natural* behavior has become *human* . . . the extent to which he in his individual existence is at the same time a social being.[7]

This relationship is put forward as the acid test of the real humanness of any and all interpersonal relationships.

In *The Holy Family,* written later the same year, Fourier is quoted at length on the subject. The context is Marx's dissection of Eugene Sue's novel *The Mysteries of Paris,* in which Marx debunks the aristocratic philanthropism of the hero, Rudolph of Geroldstein. For one thing he points out that this noble paragon of virtue is capable of pitying the lot of a servant girl but is unable "to grasp the general condition of women in modern society as an inhuman one."

It is against this bourgeois-philanthropic attitude that he quotes Fourier at some length, including the following:

"The change in a historical epoch can always be determined by the progress of women toward freedom, because in the relation of woman to man, of the weak to the strong, the victory of human nature over brutality is most evident. The degree of emancipation of woman is the natural measure of general emancipation."[8]

Thirty-four years later, in *Anti-Dühring,* Engels was again going to pay homage to Fourier as the first to express this sentiment.[9] Twenty-four years later, Marx was going to echo it, perhaps without thinking of the source:

. . . great progress was evident in the last Congress of the American "Labour Union" in that, among other things, it treated working women with complete equality. While in this respect the English, and still more the gallant French, are burdened with a spirit of narrowmindedness. Anybody who knows anything of history knows that great social changes are impossible without the feminine

[7] *Marx: Economic and Philosophic Manuscripts of 1844* (Moscow, For. Lang. Pub. House, n.d.), 101.
[8] Fourier as quoted in *ME: The Holy Family* (Moscow, For. Lang. Pub. House, 1956), 258–59.
[9] *Engels: Anti-Dühring,* 2nd ed. (Moscow, For. Lang. Pub. House, 1959), 357.

ferment. Social progress can be measured exactly by the social position of the fair sex (the ugly ones included).[10]

There was still an element of condescension in the citation from Fourier: woman is "weak," man is "strong," etc. This element is going to be eliminated by the theoretical underpinning which the later work of Marx and Engels gave to this question.

The Holy Family does not deal with the problem of the family. On the "woman question" it is still mainly a reflection of what was best in then well-known socialist opinions.

A new note about the family first appears in Engels' book *The Condition of the Working Class in England,* also written in 1844, independently of Marx. Here the facts lead him to the condition of the *working-class* family as a result of the widespread employment of women and children.

The transposition of women from home to mill and mine "breaks up the family," makes it impossible for married women to care for children or household, engenders "unbridled sexual license" and illegitimate children, even though it has not "sunk to the level of prostitution." The most pertinent passage is not any of those that assert the working-class family is "being dissolved" but that which discusses how it is "inverted," "turned upside," when the employed wife is the breadwinner and the unemployed husband must become the housekeeper.

This, says Engels, is an "insane state of things"; it "unsexes the man and takes from the woman all womanliness"; it "degrades, in the most shameful way, both sexes, and, through them, Humanity . . ." But the new note is struck when he shows that he sees this as a socially conditioned result of historically determined attitudes:

. . . we must admit that so total a reversal of the position of the sexes can have come to pass only because the sexes have been placed in a false position from the beginning. If the reign of the wife over the husband, as inevitably brought about by the factory system, is inhuman, the pristine rule of the husband over the wife must have been inhuman too. If the wife can now base her supremacy upon the fact that she supplies the greater part, nay the whole of the common possession, the necessary inference is that this community of possession is no true and rational one, since one member of the family boasts offensively of contributing the greater share. If the family of our present society is being thus dissolved, this dissolution merely shows that, at bottom, the binding tie of this family was not family affection, but private interest lurking under the cloak of a pretended community of possessions.[11]

It is not until *The German Ideology* (1845–46) that Marx and Engels begin laying the basis for a distinctive analysis, just as it is first in this work that the materialist conception of history is well developed. To be sure, Marx at this point apparently believes that some kind of family always existed, but at any rate the family is clearly viewed as a histori-

[10] *Marx: Letters to Dr. Kugelmann,* Marxist Lib., 17 (N.Y., International Pub., 1934), letter of 12 Dec. 1868, p. 83.
[11] *E: Cond. Wkg. Cl.,* in *ME: On Britain,* 2d ed. (Moscow, FLPH, 1962), 179–180; other citations are from p. 175, 177, 225, 234, 243, 287.

cally changing product of changing material conditions. It "must then be treated and analyzed according to the existing empirical data, not according to 'the concept of the family,' as is the custom in Germany"[12] —a direct hit at the Marx of 1842.

The family is taken to be the *first* form of social relationship, indeed the "only social relationship" to begin with.[13] The division of labor begins in the family, which is headed by "patriarchal family chieftains." "The slavery latent in the family only develops gradually . . ."[14] The family is made virtually responsible for the rise of private property:

the nucleus, the first form of [property] lies in the family, where wife and children are slaves of the husband. This latent slavery in the family, though still very crude, is the first property . . .[15]

This conception is also used to hit at the double standard in sexual behavior. In Prussian law, says Marx, "the sanctity of marriage is supposed to be enforced both upon men and women" but this is a juridical fantasy. The real bourgeois relationship is encoded in France: "in French practice, where the wife is regarded as the private property of her husband, only the wife can be punished for adultery . . ."[16]

"Abolishing" the Family

The family is not linked to private-property economy in *The German Ideology* anywhere near as thoroughly as Engels did later, but Marx evidently thought the connection required little "empirical data," for he had no hesitation in drawing the drastic conclusion that, with the abolition of private property, it follows that "the abolition of the family is self-evident."[17] Further on, it is taken as equally self-evident that this means "the abolition of marriage." But there is no hint of what relations are supposed to replace the present institutions, though it is made clear that "the fantasies by which Fourier tried to give himself a picture of free love" are not to be taken seriously.[18]

In Marx's "Theses on Feuerbach," written before *The German Ideology,* the fourth [thesis] already announces the opinion that the family "must . . . be destroyed in theory and in practice."[19]

So intent is Marx on the "abolition of the family," in fact, that he practically has it abolished already in 1845. He announces "the bourgeois

[12] ME: *The German Ideology* (Moscow, Progress Pub., 1964), 40. (This ed. contains all three parts, not only Parts 1 and 3.)
[13] Ibid., 40.
[14] Ibid., 33.
[15] Ibid., 44.
[16] Ibid., 369.
[17] Ibid., 40.
[18] Ibid., 564.
[19] This is what *Marx* wrote as thesis no. 4. The edited version published by Engels in 1888 softened this to the formulation that the family must be "criticized in theory and revolutionized in practice"—a change that Engels felt certain reflected the mature Marx too. This question comes up again below. (For the two formulations, see ME: *German Ideology,* 646, 652).

dissolution of the family," admitting only that the family still exists "officially" as a property relation. By this "bourgeois dissolution of the family" Marx appears to mean such things as: "The dissolute[20] bourgeois evades marriage and secretly commits adultery," etc. It is not a very convincing demonstration of dissolution. With the proletariat "the family is *actually* abolished," he emphasizes, and "There the concept of the family does not exist at all"—a proposition for which no "empirical data" are given at all.[21] Engels' book on England is not referred to as evidence, nor is the problem linked to the employment of women. In any case Engels' book had offered no ground for the extravagant claim that "the concept of the family does not exist at all" among the proletariat; just the contrary.[22]

This annunciation of the all-but-economic disappearance of the family exists in the exposition mainly as a piece of rhetoric; there is no organic explanation of why the family's existence should *already* be so tenuous, not only under capitalism but under undeveloped capitalism—quite a distance from the abolition of private property. When Marx writes, "the family still exists although its dissolution was long ago proclaimed by French and English socialists,"[23] he betrays that he is again echoing the socialism of the time, and has not yet worked it out himself.

To round off this period: there is the curious and little-known article which Marx wrote while working on *The German Ideology:* the article "Peuchet on Suicide," in which he summarizes the conclusions of a book of Jacques Peuchet on the sociological meaning of the increase in suicides in France.[24] One passage goes as follows—the emphasis is by Marx, as is the selection:

Among the reasons for the despair which leads very oversensitive, persons to seek death . . . I [Peuchet] have uncovered as a dominant factor the bad treatment, the injustices, the secret punishments which severe parents and superiors visit on people dependent on them. *The Revolution has not overthrown all tyrannies; the evils which were charged against despotic power continue to exist in the family; here they are the cause of crises analogous to those of revolutions.*

The connections between interests and feelings, true relationships among individuals, are still one day to be created among us *from the ground up,* and *suicide is only one of the thousand-and-one symptoms of the general social struggle always going on . . .*[25]

Apropos of the case of a girl driven to suicide by a man's jealousy, Marx summarizes: This was really a case of murder—"The jealous person is in want of a slave; he can be in love, but this love is only a

[20] The accidental pun involving *dissolution* and *dissolute* exists only in the English trans.
[21] *Ibid.,* 192.
[22] There is no extant record of Marx's reaction to the publication of Engels' book, though he must have read it immediately.
[23] Ibid., 193.
[24] The peculiar form and content of this article are explained in the preceding chapter. [Not reprinted here.—Ed.]
[25] *ME: Gesamtausgabe (MEGA),* I, 3:395. Also cf. A. Cornu: *Karl Marx und Friedrich Engels* (Berlin/Weimar, Aufbau-Verlag, 1968), 3:174.

feeling of luxuriating in jealousy; *the jealous person is above all a private-property owner.*"[26]

Of these analyses of 1842–46, some elements were going to be retained, some were going to be modified or refined, and some were going to be dropped, when Marx and Engels came to a maturer formulation of their historical theory.

2: The Sexual Revolution of the Past

The historical-materialist approach to the history of man showed that the current form of the family was no more "natural" than any other variable social institution, and that the family (with attendant sexual mores) had changed form along with changes in property relations. One immediate conclusion was: it can therefore be expected to change in a future society which has changed all other social institutions. Change to what?

Evolutionary View of the Family

The *Communist Manifesto* mainly announced flatly that "The bourgeois family will vanish as a matter of course" with the disappearance of capitalism.[27] It contained other echoes of 1845.

Engels' draft for the Manifesto had been more pointed:

It [communist society] will transform the relations between the sexes into a purely private matter which concerns only the persons involved and into which society has no occasion to intervene. It can do this since it does away with private property and educates children on a communal basis, and in this way removes the two bases of traditional marriage, the dependence, rooted in private property, of the woman on the man and of the children on the parents.[28]

Thus (he adds) communism will also abolish prostitution, the bourgeois form of "community of women."

In 1850 Marx and Engels had occasion to pin-prick the "woman-cult" approach, in a review of a book by one Daumer advocating a new religiosity. "Nature" and "woman" are exalted as "divine," and "the sacrifice of the male to the female" is called for in the name of virtue and piety. In both cases, Daumer is fleeing from today's threatening reality to, on the one hand, a "mere rustic idyll" (which has nothing to do with real nature) and on the other hand to "effeminate resignation" (which has nothing to do with real women).

The position as regards the worship of the female is the same as with nature worship. Mr. Daumer naturally does not say a word about the present social

[26] Ibid., 402.
[27] In *ME:SW* 1:50.
[28] Engels, "Principles of Communism," in *ME: The Communist Manifesto* [et al.] (Modern Reader Paperbacks, 1968), 80.

situation of women; on the contrary it is a question only of the female as such. He tries to console women for their social distress by making them the object of a cult in words which is as empty as it would fain be mysterious. Thus he puts them at ease over the fact that marriage puts an end to their talents through their having to take care of the children . . . by telling them that they can suckle babies until the age of sixty . . . and so on.[29]

His "ideal women characters" turn out to look very much like aristocratic patronesses of men of letters like himself. For Daumer, the abstraction of femininity is made "divine" in order to elevate the problem of real women in real society to cloudier realms—the outcome of one form of "feminism." In contrast, Marx's *Capital* takes up the profane woman.

In *Capital* Marx generalizes only at one point (though he pays much attention to the murderous exploitation of women's and children's labor, and therefore the necessity of legislative protection). He quotes an English government commission report to the effect that "against no persons do the children of both sexes so much require protection as against their parents." Parents must not have power over children. This power has been abused for exploitive purposes.

However terrible and disgusting the dissolution, under the capitalist system, of the old family ties may appear, nevertheless modern industry, by assigning as it does an important part in the process of production, outside the domestic sphere, to women, to young persons, and to children of both sexes, creates a new economic foundation for a higher form of the family and of the relations between the sexes. It is, of course, just as absurd to hold the Teutonic-Christian form of the family to be absolute and final as it would be to apply that character to the ancient Roman, the ancient Greek, or the Eastern forms which, moreover, taken together form a series in historic development. Moreover, it is obvious that the fact of the collective working group being composed of individuals of both sexes and all ages must necessarily, under suitable conditions, become a source of humane development . . .[30]

It is not possible "that the modern-bourgeois family can be torn from its whole economic foundation without changing its entire form," wrote Engels in 1878.[31] But the strongest exposition of this view came in *The Origin of the Family, Private Property and the State.* Although Engels wrote it up the year after Marx's death, this book was the result of previous close collaboration between the two; Marx had intended to do it himself, and its broad views should be considered the joint work of both men.[32]

In this book, the chapter on "The Family" closes with the words of

[29] "Review of G. Fr. Daumer's *The Religion of the New Age* . . . ," Feb. 1850, in *ME: On Religion* (Moscow, FLPH, 1957), 95.
[30] *M: Capital* (Moscow, For. Lang. Pub. House, n.d.), 1:489–90. See also Marx's remarks on the subject at the meeting of 28 July 1868 in *The General Council of the First International 1866–1868; Minutes* [v. 2] (Moscow, Progress Pub., n.d.), 232–33.
[31] *E: Anti-Dühring*, 438.
[32] *E: Pref. to Origin of the Family,* in *ME:SW* 2:170.

the anthropologist Lewis H. Morgan, on whose researches it leaned.[33] Morgan concluded that the family is the creature of the social system, and will reflect its culture. . . Should the monogamian family in the distant future fail to answer the requirements of society . . . it is impossible to predict the nature of its successor.[34]

So the family and sexual relations will change—from what, to what?

The Defeat of Woman

In *The Origin of the Family* Engels emphasizes the evidence for a primitive stage of female dominance in the family, based on the then conditions of existence.[35]

The division of labor between the two sexes is determined by causes entirely different from those that determine the status of women in society. Peoples whose women have to work much harder than we would consider proper often have far more real respect for women than our Europeans have for theirs. The social status of the lady of civilization, surrounded by sham homage and estranged from all real work, is socially infinitely lower than that of the hardworking woman of barbarism . . .[36]

He traces the transition to the dominance of the father, on the basis of the change in the nature of the main type of property held by the family (agriculture to cattle-breeding); but it is not the anthropological exposition we are interested in now. This transference of power (dominance) within the framework of the family division of labor was a "revolution"—"one of the most decisive ever experienced by mankind." It "was the *world-historic defeat of the female sex*." The woman was "degraded," in effect enslaved, turned largely into "a mere instrument for breeding children. This lowered position of women . . . has become gradually embellished and dissembled and, in part, clothed in a milder form, but by no means abolished."[37] Or in Marx's words:

[33] There is a myth, widely accepted among the half-informed, that Morgan's anthropological work is now simply "outmoded," like Ptolemaic astronomy, and is rejected by "modern anthropologists." (In part this is as true as the statement that Marx is rejected by "modern sociologists.") Before merely parroting this myth about Morgan, one should go to the article on him in the *International Encyclopedia of the Social Sciences* (1968— very modern) by Prof. Leslie White, not only for the article itself but esp. for the appended bibliography. The issue is not this or that detail or aspect of Morgan's views—in this respect Darwin and Newton are "outmoded" as well—but rather the conflict between evolutionary anthropology and the "modern" dominant anti-evolutionary school of the Boas type, which rescues established institutions from the subversive conclusions suggested by an evolutionary approach to man's prehistory. A separate issue is the extent to which particular conclusions by Engels are based on particular details in Morgan; cf. next footnote.
[34] In *ME:SW* 2:241; here corrected after L. H. Morgan, *Ancient Society* (Chicago, Kerr, n.d.), 499 (end of Chap. 5 of Part III).
[35] Engels discussed his sources in his preface to the 4th edition of 1891 (in *ME:SW* 2:172 & seq.)—J. J. Bachofen, J. F. McLennan, R. G. Latham, J. Lubbock, etc. besides Morgan. The modern reader should go to Robert Briffault's *The Mothers*. At the end of this preface, Engels distinguishes between holding to "Morgan's hypotheses pertaining to particular points" and maintaining "his principal conceptions."
[36] *E: Orig. Fam.*, in *ME:SW* 2:209–10.
[37] Ibid., 215–17.

The modern family contains in embryo not only slavery *(servitus)* but serfdom also, since from the very beginning it is connected with agricultural services. It contains within itself in *miniature* all the antagonisms which later develop on a wide scale within society and its state.[38]

The institution of monogamy arises, together with private property and class divisions:

It is based on the supremacy of the man; its express aim is the begetting of children of undisputed paternity, this paternity being required in order that these children may in due time inherit their father's wealth as his natural heirs.[39]

As a rule, only the man can dissolve the marriage, and in practice the monogamous restriction applies to the woman only. In this sense, it is not even a genuine monogamy.

It was not in any way the fruit of individual sex love, with which it had absolutely nothing in common, for the marriages remained marriages of convenience, as before. It was the first form of the family based not on natural but on economic conditions, namely, on the victory of private property . . .

Thus, monogamy does not by any means make its appearance in history as the reconciliation of man and woman, still less as the highest form of such a reconciliation. On the contrary, it appears as the subjection of one sex by the other, as the proclamation of a conflict between the sexes entirely unknown hitherto in prehistoric times.[40]

Engels then sums this up with a strong statement:

The first class antagonism which appears in history coincides with the development of the antagonism between man and woman in monogamian marriage, and the first class oppression with that of the female sex by the male. Monogamy was a great historical advance, but at the same time it inaugurated, along with slavery and private wealth, that epoch, lasting until today, in which every advance is likewise a relative retrogression, in which the well-being and development of the one group are attained by the misery and repression of the other. It is the cellular form of civilized society, in which we can already study the nature of the antagonisms and contradictions which develop fully in the latter.[41]

This "cellular" form of the social struggle produces its characteristic counter-institutions, symbolized by "the wife's paramour and the cuckold" on the one hand and prostitution (in various forms) on the other. The former is the oppressed group's "revenge" for the masculine double-standard; the latter "demoralizes the men far more than it does the woman."[42]

Thus, in the monogamian family, in those cases that faithfully reflect its historical origin and that clearly bring out the sharp conflict between man and

[38] Marx, "Abstract of Morgan's *Ancient Society*," quoted by Engels in *Orig. Fam.*, ibid., 217.
[39] E: *Orig. Fam.*, in *ME:SW* 2:221.
[40] Ibid., 224.
[41] Ibid., 224–25.
[42] Ibid., 233.

woman resulting from the exclusive domination of the male, we have a picture in miniature of the very antagonisms and contradictions in which society, split up into classes since the commencement of civilization, moves, without being able to resolve and overcome them.[43]

Love and Equality

Out of this development, in which "every advance is likewise a relative retrogression," a new step emerges in Europe out of the breakdown of the Roman world:

This, for the first time, created the possibility for the greatest moral advance which we derive from and owe to monogamy—a development taking place within it, parallel with it, or in opposition to it, as the case might be—namely, modern individual sex love, previously unknown to the whole world.[44]

It arises contradictorily. On the one hand, the dominance of bourgeois private property reinforces the prevalence of the marriage of convenience, and of "marriage . . . determined by the class position of the participants."[45] On the other hand, bourgeois *ideology,* especially in the Protestant countries, emphasizes freedom of contract and equality of status for the freely contracting parties. As happened with "Liberty, Equality, Fraternity," not to speak of "democracy," the ideological extrapolation is in conflict with the economic reality—of bourgeois society. The ideology reinforces at least lip-service to individual sex love, freely and equally accorded, as the foundation of monogamy. But the bourgeois economic reality, in which the man is still the economic master, maintains the marriage of convenience, the limitation of possible partners by class strata, the restriction of women's economic independence and therefore their independence as human beings, etc.[46]

Literary history reflects the advance of individual sex love mainly in channels *outside* of bourgeois matrimony, that "wedded life of leaden boredom, which is described as domestic bliss"—from the "chivalrous" love stories of the Middle Ages to the French novel of institutionalized adultery. Engels especially emphasizes the view that individual sex love could develop most easily among the propertiless working classes; and here also working-women could begin to assert first steps in economic independence. And a marriage with a woman who "has regained the right of separation," because she can leave and support herself economically, is "monogamian in the etymological sense of the word, but by no means in the historic sense."[47]

To be sure, this does not yet change the juridical situation. "The inequality of the two before the law, which is a legacy of previous social conditions, is not the cause but the effect of the economic oppression of women."[48]

[43] Ibid., 226.
[44] Ibid., 227–28; for Engels' differentiation of this from the ancient *eros,* ibid., 235.
[45] Ibid., 229.
[46] Ibid., 237–38.
[47] Ibid., 228–30.
[48] Ibid., 231.

The wife became the first domestic servant, pushed out of participation in social production. . . . Today [1884], in the great majority of cases, the man has to be the earner, the bread-winner of the family, at least among the propertied classes, and this gives him a dominating position which requires no special legal privileges. In the family, he is the bourgeois; the wife represents the proletariat.[49]

(That last sentence became one of the watchwords of the German socialist women's movement—as a strong metaphor, of course.)

Modern industry technologically undermines this pattern, as it technologically undermines capitalism itself. Then: "What applies to the woman in the factory applies to her in all the professions, right up to medicine and law." But the advance of legal equality between the sexes, even when achieved, will not yet establish real quality. A comparison (Engels'): bourgeois democracy only provides the field on which the class struggle is fought out—

And, similarly, the peculiar character of man's domination over woman in the modern family, and the necessity as well as the manner of establishing real social equality between the two, will be brought out into full relief only when both are completely equal before the law. It will then become evident that the first premise for the emancipation of women is the reintroduction of the entire female sex into public industry; and that this again demands that the quality possessed by the individual family of being the economic unit of society be abolished.[50]

Let us note that the outcome is now posed not as the "abolition of the family" but as the abolition of the family *as the economic unit of society*, through the change in the role of women in the economy. The road to women's liberation then runs through the same field as saw their "world-historic defeat"—the process of production and the women's relation to it—and cannot be basically changed simply by ideological (including psychiatric) exhortations.

3: Monogamy and/or Love: The Future of the Family

What then happens to monogamy and the family under the impact of a socialist transformation?

The fact that monogamy did not always exist naturally raises—but does not settle—the question whether it will always continue to exist in the future.[51] Engels considers two possibilities, though clearly he personally expects the second.

[49] Ibid., 232.
[50] Ibid., 232, 310.
[51] For the importance Engels attached to the historically limited character of monogamy, see his sharp reaction against the articles published by Karl Kautsky in 1882–83 on the prehistory of marriage, in which Kautsky suggested that at least a "loose" monogamy had always existed; it is ascribed to the psychological motive of jealousy, which is apparently taken as an instinct. (So also Westermarck was going to promote the counter-revolution in anthropology by the theory of the "monogamous instinct.") See Engels' letters to Kautsky of 10 Feb. and 2 March 1883, in *ME:W* 35:432–33, 447–49. He wrote and published his *Origin of the Family* a year later.

The approaching social revolution will do away with "the hitherto existing economic foundations of monogamy" as well as its accompaniment, prostitution. The bourgeois anxiety about inheritance is reduced to a minimum. "Since monogamy arose from economic causes, will it disappear when these causes disappear?" Clearly the first answer is: *maybe.*

With the passage of the means of production into common property, the individual family ceases to be the economic unit of society. Private housekeeping is transformed into a social industry. The care and education of the children become a public matter. Society takes care of all children equally, irrespective of whether they are born in wedlock or not. Thus, the anxiety about the "consequences," which is today the most important social factor—both moral and economic—that hinders a girl from giving herself freely to the man she loves disappears. Will this not be cause enough for a gradual rise of more unrestrained sexual intercourse, and along with it, a more lenient public opinion regarding virginal honor and feminine shame? . . . Can prostitution disappear without dragging monogamy with it into the abyss?[52]

That there is bound to be a basic change in the nature of the man-woman relationship is not in question. (That would be so even without the Pill.) But is that change bound to be the disappearance of the monogamous family in any form?

To make a comparison (not Engels' this time): modern democracy arose with the bourgeoisie; but the abolition of capitalism does not therefore mean the disappearance of democracy. On the contrary, as we have seen, it means, to Marxists, the full flowering of genuine and complete democracy, a new type of democracy. In effect, Engels' answer on monogamy is similar.[53]

For one thing: "monogamy, instead of declining, finally becomes a reality—for the men as well."[54] The double-standard goes first of all.

But more basically, Engels puts the emphasis on what we have already noted (in the preceding chapter) [Not reprinted here—Ed.] about the transformation of society at large: *the future lies with a new individualism.*

Here a new factor comes into operation, a factor that, at most, existed in embryo at the time when monogamy developed, namely, individual sex love.[55]

Our comparison was with "the full flowering of genuine and complete democracy, a new type of democracy." For "democracy" in this proposition, substitute *individual sex love*; and this is Engels' approach. In

---

[52] Ibid., 234.
[53] The argument for monogamy that Engels vigorously rejects is that it is sanctified as the "highest" historical stage, etc. After which he philosophizes: "And if strict monogamy is to be regarded as the acme of all virtue, then the palm must be given to the tapeworm, which possesses a complete male and female sexual apparatus in every one of its 50 to 200 proglottides or segments of the body, and passes the whole of its life in cohabiting with itself in every one of these segments." (*Ibid.,* 194.)
[54] Ibid., 234.
[55] Ibid., 234.

both cases, the best of bourgeois thought has done enough trumpeting; a socialist transformation of society is needed to open the gates of the City of Humanity.

Thus, full freedom in marriage can become generally operative only when the abolition of capitalist production, and of the property relations created by it, has removed all those secondary economic considerations which still exert so powerful an influence on the choice of a partner. Then, no other motive remains than mutual affection.

Since sex love is by its very nature exclusive—although this exclusiveness is fully realized today only in the woman—then marriage based on sex love is by its very nature monogamy.[56]

The crux of Engels' argument for this expectation, then, is the inherent exclusiveness of individual love. Obviously this is a highly controversial area, and it is quite certain that Engels would *not* claim that this is the sole and inevitable conclusion from Marxist theory. It is his opinion; and it invites a short excursus on—[Marxism and love].

Marxism and Love

For is it not "un-Marxist" to lay so much store by, and assign such a basic role to, such a thing of the mind as "love," which cannot be summed up in economic formulas and may even evade sociological analysis?

The answer is a flat no; for, as we shall see (in the next chapter) [Not reprinted here—Ed.], one of the consequences of the ascent "from necessity to freedom" in a completely transformed society is precisely the pushing of economic and social factors into the background, and the emergence of the freed human spirit as a history-maker (social determinant) for the *first* time. Of course, we must still keep in mind that the "human spirit" in any given epoch is the product of a long material (bio-social) evolution.

But even today, in advance of such a social transformation, the fact that this element of the human spirit is prevented from being a decisive social determinant does not mean that it is not an active factor for individuals. "Sex love in particular," remarked Engels, "has undergone a development and won a place during the last eight hundred years which has made it a compulsory pivotal point of all poetry during this period."[57] Of poetry—yes; but despite Shelley, poets are not the legislators of the world; they are individuals who more often belong to the anticipative department than the legislative. The further development is still ahead.

Nor is it "Marxist" to reduce love to physical sex alone. This reductionism is a classic example of vulgar mechanical-materialism, and in denying the efficacy of *ideas,* it is quite alien to the Marxist outlook. So much for the theoretical side.

[56] Ibid., 239.
[57] *Engels: Ludwig Feuerbach,* in *ME:SW* 2:377.

Marx himself had no more doubt about it than Engels. As is well known, he did not consider his own love for his wife as a petty-bourgeois deviation from orthodoxy. On the contrary, he took the emotional need—over and above the sexual need—as an integral part of the complete human spirit. "In the case of that which I truly love," he wrote in his first published article in 1842, "I feel its existence to be a necessary one, one of which I am in need, without which my being cannot have a fulfilled, satisfied and complete life."[58]

This insight, set down before he became a socialist, was written up at much greater length afterward, in *The Holy Family*. One of the Bauer brothers, who are the butt of this book, had decried "childishness like so-called love." Love, replied Marx, is neither a goddess nor a devil, but simply an inseparable part of man as he is, "which first really teaches man to believe in the objective world outside himself"—hence is an "unchristian materialist." The trouble with Bauer is that he "is not against love alone, but against everything living, everything which is immediate, every sensuous experience, any and every *real* experience the 'Whence' and the 'Whither' of which is not know beforehand."[59]

Nor did Marx change his mind about this later, though he wrote no manifesto on the subject. In a letter to Jenny, written after thirteen years of marriage, he completely echoed his earlier words, in an unusual passage of theorization for a personal letter:

My love for you, when you are away, emerges as what it is, as a giant, in which all the force of my spirit and all the character of my heart concentrates itself. I feel myself again a man, because I feel a great passion; and the complexities in which we are entangled by study and modern education, and the skepticism which necessarily makes us critical of all subjective and objective impressions, are wholly designed to make us all small and weak and querulous and indecisive. But love—not love for the Feuerbachian Man nor for the Moleschottian metabolism,[60] nor for the proletariat—but love for the loved one, and in particular for you, makes a man a man again.
You will laugh, my sweetheart, and ask how I suddenly break out with all this rhetoric . . .[61]

The other side of this viewpoint we have discussed in a previous chapter: rejection of rhetoric about abstract "love" (of Humanity, etc.) as a type of reformist ideology. For love cannot be a social determinant *today*, in this society—a society which love cannot reform but which rather deforms love. When "love" is abstractionalized into a social ideology of general reconciliation, it is also emptied of all real content, in order to turn into its opposite: hatred of class struggle.

[58] Marx, "Debatten über Pressfreiheit [&c.]," in *Rhein. Zeit.*, 5 May 1842, in *ME:W* 1:33. He has just remarked that one must love freedom of the press in order to defend it.
[59] *ME: Holy Fam.*, 32–34. I take it that Marx is making a similar point in a woolly passage in *Econ. Phil. Mss.*, 141 (end of "The Power of Money in Bourgeois Society").
[60] The reference to Feuerbach is to his abstract "humanism"; cf. Marx's first thesis on Feuerbach, and Engels' *Feuerbach*, in *ME:SW* 2:402, 380–84. The reference to Moleschott hits at mechanical-materialism; cf. Engels' *Feuerbach*, ibid., 372, 374; also Marx's anonymous reference in *Capital*, 1:373 fn.3.
[61] Letter of 21 June 1856, in *ME:W* 29:535.

The Revolutionization of Monogamy

If individual sex love implies the retention of monogamy in some form, yet that form will certainly not be the same as today's. Some of the consequences Engels looked to are touched on in the following passage:

What will most definitely disappear from monogamy, however, is all the characteristics stamped on it in consequence of its having arisen out of property relationships. These are, first, the dominance of the man, and secondly, the indissolubility of marriage. The predominance of the man in marriage is simply a consequence of his economic predominance and will vanish with it automatically. The indissolubility of marriage is partly the result of the economic conditions under which monogamy arose, and partly a tradition from the time when the connection between these economic conditions and monogamy was not yet correctly understood and was exaggerated by religion. Today it has been breached a thousandfold. If only marriages that are based on love are moral, then also only those are moral in which love continues. The duration of the urge of individual sex love differs very much according to the individual, particularly among men; and a definite cessation of affection, or its displacement by a new passionate love, makes separation a blessing for both parties as well as for society. People will only be spared the experience of wading through the useless mire of divorce proceedings.[62]

It would appear, from the rejection of "divorce proceedings," that Engels is taking for granted something akin to simple registration of marriage and divorce; and even registration would depend on its relevance to some other matter of proper societal concern. Otherwise, Engels' general principle of 1847 would hold good—undoubtedly for him: "the relations between the sexes [will be] a purely private matter which concerns only the persons involved and into which society has no occasion to intervene." In his book *Ludwig Feuerbach*, Engels delivers a passing thrust at the very notion of "state-regulated sex love, that is . . . the marriage laws"—"which could all disappear tomorrow without changing in the slightest the practice of love and friendship."[63]

All this has been Engels' opinion. Very much the same picture of a transformation in sex morals, marriage forms and the place of women in society had been published in the book by the leader of the German party, August Bebel, *Woman and Socialism*, especially Chap. 28, "Woman in the Future."[64] Bebel emphasized that much of this was already taken for granted by advanced people for special cases like George Sand—"But why should only 'great souls' lay claim to this right . . . ?"

For the rest, however, Engels inevitably winds up on the same note as on other speculations about future society. He leaves the question

[62] *E: Orig. Fam.*, in *ME:SW* 2:240.
[63] *E: Feuerbach*, in *ME:SW* 2:377.
[64] Bebel's *Die Frau und der Sozialismus* was first pub. 1879; his title *Die Frau in der Vergangenheit, Gegenwart und Zukunft* in 1883. An English trans. under title *Women in the Past, Present and Future* was pub. London, 1885. References in this article are based on the English trans. *Woman and Socialism* (N.Y., 1910, "Jubilee 50th ed.," trans. by M. L. Stern).

open to solution by those more qualified than himself, viz. the men and women to come:

Thus, what we can conjecture at present about the regulation of sex relationships after the impending effacement of capitalist production is, in the main, of a negative character, limited mostly to what will vanish. But what will be added? That will be settled after a new generation has grown up: a generation of men who never in all their lives have had occasion to purchase a woman's surrender either with money or with any other means of social power, and of women who have never been obliged to surrender to any man out of any consideration other than that of real love, or to refrain from giving themselves to their beloved for fear of the economic consequences. Once such people appear, they will not care a rap about what we today think they should do. They will establish their own practice and their own public opinion, conformable therewith, on the practice of each individual—and that's the end of it.[65]

4: Problems of Women's Liberation

Looking a little nearer than the dim future, we have already mentioned that legal equality is a necessary, but not sufficient, precondition for the full emancipation of women. Of course, that includes first of all the right to vote and hold office.[66]

Emancipation demands have also included opposition to any discrimination against women on bourgeois-moral grounds. A typical example came up in the Paris Commune of 1871 (in which the working-women played a prominent and militant role), and was noted by Marx in an early draft of his *Civil War in France* as one of the progressive acts of the revolutionary government:

Commune has given order to the *mairies* to make no distinction between the *femmes* called illegitimate, the mothers and widows of national guards, as to the indemnity . . .[67]

Beginning at Home

In addition, socialist women militants have always pointed out that equality begins at home, i.e., in the socialist movement itself.[68] In 1868

---

[65] *E: Orig. Fam.*, in *ME:SW* 2:240.
[66] For ex., see letter, Engels to Ida Pauli, 14 Feb. 1877, in *ME:W* 34:253.
[67] First Draft of *The Civil War in France*, in *Arkhiv Marksa i Engel'sa*, v.3 (8), 1934, p. 302. (The English is Marx's.)
[68] Less important is the fact that socialist women have also had to be reminded that equality cuts two ways. The old society's tradition of "chivalry" and "gentlemanly behavior," which assumes the inferiority of women, dies hard. After his visit to America, Engels related in a letter: "Mother Wischnewetzky is very much hurt because I did not visit her in Long Branch instead of getting well . . . She seems to be hurt by a breach of etiquette and lack of gallantry towards ladies. But I do not allow the little women's-rights ladies to demand gallantry from us; if they want men's rights, they should also let themselves be treated as men."—Letter to Sorge, 12 Jan. 1889, in *ME: Letters to Americans* (New York: Internat'l. Pub., 1953), 209.

Marx had to assure a correspondent that "of course" women could join the First International the same as men.[69] (In fact, not long after the formation of the International his correspondence shows him urging a couple of women to join the International as individual members independently of their husbands.[70] In the 1860s this could hardly be taken for granted.) Another letter anticipated another question: "In any case ladies cannot complain of the *International,* for it has elected a lady, Madame [Harriet] Law, to be a member of the General Council."[71]

Later, it was Marx who proposed a resolution to the General Council calling for the "formation of working women's branches," or "female branches among the working class," without however interfering "with the existence or formation of branches composed of both sexes." At the 1871 Conference of the International, Marx moved this in the name of the General Council, stressing "the need for founding women's sections in countries whose industries engage many women."[72]

Writing to Liebknecht's wife Natalie while her husband was in jail, Engels urged that women have the same struggle to carry on as men:

Fortunately our German women do not let themselves be confused and show by deeds that the much renowned soft sentimentality is only a characteristic class-disease of the bourgeois woman.[73]

The socialist women's movement blossomed, under the encouragement of Engels and Bebel especially, with an autonomous leadership and press of its own. (In Germany, Clara Zetkin's organ *Gleichheit* eventually reached a circulation of 100,000.) In Germany it was the Lassallean wing which opposed socialist agitation for the emancipation of women and argued against the increasing entrance of women into industry. At the unity congress at Gotha in 1875 between the Lassallean and the semi-Marxist groups, the proposal of the Marxist wing (moved by Bebel) that the party go on record as favoring equal rights for women was rejected by the majority, on the traditional ground that women were "not prepared" for the step. But Bebel's book on woman was very influential. At the Erfurt (1891) congress of the Social-Democracy, which finally adopted a formally Marxist program, the majority also finally came out in support of women's-rights demands, at least the demand for legal equality. Yet the same year, at the Second International congress, the Marxist position was still opposed by that very embodiment of social-democratic reformism, Emile Vandervelde.[74]

In England, the most promising socialist women's leader at the time of Engels' death was Eleanor Marx, whose remarkable career as a revo-

[69] Letter, Marx to Kugelmann, 12 Oct. 1868, in *M: Lett. Kugelm.,* 78.
[70] Letter, Marx to Engels, 25 Jan. and 13 Feb. 1865, in *ME:W* 31:43, 72.
[71] Letter, Marx to Kugelmann, 12 Dec. 1868, in *M: Lett. Kugelm.,* 83.
[72] *Gen. Counc. F.I. 1870–71* [v.4], 442, 460, 541 (n.320).
[73] Letter of 31 July 1877, in *ME:W* 34:284.
[74] B. J. Stern, article "Woman, Position in Society—History," in the *Encyclopedia of the Social Sciences,* 1937.

New York, early 1900s: socialist women march in May Day parade

lutionary organizer and agitator has been obscured by the label "daughter of Karl Marx" and by the tragic circumstances of her suicide in 1898.[75] Not only was she an extraordinarily effective political activist, working by preference among the most exploited workers of London's East End, she was also the ablest woman trade-union organizer in the "New Unionism" movement. After playing an active role in the building of the new-type Gas Workers' and General Labourers Union, which organized the unskilled into a militant mass organization—"by far the best union" in Engels' opinion[76]—she also became the acknowledged leader of the women workers in the movement, whom she organized into what were the first women's trade-union sections in the country.[77]

In addition she participated in discussions on women's-liberation policy in the socialist women's movement on the Continent,[78] and co-authored a pamphlet for England on "The Woman Question."[79] In the intellectual circles of the decade, the "woman question" was often spelled *Ibsenism*; Eleanor was one of the pioneers in spreading the reputation of the dramatist of the "New Woman," and she was one of the first translators of both Ibsen and his fellow Norwegian Kielland.

Typically, Engels, already over 70, began to study Norwegian in order to read both of these writers in the original.[80] It is perhaps as a result of Nora's door-slamming in *The Doll House* that Engels remarked, in a letter of 1893, on hearing that Hermann Schlüter's wife had left him: "it is always gratifying to hear that a woman whom one knows has had the courage to go independent. . . . But what a prodigal waste of energy is bourgeois marriage—first till one gets that far; then as long as the business lasts; and then till one is rid of it again."[81]

Opposition to Bourgeois Feminism

But, like the socialist women's movements in the main, Engels had little use for the bourgeois women's-rights leagues. For one thing, the latter (then as now) commonly counterposed abstract equality to the pro-

---

[75] With the publication of C. Tsuzuki's *The Life of Eleanor Marx* (Oxford, 1967) a modicum of justice has been done at least to the facts about her work as a revolutionary socialist —all the more strikingly since Tsuzuki's own ideas are utterly alien to her Marxism.
[76] Cf. Engels' letters: to Laura (Marx) Lafargue, 10 May 1890, in *Engels-Lafargue: Correspondence* (Moscow, FLPH, n.d.), 2:375; to Sorge, 19 Apr. 1890, in *ME: Lett. Amer.*, 230; to Bebel, 9 May 1890, in *ME:W* 37:401.
[77] For Eleanor's work as trade-union organizer among women, see (besides letters listed in n.76) Tsuzuki, *Life*, 198–99, 202–03; Engels' article "May 4 in London," 1890, in *ME: On Britain*, 2d ed. (Moscow, FLPH, 1962), 522–23; and his letters as follows: to Guesde, 20 Nov. 1889, in *ME:W* 37:312, to Sorge, 7 Dec. 1889, in *ME: Selected Correspondence* (Moscow, FLPH, n.d.), 490; to Natalie Liebknecht, 24 Dec. 1889, in *ME:W* 37:330; to Sorge, 30 Apr. 1890, in *ME:W* 37:396.
[78] Cf. letter, Engels to Laura (Marx) Lafargue, 2 Oct. 1891, in *E-Lafargue: Corr.*, 3:109.
[79] Published London, 1886; cf. Tsuzuki, *Life*, 124–25.
[80] F. Lessner, in *Reminiscences of Marx and Engels* (Moscow, n.d.), 180.
[81] Letter, Engels to Bebel, 12 Oct. 1893, in *ME:W* 39:142.

tection of women workers in industry. Engels explained to a feminist:[82]

Equal wages for equal work to either sex are, until [wages are] abolished in general, demanded, as far as I know, by all Socialists. That the working woman needs special protection against capitalist exploitation because of her special physiological functions seems obvious to me. The English women who championed the formal rights of members of their sex to permit themselves to be as thoroughly exploited by the capitalists as the men are mostly, directly or indirectly, interested in the capitalist exploitation of both sexes. I admit I am more interested in the health of the future generation than in the absolute formal equality of the sexes during the last years of the capitalist mode of production. It is my conviction that real equality of women and men can come true only when the exploitation of either by capital has been abolished and private housework has been transformed into a public industry.[83]

Besides, on this question Marx had pointed out very early (1847) that gains made on behalf of women and children in the factories were then more easily won for men too. Writing of "the dogged resistance which the English factory owners put up to the Ten Hours' Bill," he explained:

They knew only too well that a two hours' reduction of labor granted to women and children would carry with it an equal reduction of working hours for adult men. It is in the nature of large-scale industry that working hours should be equal for all.[84]

Opposition to protective legislation for women has, in the course of time, come from many different quarters besides the capitalist class itself; every ruling class learns to mobilize not only its beneficiaries but also its victims. Just as in *Capital* Marx had pilloried parents who exploited their children's labor, so also he had noted the resistance of poor working-women to a limitation of the working day out of fear of reducing their already meager earnings.[85] Resistance had come from pure-and-simple unionists who did not want "meddling" legislation. Resistance had naturally come from anarchist rhetoricians of revolution: in an 1873 article Marx ridiculed the anarchist arguments that one "must not take the trouble to obtain legal prohibition of the employment of girls under 10 in factories because a stop is not thereby put to the exploitation of boys under 10"—hence was a "compromise which damages the purity of the eternal principles."[86] The bourgeois women's-righters took their place in this serried phalanx.

[82] This was Gertrud Guillaume-Schack (*née* Countess Schack). She had been a leader of the bourgeois women's movement in Germany, then was active in the socialist women's movement for a while (a blow from which it recovered), went to England where she moved on to anarchism and was active in blighting William Morris's Socialist League; also in the Anti-Contagious Diseases Acts Agitation. Cf. Engels' account of her in a number of letters in *ME:W* 36, esp. 667, 723–24.
[83] Letter, Engels to G. Guillaume-Schack, ab. 5 July 1885, in *ME: Sel. Corr. (FLPH)*, 461–62, corrected after *ME:W* 36:341.
[84] *Marx: The Poverty of Philosophy* (Moscow, FLPH, n.d.), 77.
[85] *M: Capital*, 1:554 and n.4 on same page; cf. also Marx's letter to Kugelmann, 17 March 1868, in *M: Lett. Kugelm.*, 66.
[86] Marx, "Indifference in Political Affairs," in *ME: Scritti Italiani* (Rome, Ed.Avanti, 1955), 98.

In general, Engels—like the revolutionary Marxist women leaders, such as Clara Zetkin in Germany, and Eleanor Marx in England—vigorously supported the organization of *socialist* women's movements and working-women's movements in the fight for full sexual equality, as against the bourgeois women's-rights groups for whom "the separate women's-rights business" was "a purely bourgeois pastime."[87] In the First International, Marx had had to fight the notorious crackpottery of the American "Section 12," led by Victoria Woodhull, which combined a pro-middle-class and anti-working-class "socialism" with "free love" cultism, spiritualism, "funny money" schemes, and almost every other fad of the time.[88] Referring to a group of British counterparts, Marx summed it up as "follies and crotchets, such as currency quackery, false emancipation of women, etc."[89]

Social Revolution Comes First

As we have seen, it was not the demand or aspiration for extension of sexual freedom ("free love" or whatever the fashionable term of the moment might be) that was in question, but rather the social ideology in which this is embedded and the strategic place this is given in the over-all work of the socialist movement. Writing of the similarities between the modern socialist movement and the first Christian communities in the days when the new religion was still subversive doctrine,[90] Engels commented wryly on the Bible's evidence for the proliferation of Christian sects and their mutual recriminations, such as charges of sexual immorality:

It is a curious fact that with every great revolutionary movement the question of "free love" comes into the foreground. With one set of people as a revolutionary progress, as a shaking off of old traditional fetters, no longer necessary; with others as a welcome doctrine, comfortably covering all sorts of free and easy practices between man and woman. The latter, the philistine sort, appear here soon to have got the upper hand . . .[91]

The "curious fact" is due to

a phenomenon common to all times of great agitation, that the traditional bonds

---

[87] Cf. letter, Engels to Bebel, 1 Oct. 1891, in *ME:W* 38:164; and to Laura (Marx) Lafargue, 2 Oct. 1891, in *E-Lafargue: Corr.*, 3:109. Early in 1892, both Eleanor and Laura as well as Louise Kautsky had articles in the Vienna *Arbeiterinnenzeitung* on disputed issues.

[88] For the story of the Woodhull-Claflin "Section 12" in general, see Samuel Bernstein: *The First International in America* (N.Y., 1962). For Marx's documentation on the anti-proletarian politics of the group, see his notes "American Split," in *Gen. Counc. F.I. 1871–72* [v.5], 323–32.

[89] Letter, Marx to F. Bolte, 23 Nov. 1871, in *ME:W* 33:328, referring to the "O'Brienite" sect.

[90] Engels liked to quote Ernest Renan's statement that anyone who wanted a good idea of what the first Christian communities were like should look up a local section of the First International. (See *ME: On Relig.*, 204–05, 315.)

[91] Engels, "The Book of Revelation," in *ME: On Religion* (Moscow, FLPH, 1957), 205.

of sexual relations, like all other fetters, are shaken off. In the first centuries of Christianity, too, there appeared often enough, side by side with ascetics which mortified the flesh, the tendency to extend Christian freedom to a more or less unrestrained intercourse between man and woman. The same thing was observed in the modern socialist movement.[92]

Saint-Simon (Engels goes on) called for "the rehabilitation of the flesh" and Fourier was even more horrifying to the ruling philistines. "With the overcoming of utopianism these extravagances yielded to a more rational and in reality far more radical conception"—to "the hypocritical indignation of the distinguished pious world."[93]

In Marx and Engels, then, there is nothing of the later social-democratic cringing from the "accusation" that social revolution entails sexual revolution. What irked them and others from time to time was the ideological package that so often accompanied obsession with the sexual side of a world that is out of joint in general. On this, too, Engels consoled himself with the observation that the subversive Christian sects had had to go through the same problem:

And just as the working-class parties in all countries are besieged by all the types who have nothing to look forward to from the official world or have been enervated by it—anti-vaccinationists, temperance advocates, vegetarians, anti-vivisectionists, nature-healers, free-community preachers whose communities have collapsed, creators of new world-genesis theories, unsuccessful or unlucky inventors, victims of real or imaginary injustices labeled "good-for-nothing cranks" by the bureaucracy, honest fools and dishonest swindlers—so it was also with the first Christians. All the elements set free, i.e. at a loose end, by the process of the old world's dissolution came one after the other into the orbit of Christianity as the only element resisting that process of dissolution . . .[94]

What was primary was the movement for social revolution, not the many and various reform movements directed against *symptoms* of social dissolution.

This attitude did not counterpose socialism to the fight for women's rights, any more than Marxism counterposed socialism to the fight for reforms, but it established a relationship between them. In this field, reforms were just as necessary as in economics or politics, and socialists would fight for them in the same spirit. But in the last analysis, the historic forms of the division of labor between the sexes could be uprooted for good and all only by as profound an upheaval as it had originally taken to impose "the world-historic defeat of the female sex" of which Engels had written.

[92] Engels, "On the History of Early Christianity," in *ME: On Relig.*, 239.
[93] Ibid., 330.
[94] Ibid., 319–20.

THE HOME: ITS WORK AND INFLUENCE

Charlotte Perkins Gilman

The world of science and invention may change; art, religion, government may change; industry, commerce and manufacturing may change; but women and the home are supposed to remain as they are, forever . . . the home is the most unalterably settled in its ideals and convictions; the slowest and last to move . . . [and] a peculiar condition of women is that their environment has been almost wholly that of the home.

> Charlotte Perkins Gilman, "Economic Basis of the Woman Question,"
> *Woman's Journal,* October 1, 1898.

Charlotte Perkins Gilman (1860–1935) has been called "the leading intellectual in the woman's movement in the United States during the first two decades of the twentieth century."[1] Born in Connecticut into a family already famous for feminist activities—Henry Ward Beecher was her great-uncle and Harriet Beecher Stowe her great-aunt—Charlotte Perkins' childhood was nevertheless scarred by poverty and unhappiness. Soon after Charlotte's birth, Frederic Perkins deserted his wife and children, leaving them to roam about for years in financial and emotional uncertainty. Thus Charlotte had no regular schooling until she attended the Rhode Island School for Design for a year at the age of eighteen (subsequently she occasionally earned money as a commercial artist). What is most notable about Charlotte Perkins Gilman is her strength of character, defiance, and self-discipline. Overcoming family and social pressures she became, as she says in her autobiography, "My own mistress at last. No one on earth had a right to ask obedience of me. I was self-supporting . . ."[2] She wrote over twenty books—social criticism, poetry, fiction.[3] Between 1909 and 1916 she wrote, edited, owned, and published a journal, *The Forerunner.* And all by dint of a strong will: since she was almost completely self-educated and suffered poor health most of her adult life. Since she always demanded top performance from herself, when cancer prevented her from continuing her studies and writings, she committed suicide.

Charlotte Perkins Gilman, *The Home: Its Work and Influence* (New York: McClure, Phillips & Co., 1903), pp. 30–34, 64–65, 69, 70–73, 161–163, 165–167, 169–170, 176–180, 301, 314–318, 320–322. Reprinted by permission.

[1] In Carl N. Degler's introduction to *Women and Economics* (New York: Harper Torchbooks, 1966), p. xiii. This is an intelligent summary of Gilman's life and works. Less intelligent—in fact, somewhat misleading—is the brief discussion of Charlotte Gilman by William L. O'Neill in *Everyone Was Brave: Rise and Fall of Feminism in America* (New York: Quadrangle, 1969, pp. 130–133) where the analysis centers on Gilman's failure to be a good mother and on her "low level of sexual intensity."

[2] *The Living of Charlotte Perkins Gilman* (New York: 1935), p. 5.

[3] Her best-known works are *Women and Economics* (1898), *The Home: Its Work and Influence* (1902), and *The Man-Made World: Or Our Androcentric Culture* (1911). Today her novels (such as *What Diantha Did, The Crux*) and books of poetry (*In This Our World*) have been all but forgotten.

Gilman's contribution to the women's movement was theoretical; she was an intellectual socialist and feminist, not a political activist. For her, the woman question was far wider than suffrage. In her most important works, *Women and Economics* and *The Home: Its Work and Influence* (excerpts from which follow), she stresses two major points. First, she argues, a woman's economic independence is the basis of her freedom—as long as a woman depends on a father, brother, or husband for material support, she will depend on him intellectually and emotionally as well. Second, Gilman argues that the traditional concept of family life and motherhood, which she calls the "domestic ethic," is the major deterrent to female independence. If women are taught that they are only suited for marriage and child-bearing, then it is logical that they will be primarily concerned with acquiring those attributes that help them obtain husbands and a "free" livelihood. "Women are not underdeveloped men," Gilman stated, "but the feminine half of humanity is underdeveloped human."[4]

Like Emma Goldman (see Part 2 of this book), Gilman equated traditional marriage and prostitution: both are relationships in which women exchange sexual services for financial recompense. However, unlike Goldman, who supported a blanket rejection of the institution of marriage, Gilman was willing to accept matrimony and motherhood providing women were released from their conventionally defined and limited roles. In 1902 she advocated socialization of the most sacred of American private institutions, the home. And as the following selection shows, she pointed to the establishment of community child care and food preparation as a crucial step in freeing women from domestic drudgery.

Evolution of the Home

. . . the least evolved of all our institutions is the home. Move it must, somewhat, as part of human life, but the movement has come from without, through the progressive man, and has been sadly retarded in its slow effect on the stationary woman.

This difference in rate of progress may be observed in the physical structure of the home, in its industrial processes, and in the group of concepts most closely associated with it. We have run over, cursorily enough, the physical evolution of the home-structure, yet wide as have been its changes they do not compare with the changes along similar lines in the ultra-domestic world. Moreover, such changes as there are have been introduced by the free man from his place in the more rapidly progressive world outside.

The distinctively home-made product changes far less. We see most progress in the physical characteristics of the home, its plan, building, materials, furnishings, and decoration, because all these are part of the world growth outside. . . .

Least of all do we see progress in the home ideas. The home has

---

[4]*The Forerunner* (New York), I (1910), 12.

changed much in physical structure, in spite of itself. It has changed somewhat in its functions, also in spite of itself. But it has changed very little—painfully little—dangerously little, in its governing concepts. Naturally ideas change with facts, but if ideas are held to be sacred and immovable, the facts slide out from under and go on growing because they must, while the ideas lag further and further behind. . . .

. . .

What progress has been made in our domestic concepts? The oldest, —the pre-human,—shelter, safety, comfort, quiet, and mother love, are still with us, still crude and limited. Then follow gradually later sentiments of sanctity, privacy, and sex-seclusion; and still later, some elements of personal convenience and personal expression. How do these stand as compared with the facts? Our safety is really insured by social law and order, not by any system of home defence. Against the real dangers of modern life the home is no safeguard. It is as open to criminal attack as any public building, yes, more. A public building is more easily and effectively watched and guarded than our private homes. Sewer gas invades the home; microbes, destructive insects, all diseases invade it also; so far as civilised life is open to danger, the home is defenceless. So far as the home is protected it is through social progress —through public sanitation enforced by law and the public guardians of the peace. If we would but shake off the primitive limitations of these old concepts, cease to imagine the home to be a safe place, and apply our ideas of shelter, safety, comfort, and quiet to the City and State, we should then be able to ensure their fulfilment in our private homes far more fully.

The mother-love concept suffers even more from its limitations. As a matter of fact our children are far more fully guarded, provided for, and educated, by social efforts than by domestic; compare the children of a nation with a system of public education with children having only domestic education; or children safeguarded by public law and order with children having only domestic protection. The home-love and care of the Armenians for their children is no doubt as genuine and strong as ours, but the public care is not strong and well organised, hence the little Armenians are open to massacre as little Americans are not. Our children are largely benefited by the public, and would be much more so if the domestic concept did not act too strongly in limiting mother love to so narrow a field of action.

The later sentiments of sanctity and the others have moved a little, but not much. *Why* it is more sacred to make a coat at home than to buy it of a tailor, to kill a cow at home than to buy it of a butcher, to cook a pie at home than to buy it of a baker, or to teach a child at home than to have it taught by a teacher, is not made clear to us, but the lingering weight of those ages of ancestor-worship, of real sacrifice and libation at a real altar, is still heavy in our minds. We still by race-habit regard the home as sacred, and cheerfully profane our halls of justice and marts of trade, as if social service were not at least as high a thing as domestic service. This sense of sanctity is a good thing, but it should grow, it should evolve along natural lines till it includes all human functions, not be forever confined to its cradle, the home.

The concept of sex-seclusion is, with us, rapidly passing away. Our millions of wage-earning women are leading us, by the irresistible force of accomplished fact, to recognise the feminine as part of the world around us, not as a purely domestic element. The foot-binding process in China is but an extreme expression of this old domestic concept, the veiling process another. We are steadily leaving them all behind, and an American man feels no jar to his sexuo-domestic sentiments in meeting a woman walking freely in the street or working in the shops.

· · ·

Present Conditions

. . . An average home of to-day, in this sense, is one of good social position, wherein the husband has sufficient means and the wife sufficient education to keep step with the march of events; one which we should proudly point out to a foreign visitor as "a typical American home."

Now, how does this home really stand under dispassionate observation?

The ideal which instantly obtrudes itself is this: A beautiful, comfortable house meeting all physical needs; a happy family, profoundly enjoying each other's society; a father, devotedly spending his life in obtaining the wherewithal to maintain this little heaven; a mother, completely wrapped up in her children and devotedly spending her life in their service, working miracles of advantage to them in so doing; children, happy in the home and growing up beautifully under its benign influence—everybody healthy, happy, and satisfied with the whole thing.

· · ·

Now for our happy family. Let it be carefully borne in mind that no question is raised as to the happiness of husband and wife; or of parent and child in their essential relation; but of their happiness as affected by the home.

The effect of the home, as it now is, upon marriage is a vitally interesting study. Two people, happily mated, sympathetic physically and mentally, having many common interests and aspirations, proceed after marrying to enter upon the business of "keeping house," or "homemaking." This business is not marriage, it is not parentage, it is not child-culture. It is the running of the commissary and dormitory departments of life, with elaborate lavatory processes.

The man is now called upon to pay, and pay heavily, for the maintenance of this group of activities; the woman to work, either personally, by deputy, or both, in its performance.

Then follows one of the most conspicuous of conditions in our present home: the friction and waste of its supposedly integral processes. The man does spend his life in obtaining the wherewithal to maintain—not a "little heaven," but a bunch of ill-assorted trades, wherein everything costs more than it ought to cost, and nothing is done as it should be done—on a business basis.

How many men simply hand out a proper sum of money for "living expenses," and then live, serene and steady, on that outlay?

Home expenses are large, uncertain, inexplicable. In some families an exceptional "manager," provided with a suitable "allowance," does keep the thing in comparatively smooth running order, at considerable cost to herself; but in most families the simple daily processes of "housekeeping" are a constant source of annoyance, friction, waste, and loss. Housekeeping, as a business, is not instructively successful. As the structure of the home is not what we so readily took for granted in our easily fitting ideals, so the functions of the home are not, either. We are really struggling and fussing along, trying to live smoothly, healthfully, peacefully; studying all manner of "new thought" to keep us "poised," pining for a "simpler life"; and yet all spending our strength and patience on the endless effort to "keep house," to "make a home"—to live comfortably in a way which is not comfortable; and when this continuous effort produces utter exhaustion, we have *to go away from home* for a rest! Think of that, seriously.

The father is so mercilessly overwhelmed in furnishing the amount of money needed to maintain a home that he scarce knows what a home is. Time, time to sit happily down with his family, or to go happily out with his family, this is denied to the patient toiler on whose shoulders this ancient structure rests. The mother is so overwhelmed in her performance or supervision of all the inner workings of the place that she, too, has scant time for the real joys of family life.

The home is one thing, the family another; and when the home takes all one's time, the family gets little. So we find both husband and wife overtaxed and worried in keeping up the institution according to tradition; both father and mother too much occupied in home-making to do much toward child-training, man-making!

What is the real condition of the home as regards children—its primal reason for being? How does the present home meet their needs? How does the homebound woman fill the claims of motherhood? As a matter of fact, *are* our children happy and prosperous, healthy and good, at home? Again the ideal rises; picture after picture, tender, warm, glowing; again we must push it aside and look at the case as it is. In our homes to-day the child grows up—when he does not die—not at all in that state of riotous happiness we are so eager to assume as the condition of childhood. The mother loves the child, always and always; she does what she can, what she knows how; but the principal work of her day is the care of the house, not of the child; the construction of clothes—not of character.

Follow the hours in the day of the housewife: count the minutes spent in the care and service of the child, as compared with those given to the planning of meals, the purchase of supplies, the labour either of personally cleaning things or of seeing that other persons do it; the "duties" to society, of the woman exempt from the actual house-labour.

"But," we protest, "all this is for the child—the meals, the well-kept house, the clothes—the whole thing!"

Yes? And in what way do the meals we so elaborately order and prepare, the daintily furnished home, the much-trimmed clothing, contribute to the body-growth, mind-growth, and soul-growth of the child? The conditions of home life are not those best suited to the right growth of children. Infant discipline is one long struggle to coerce the growing creature into some sort of submission to the repressions, the exactions, the arbitrary conventions of the home.

In broad analysis, we find in the representative homes of to-day a condition of unrest. The man is best able to support it because he is least in it; he is part and parcel of the organised industries of the world, he has his own special business to run on its own lines; and he, with his larger life-basis, can better bear the pressure of house-worries. The wife is cautioned by domestic moralists not to annoy her husband with her little difficulties; but in the major part of them, the economic difficulties, she must consult, because he pays the bills.

. . .

Home-life, as such, does in itself tend to produce certain ethical qualities; qualities not produced, or not in any such degree, by other fields of life. Constant association with helpless infancy develops a generous care and kindness—that is, it does so when the helpless infants are one's own. The managers of foundling and orphan asylums do not seem always to be so affected. Constant association with the inevitable errors and mistakes of childhood develops patience and sympathy, or tends to do so. There are qualities brought out in home life which extend their influence into the life of the world. The young man or woman who has had good home influence shows that advantage all through life. But there are also qualities brought out in the world's life apart from the home; and the man or woman affected by these shows them in the home life. We find in our homes the gathered flowers of civilisation, of Christianity, of progress in general; and unconsciously accredit the homes with the production of these beautiful results—quite erroneously.

. . .

The home as a permanent institution in society, if rightly placed and understood, works for good. The home in its non-essential conditions, if wrongly placed in our scheme of thought, if misunderstood, if out of proportion and loaded with anachronisms, works evil. In the complex group of qualities which make up the human character to-day, for good and ill, many influences are traceable; and we wish here to disentangle from among them some lines of influence, and show what place is held by the home in making us what we are and what we wish to be.

· · ·

. . . Mother-love is the foundation and permanent force of home life; and, mother-love is, indeed, the parent of all the love we know. Altruism was born of babyhood. The continued existence of the child—of a succession of children; the permanent presence of helplessness and its irresistible demands for care; this forced up into a widening of the sympathies, a deepening of sensitiveness to others' needs; this laid the foundations of human love. In this sense, the home is the cradle of one of our very greatest virtues. Love began with the mother; but it should not stop with her. "Mother-love" is precisely limited to its own children.

Few, indeed, are the mothers who love other women's children. As "mother" is a synonym for all kindness, so "stepmother" is a synonym for all unkindness. Folklore and fairy-tale indicate old fact. Infant helplessness and orphan need are not only what appeals to the mother—it is most the blood-tie, the physical relation.

Civilisation and Christianity teach us to care for "the child," motherhood stops at "my child."

Still, in the home we do find the nursery of all the lines of family affection, parental, filial, fraternal, and these are good. Hearts able to love ten could more easily take in twenty; the love of one's own parents spread to our present care for the aged; the power of loving grew, and, as soon as it overstepped the limits of the home, it grew more rapidly. We have learned to love our neighbors—if not as ourselves, at least, better than strangers. We have learned to love our fellow-citizens, fellow-craftsmen, fellow-countrymen. To-day the first thrills of international good-will are stealing across the world—and we are extending our sympathy even to the animals.

All this beautiful growth of love began at home; but the influence of the home, as it now exists upon the growth, is not so wholly gratifying. The love that we call human, the love of one another, the love Christ teaches us, is extra-domestic. We are not told, "Inasmuch as you have done it to your own families you have done it unto me." We are not exhorted to an ever-increasing intensity of devotion to our own blood-relations.

Both the teaching of our religion and the tendency of social progress call for a larger love, and the home, in its position of arrested development, primitive industry, and crippled womanhood, tends rather to check that growth than to help it. The man's love for his family finds expression in his labour for other people—he serves society, and society provides for him and his dear ones; so good will spreads and knits; comradeship and fellow-feeling appear, friendship brings its pure height of affection; this is the natural line of development in the great social virtue, love.

But the woman, still expressing her love for her family in direct personal service, misses all that.

. . .

The cowardice of women is a distinctly home product. It is born of weakness and ignorance; a weakness and an ignorance by no means essential feminine attributes, but strictly domestic attributes. Keep a man from birth wrapped in much cloth, shut away from sky and sun, wind and rain, continually exhausting his nervous energy by incessant activity in monotonous little things, and never developing his muscular strength and skill by suitable exercise of a large and varied nature, and he would be weak. Savage women are not weak. Peasant women are not weak. Fishwives are not weak. The home-bound woman is weak, as would be a home-bound man. Also, she is ignorant. Not, at least not nowadays, ignorant necessarily of books, but ignorant of general life.

It is this ignorance and this weakness which makes women cowards; cowards frank and unashamed; cowards accustomed to be petted and praised, to be called "true woman" because they scream at that arch-terror of the home—a mouse.

. . .

The man, accustomed to meet all sorts of people in many ways, has a far larger and easier adjustment. The woman, used only to the close contact of a few people in a few relations, as child, parent, servant, tradesman; or to the set code of "company manners," has no such healthy human plane of contact.

"I never was so treated in my life!" she complains—and she never was—at home. This limits the range of life, cuts off the widest channels of growth, overdevelops the few deep ones; and does not develop self-control. The dressing-gown-and-slippers home attitude is temporarily changed for that of "shopping," or "visiting," but the childish sensitive-ness, the disproportionate personality, remain dominant.

A too continuous home atmosphere checks in the woman the valuable social faculties. It checks it in the man more insidiously, through his position of easy mastery over these dependents, wife, children, serv-ants; and through the constant catering of the whole *ménage* to his special tastes. If each man had a private tailor shop in his back yard he would be far more whimsical and exacting in his personal taste in clothes. Every natural tendency to self-indulgence is steadily increased by the life service of an entire wife. This having one whole woman devoted to one's direct personal service is about as far from the culti-vation of self-control as any process that could be devised.

The man loves the woman and serves her—but he serves her *through his service of the world*—and she serves him direct.

. . .

What does the morbid, disproportioned, overgrown home life do? It tends to develop a domineering selfishness in man and a degrading abnegation in woman—or sometimes reverses this effect. The smooth, unconscious, all-absorbing greed which the unnaturally developed home of to-day produces in some women, is as evil a thing as life shows. Here is a human creature who has all her life been loved and cared for, sheltered, protected, defended; everything provided for her and nothing demanded of her except the exercise of her natural feminine functions, and some proficiency in the playground regulations of "society."

The degree of sublimated selfishness thus produced by home life is quite beyond the selfishness we so deplore in men. A man may be—often is—deplorably selfish in his home life; but he does not expect all the world to treat him with the same indulgence. He has to give as well as take in the broad, healthy, growing life of the world.

The woman has her home-life to make her selfish, and has no world life to offset it. Men are polite to her on account of her sex—not on account of any power, any achievement, any distinctive human value, but simply because she is a woman. The guests are necessarily polite to her. Her hosts are necessarily polite to her, and so are her fellow-guests. Her servants are necessarily polite to her. Her children also; if they are not she feels herself abused, denied a right.

The home and its social tributaries steadily work to develop a limitless personal selfishness in which the healthy power of self-control is all unknown. One way or the other swings the pendulum; here the woman pours out her life in devotion to her husband and children; in which case she is developing selfishness in them with as much speed and efficacy as if she were their worst enemy; and here again the woman sits, plump and fair, in her padded cage, bedizening its walls with every decoration; covering her own body with costly and beautiful things; feeding herself, her family, her guests; running from meal to meal as if eating were really the main business of a human being. This is the extreme.

Our primitive scheme requires that the entire time of the woman-who-does-her-own-work shall be spent in ministering to the physical needs of her family; and in the small minority who have other women to do it for them, that she shall still have this ministry her main care—and shall have no others. It is this inordinate demand for the life and time of a whole woman to keep half a dozen people fed, cleaned, and waited on, which keeps up in us a degree of self-indulgence we should, by every step of social development, have long since outgrown.

· · ·

Home and Social Progress

Human nature has changed and improved in tremendous ratio; and, if its improvement has been strangely irregular, far greater in social life than in personal life, it is for a very simple reason. All these large social processes which show such marked improvements are those wherein people work together in legitimate specialised lines in the world. These personal processes which have not so improved, the parts of life which are still so limited and imperfectly developed, may be fully accounted for by their environment—the ancient and unchanging home. Bring the home abreast of our other institutions; and our personal health and happiness will equal our public gains.

. . .

In what way does a woman best benefit her family? By staying at home and doing what she can with her own two hands—whereby no family ever has more than the labour of one affectionate amateur can provide —or by enlarging her motherhood as man has enlarged his fatherhood, and giving to her family the same immense advantages that he has given it? We have always assumed that the woman could do most by staying at home. Is this so? Can we prove it? Why is that which is so palpably false of a man held to be true of a woman? "Because men and woman are different!" will be stoutly replied. Of course they are different —in sex, *but not in humanity.* In every human quality and power they are alike; and the right service of the home, the right care and training of the child, call for human qualities and powers, not merely for sex-distinctions.

The home, in its arbitrary position of arrested development, does not properly fulfill its own essential functions—much less promote the social ones. Among the splendid activities of our age it lingers on, inert and blind, like a clam in a horse-race.

It hinders, by keeping woman a social idiot, by keeping the modern child under the tutelage of the primeval mother, by keeping the social conscience of the man crippled and stultified in the clinging grip of the domestic conscience of the woman. It hinders by its enormous expense; making the physical details of daily life a heavy burden to mankind; whereas, in our stage of civilisation, they should have been long since reduced to a minor incident.

Consider what the mere protection and defense of life used to cost, when every man had to be fighter most of his life. Ninety per cent., say, of masculine energy went to defend life; while the remaining ten, and the women, in a narrow, feeble way, maintained it. They lived, to be sure, fighting all the time for the sorry privilege. Now we have systematised military service so that only a tiny fraction of our men, for a very short period of life, need be soldiers; and peace is secured, not by constant painful struggles, but by an advanced economic system. "Eternal vigilance" may be "the price of liberty," but it is a very high price; and paid only by the barbarian who has not risen to the stage of civilised service.

Organisation among men has reduced this wasteful and crippling habit of being every-man-his-own-soldier. We do not have to carry a rifle and peer around every street-corner for a hidden foe. As a result the released energy of the ninety per cent. men, a tenth being large allowance for all the fighting necessary, is now poured into the channels that lead to wealth, peace, education, general progress.

Yet we are still willing that the personal care of life, the service of daily physical needs, shall monopolise as many women as that old custom of universal warfare monopolised men! Ninety per cent. of the feminine energy of the world is still spent in ministering laboriously to the last details of bodily maintenance; and the other tenth is supposed to do nothing but supervise the same tasks, and flutter about in fruitless social amusement. This crude waste of half the world's force keeps back human progress just as heavily as the waste of the other half did.

· · ·

The omnipresent domestic ideal is a deadly hinderance to the social ideal. When half our population honestly believe that they have no duties outside the home, the other half will not become phenomenal statesmen. This cook-and-housemaid level of popular thought is the great check. The social perspective is entirely lost; and a million short-sighted homes, each seeing only its own interests, cannot singly or together grasp the common good which would benefit them all.

That the home has improved as much as it has is due to the freedom of man outside it. That it is still so clumsy, so inadequate, so wickedly wasteful of time, of money, of human life, is due to the confinement of woman inside it.

What sort of citizens do we need for the best city—the best state— the best country—the best world? We need men and women who are sufficiently large-minded to see and feel a common need, to work for a common good, to rejoice in the advance of all, and to know as the merest platitude that their private advantage is to be assured *only* by the common weal. That kind of mind is not bred in the kitchen.

· · ·

The position is this: the home, as now existing, costs three times what is necessary to meet the same needs. It involves the further waste of nearly half the world's labour. It does not fulfill its functions to the best advantage, thus robbing us again. It maintains a low grade of womanhood, overworked or lazy; it checks the social development of men as well as women, and, most of all, of children. The man, in order to meet this unnecessary expense, must cater to the existing market; and the existing market is mainly this same home, with its crude tastes and limitless appetites. Thus the man, to maintain his own woman in idleness, or low-grade labour, must work three times as hard as is needful, to meet the demands of similar women; the home-bound woman clogging the whole world.

Change this order. Set the woman on her own feet, as a free, intelligent, able human being, quite capable of putting into the world more than she takes out, of being a producer as well as a consumer. Put these poor antiquated "domestic industries" into the archives of past history; and let efficient modern industries take their place, doing far more work, far better work, far cheaper work in their stead.

With an enlightened system of feeding the world we shall have better health—and wiser appetites. The more intelligent and broad-minded woman will assuredly promote a more reasonable, healthful, beautiful, and economical system of clothing, for her own body and that of the child. The wiser and more progressive mother will at last recognise child-culture as an art and science quite beyond the range of instinct, and provide for the child such surroundings, such training, as shall allow of a rapid and enormous advance in human character.

The man, relieved of two-thirds of his expenses; provided with double supplies; properly fed and more comfortable at home than he ever dreamed of being, and associated with a strong, free, stimulating companion all through life, will be able to work to far better purposes in the social service, and with far greater power, pride, and enjoyment.

The man and woman together, both relieved of most of their personal cares, will be better able to appreciate large social needs and to meet them. Each generation of children, better born, better reared, growing to their full capacity in all lines, will pour into the world a rising flood of happiness and power. Then we shall see social progress.

ANARCHISM AND OTHER ESSAYS

Emma Goldman

Emma Goldman was born in a Jewish ghetto in Russia in 1869. Fleeing a tyrannical father who wanted her to marry the proverbial good Jewish boy and breed lots of sons, she arrived in New York City in 1889. Thirty years later she was exiled from the United States as a "criminal anarchist." She devoted the rest of her life to political struggle, which included fighting on the side of the anarchists in the Spanish Civil War. She died in Canada in 1940.

In her autobiography and in five essays concerning women,[1] Goldman makes her position on feminism clear. She was, in the words of Alix Shulman, "one of the few people in the feminist movement who insisted there was a difference between women's liberation and women's rights. She knew that 'traditions of

Emma Goldman, *Anarchism and Other Essays* (New York: Mother Earth Publishing Association, 1911). "Woman Suffrage," pp. 201–218; "Marriage and Love," pages 233–246. Reprinted by permission. Footnotes have been renumbered.

[1] *Living My Life,* 2 vols. Originally published in 1931 and reprinted in 1970 by Dover Publications, New York. The five essays include "The Hypocrisy of Puritanism," "The Traffic in Women," "Woman Suffrage," "The Tragedy of Woman's Emancipation," and "Marriage and Love," in *Anarchism and Other Essays* (New York: Mother Earth Publishing Association, 1911).

centuries' could never be wiped out by outward reforms, however urgent or numerous or sweeping."[2]

Emma Goldman's essays courageously and brilliantly attack the hypocrisy, stupidity, and cultural and sensual barrenness of American puritanism. She defended every woman's right to sex and love outside of marriage and denounced matrimony as an efficient way to enslave women, as well as a deterrent to love and sensual enjoyment. In her essay "The Traffic in Women" she claimed that the economic and social inferiority of women was responsible for prostitution and advocated sex education and birth control:

It is a conceded fact that woman is being reared as a sex commodity, and yet she is kept in absolute ignorance of the meaning and importance of sex. Everything dealing with that subject is suppressed, and persons who attempt to bring light into this terrible darkness are persecuted and thrown into prison. Yet it is nevertheless true that so long as a girl is not to know how to take care of herself, not to know the function of the most important part of her life, we need not be surprised if she becomes an easy prey to prostitution, or to any other form of a relationship which degrades her to the position of an object for mere sex gratification.[3]

In New York in 1915 she publicly explained how to use a contraceptive; this was a first for American audiences. She also vigorously attacked the "double standard" treatment of women that even radical males practiced; this caused her to quarrel with such political comrades as anarchist leaders Johann Most and Peter Kropotkin.

Emma Goldman's criticism of the middle class prudishness of the suffragists is, to a large degree, valid. Furthermore, her direct experience with the misery and degradation females suffer as factory workers and her life-long contact with working class women in Europe and America made her justifiably impatient with the single-minded concern for enfranchisement that dominated the American woman's movement in the 1880s and 1890s. Also, her generous, sensual nature caused her to scorn the restrained "ladylike" quality of many American feminists. Nevertheless, Goldman's analysis of the first women's movement and the situation of women in general was incorrect in several respects.

First of all, Goldman was incorrect in blaming women for behavior that was the result of a particular system of education or socialization. She faults women for supporting religion, which "has condemned woman to the life of an inferior, a slave" and for worshipping war, which "robs woman of all that is precious to her." Her complaint is thus with the manifestation rather than with the cause, and she thus failed to condemn the complex network of forces that created the social ethic that, in fact, trained women to behave this way. Women, then as now, are schooled to perpetuate the dominant ideology; they are never given the chance to create a new one.

Secondly, she tended to think of suffragists as overly harsh judges of men.

[2] "Emma Goldman, Feminist and Anarchist," in *Women: A Journal of Liberation*. Baltimore (Spring 1970), p. 24.
[3] Goldman, *Anarchism and Other Essays, op. cit.*, p. 190.

120

"Their narrow, Puritanical vision banished man, as a disturber and doubtful character, out of their emotional life. Man was not to be tolerated at any price, except perhaps as the father of a child. . . . Fortunately, the most rigid Puritans never will be strong enough to kill the innate craving for motherhood."[4] This belief in the "innate craving for motherhood" led Emma Goldman to make statements such as life's greatest treasure was love for a man and that woman's most glorious privilege was the right to give birth to a child—and she justified these beliefs in the name of anarchism, "unrestricted freedom." However, men as much as women were responsible for the hypocritical respectability of puritan American life; Goldman unjustly blames the suffragists more than any other group. And she does this, I think, because she believes that love is *innately* more important to a woman than to a man and thus somehow women are more responsible for the condition of male-female relationships. She understands that women have to fight for their own total liberation, that it cannot simply be legislated, but she does not point out that men must undergo enormous changes if the very human needs for equality and love are ever to be reciprocally enjoyed.

Finally, because she did not believe any organized political system was valid, Goldman incorrectly invalidates a law or body of laws (such as the right to vote) that would empower one set of people to coerce another to obey. She correctly prophesied that the struggle for "women's rights" in nineteenth-century America would ultimately be reformist in nature, that is, that legal improvements such as enfranchisement were measures that served only to *mitigate* woman's oppression, not eliminate it.

Woman Suffrage

We boast of the age of advancement, of science, and progress. Is it not strange, then, that we still believe in fetich worship? True, our fetiches have different form and substance, yet in their power over the human mind they are still as disastrous as were those of old.

Our modern fetich is universal suffrage. Those who have not yet achieved that goal fight bloody revolutions to obtain it, and those who have enjoyed its reign bring heavy sacrifice to the altar of this omnipotent deity. Woe to the heretic who dare question that divinity!

Woman, even more than man, is a fetich worshipper, and though her idols may change, she is ever on her knees, ever holding up her hands, ever blind to the fact that her god has feet of clay. Thus woman has been the greatest supporter of all deities from time immemorial. Thus, she has had to pay the price that only gods can exact,—her freedom, her heart's blood, her very life.

Nietzsche's memorable maxim, "When you go to woman, take the whip along," is considered very brutal, yet Nietzsche expressed in one sentence the attitude of woman towards her gods.

Religion, especially the Christian religion, has condemned woman to

[4]"The Tragedy of Woman's Emancipation," in *Anarchism and Other Essays*, p. 225.

the life of an inferior, a slave. It has thwarted her nature and fettered her soul, yet the Christian religion has no greater supporter, none more devout, than woman. Indeed, it is safe to say that religion would have long ceased to be a factor in the lives of the people, if it were not for the support it receives from woman. The most ardent churchworkers, the most tireless missionaries the world over, are women, always sacrificing on the altar of the gods that have chained her spirit and enslaved her body.

The insatiable monster, war, robs woman of all that is dear and precious to her. It exacts her brothers, lovers, sons, and in return gives her a life of loneliness and despair. Yet the greatest supporter and worshipper of war is woman. She it is who instills the love of conquest and power into her children; she it is who whispers the glories of war into the ears of her little ones, and who rocks her baby to sleep with the tunes of trumpets and the noise of guns. It is woman, too, who crowns the victor on his return from the battlefield. Yes, it is woman who pays the highest price to that insatiable monster, war.

Then there is the home. What a terrible fetich it is! How it saps the very life-energy of woman,—this modern prison with golden bars. Its shining aspect blinds woman to the price she would have to pay as wife, mother, and housekeeper. Yet woman clings tenaciously to the home, to the power that holds her in bondage.

It may be said that because woman recognizes the awful toll she is made to pay to the Church, State, and the home, she wants suffrage to set herself free. That may be true of the few; the majority of suffragists repudiate utterly such blasphemy. On the contrary, they insist always that it is woman suffrage which will make her a better Christian and homekeeper, a staunch citizen of the State. Thus suffrage is only a means of strengthening the omnipotence of the very Gods that woman has served from time immemorial.

What wonder, then, that she should be just as devout, just as zealous, just as prostrate before the new idol, woman suffrage. As of old, she endures persecution, imprisonment, torture, and all forms of condemnation, with a smile on her face. As of old, the most enlightened, even, hope for a miracle from the twentieth-century deity,—suffrage. Life,

Emma Goldman

happiness, joy, freedom, independence,—all that, and more, is to spring from suffrage. In her blind devotion woman does not see what people of intellect perceived fifty years ago: that suffrage is an evil, that it has only helped to enslave people, that it has but closed their eyes that they may not see how craftily they were made to submit.

Woman's demand for equal suffrage is based largely on the contention that woman must have the equal right in all affairs of society. No one could, possibly, refute that, if suffrage were a right. Alas, for the ignorance of the human mind, which can see a right in an imposition. Or is it not the most brutal imposition for one set of people to make laws that another set is coerced by force to obey? Yet woman clamors for that "golden opportunity" that has wrought so much misery in the world, and robbed man of his integrity and self-reliance; an imposition which has thoroughly corrupted the people, and made them absolute prey in the hands of unscrupulous politicians.

The poor, stupid, free American citizen! Free to starve, free to tramp the highways of this great country, he enjoys universal suffrage, and, by that right, he has forged chains about his limbs. The reward that he receives is stringent labor laws prohibiting the right of boycott, of picketing, in fact, of everything, except the right to be robbed of the fruits of his labor. Yet all these disastrous results of the twentieth-century fetich have taught woman nothing. But, then, woman will purify politics, we are assured.

Needless to say, I am not opposed to woman suffrage on the conventional ground that she is not equal to it. I see neither physical, psychological, nor mental reasons why woman should not have the equal right to vote with man. But that can not possibly blind me to the absurd notion that woman will accomplish that wherein man has failed. If she would not make things worse, she certainly could not make them better. To assume, therefore, that she would succeed in purifying something which is not susceptible of purification, is to credit her with supernatural powers. Since woman's greatest misfortune has been that she was looked upon as either angel or devil, her true salvation lies in being placed on earth; namely, in being considered human, and therefore subject to all human follies and mistakes. Are we, then, to believe that two errors will make a right? Are we to assume that the poison already inherent in politics will be decreased, if women were to enter the political arena? The most ardent suffragists would hardly maintain such a folly.

As a matter of fact, the most advanced students of universal suffrage have come to realize that all existing systems of political power are absurd, and are completely inadequate to meet the pressing issues of life. This view is also borne out by a statement of one who is herself an ardent believer in woman suffrage, Dr. Helen L. Sumner. In her able work on *Equal Suffrage,* she says: "In Colorado, we find that equal suffrage serves to show in the most striking way the essential rottenness and degrading character of the existing system." Of course, Dr. Sumner has in mind a particular system of voting, but the same applies with equal force to the entire machinery of the representative system. With such a basis, it is difficult to understand how woman, as a political factor, would benefit either herself or the rest of mankind.

But, say our suffrage devotees, look at the countries and States where female suffrage exists. See what woman has accomplished—in Australia, New Zealand, Finland, the Scandinavian countries, and in our own four States, Idaho, Colorado, Wyoming, and Utah. Distance lends enchantment—or, to quote a Polish formula—"it is well where we are not." Thus one would assume that those countries and States are unlike other countries or States, that they have greater freedom, greater social and economic equality, a finer appreciation of human life, deeper understanding of the great social struggle, with all the vital questions it involves for the human race.

The women of Australia and New Zealand can vote, and help make the laws. Are the labor conditions better there than they are in England, where the suffragettes are making such a heroic struggle? Does there exist a greater motherhood, happier and freer children than in England? Is woman there no longer considered a mere sex commodity? Has she emancipated herself from the Puritanical double standard of morality for men and women? Certainly none but the ordinary female stump politician will dare answer these questions in the affirmative. If that be so, it seems ridiculous to point to Australia and New Zealand as the Mecca of equal suffrage accomplishments.

On the other hand, it is a fact to those who know the real political conditions in Australia, that politics have gagged labor by enacting the most stringent labor laws, making strikes without the sanction of an arbitration committee a crime equal to treason.

Not for a moment do I mean to imply that woman suffrage is responsible for this state of affairs. I do mean, however, that there is no reason to point to Australia as a wonder-worker of woman's accomplishment, since her influence has been unable to free labor from the thraldom of political bossism.

Finland has given woman equal suffrage; nay, even the right to sit in Parliament. Has that helped to develop a greater heroism, an intenser zeal than that of the women of Russia? Finland, like Russia, smarts under the terrible whip of the bloody Tsar. Where are the Finnish Perovskaias, Spiridonovas, Figners, Breshkovskaias? Where are the countless numbers of Finnish young girls who cheerfully go to Siberia for their cause? Finland is sadly in need of heroic liberators. Why has the ballot not created them? The only Finnish avenger of his people was a man, not a woman, and he used a more effective weapon than the ballot.

As to our own States where women vote, and which are constantly being pointed out as examples of marvels, what has been accomplished there through the ballot that women do not to a large extent enjoy in other States; or that they could not achieve through energetic efforts without the ballot?

True, in the suffrage States women are guaranteed equal rights to property; but of what avail is that right to the mass of women without property, the thousands of wage workers, who live from hand to mouth?

That equal suffrage did not, and cannot, affect their condition is admitted even by Dr. Sumner, who certainly is in a position to know. As an ardent suffragist, and having been sent to Colorado by the Collegiate Equal Suffrage League of New York State to collect material in favor of suffrage, she would be the last to say anything derogatory; yet we are informed that "equal suffrage has but slightly affected the economic conditions of women. That women do not receive equal pay for equal work, and that, though woman in Colorado has enjoyed school suffrage since 1876, women teachers are paid less than in California." On the other hand, Miss Sumner fails to account for the fact that although women have had school suffrage for thirty-four years, and equal suffrage since 1894, the census in Denver alone a few months ago disclosed the fact of fifteen thousand defective school children. And that, too, with mostly women in the educational department, and also notwithstanding that women in Colorado have passed the "most stringent laws for child and animal protection." The women of Colorado "have taken great interest in the State institutions for the care of dependent, defective, and delinquent children." What a horrible indictment against woman's care and interest, if one city has fifteen thousand defective children. What about the glory of woman suffrage, since it has failed utterly in the most important social issue, the child? And where is the superior sense of justice that woman was to bring into the political field? Where was it in 1903, when the mine owners waged a guerilla war against the Western Miners' Union; when General Bell established a reign of terror, pulling men out of bed at night, kidnapping them across the border line, throwing them into bull pens, declaring "to hell with the Constitution, the club is the Constitution"? Where were the women politicians then, and why did they not exercise the power of their vote? But they did. They helped to defeat the most fair-minded and liberal man, Governor Waite. The latter had to make way for the tool of the mine kings, Governor Peabody, the enemy of labor, the Tsar of Colorado. "Certainly male suffrage could have done nothing worse." Granted. Wherein, then, are the advantages to woman and society from woman suffrage? The oft-repeated assertion that woman will purify politics is also but a myth. It is not borne out by the people who know the political conditions of Idaho, Colorado, Wyoming, and Utah.

Woman, essentially a purist, is naturally bigoted and relentless in her effort to make others as good as she thinks they ought to be. Thus, in Idaho, she has disfranchised her sister of the street, and declared all women of "lewd character" unfit to vote. "Lewd" not being interpreted, of course, as prostitution in marriage. It goes without saying that illegal prostitution and gambling have been prohibited. In this regard the law must needs be of feminine gender: it always prohibits. Therein all laws are wonderful. They go no further, but their very tendencies open all the floodgates of hell. Prostitution and gambling have never done a more flourishing business than since the law has been set against them.

In Colorado, the Puritanism of woman has expressed itself in a more drastic form. "Men of notoriously unclean lives, and men connected with saloons, have been dropped from politics since women have the vote."[1] Could Brother Comstock do more? Could all the Puritan fathers have done more? I wonder how many women realize the gravity of this would-be feat. I wonder if they understand that it is the very thing which, instead of elevating woman, has made her a political spy, a contemptible pry into the private affairs of people, not so much for the good of the cause, but because, as a Colorado woman said, "they like to get into houses they have never been in, and find out all they can, politically and otherwise."[2] Yes, and into the human soul and its minutest nooks and corners. For nothing satisfies the craving of most women so much as scandal. And when did she ever enjoy such opportunities as are hers, the politician's?

"Notoriously unclean lives, and men connected with the saloons." Certainly, the lady vote gatherers can not be accused of much sense of proportion. Granting even that these busybodies can decide whose lives are clean enough for that eminently clean atmosphere, politics, must it follow that saloon-keepers belong to the same category? Unless it be American hypocrisy and bigotry, so manifest in the principle of Prohibition, which sanctions the spread of drunkenness among men and women of the rich class, yet keeps vigilant watch on the only place left to the poor man. If no other reason, woman's narrow and purist attitude toward life makes her a greater danger to liberty wherever she has political power. Man has long overcome the superstitions that still engulf woman. In the economic competitive field, man has been compelled to exercise efficiency, judgment, ability, competency. He therefore had neither time nor inclination to measure everyone's morality with a Puritanic yardstick. In his political activities, too, he has not gone about blindfolded. He knows that quantity and not quality is the material for the political grinding mill, and, unless he is a sentimental reformer or an old fossil, he knows that politics can never be anything but a swamp.

Women who are at all conversant with the process of politics, know the nature of the beast, but in their self-sufficiency and egotism they make themselves believe that they have but to pet the beast, and he will become as gentle as a lamb, sweet and pure. As if women have not sold their votes, as if women politicians cannot be bought! If her body can be bought in return for material consideration, why not her vote? That it is being done in Colorado and in other States, is not denied even by those in favor of woman suffrage.

As I have said before, woman's narrow view of human affairs is not the only argument against her as a politician superior to man. There are others. Her life-long economic parasitism has utterly blurred her conception of the meaning of equality. She clamors for equal rights with man, yet we learn that "few women care to canvass in undesirable districts."[3] How little equality means to them compared with the Russian women, who face hell itself for their ideal!

[1] *Equal Suffrage*, Dr. Helen Sumner.
[2] *Equal Suffrage*.
[3] Dr. Helen A. Sumner.

Woman demands the same rights as man, yet she is indignant that her presence does not strike him dead: he smokes, keeps his hat on, and does not jump from his seat like a flunkey. These may be trivial things, but they are nevertheless the key to the nature of American suffragists. To be sure, their English sisters have outgrown these silly notions. They have shown themselves equal to the greatest demands on their character and power of endurance. All honor to the heroism and sturdiness of the English suffragettes. Thanks to their energetic, aggressive methods, they have proved an inspiration to some of our own lifeless and spineless ladies. But after all, the suffragettes, too, are still lacking in appreciation of real equality. Else how is one to account for the tremendous, truly gigantic effort set in motion by those valiant fighters for a wretched little bill which will benefit a handful of propertied ladies, with absolutely no provision for the vast mass of workingwomen? True, as politicians they must be opportunists, must take halfmeasures if they can not get all. But as intelligent and liberal women they ought to realize that if the ballot is a weapon, the disinherited need it more than the economically superior class, and that the latter already enjoy too much power by virtue of their economic superiority.

The brilliant leader of the English suffragettes, Mrs. Emmeline Pankhurst, herself admitted, when on her American lecture tour, that there can be no equality between political superiors and inferiors. If so, how will the workingwomen of England, already inferior economically to the ladies who are benefited by the Shackleton bill,[4] be able to work with their political superiors, should the bill pass? Is it not probable that the class of Annie Keeney, so full of zeal, devotion, and martyrdom, will be compelled to carry on their backs their female political bosses, even as they are carrying their economic masters. They would still have to do it, were universal suffrage for men and women established in England. No matter what the workers do, they are made to pay, always. Still, those who believe in the power of the vote show little sense of justice when they concern themselves not at all with those whom, as they claim, it might serve most.

The American suffrage movement has been, until very recently, altogether a parlor affair, absolutely detached from the economic needs of the people. Thus Susan B. Anthony, no doubt an exceptional type of woman, was not only indifferent but antagonistic to labor; nor did she hesitate to manifest her antagonism when, in 1869, she advised women to take the places of striking printers in New York.[5] I do not know whether her attitude had changed before her death.

There are, of course, some suffragists who are affiliated with workingwomen—the Women's Trade Union League, for instance; but they are a small minority, and their activities are essentially economic. The rest look upon toil as a just provision of Providence. What would become of the rich, if not for the poor? What would become of these idle, parasitic

---

[4] Mr. Shackleton was a labor leader. It is therefore self-evident that he should introduce a bill excluding his own constituents. The English Parliament is full of such Judases.
[5] *Equal Suffrage*, Dr. Helen A. Summer.

ladies, who squander more in a week than their victims earn in a year, if not for the eighty million wage-workers? Equality, who ever heard of such a thing?

Few countries have produced such arrogance and snobbishness as America. Particularly is this true of the American woman of the middle class. She not only considers herself the equal of man, but his superior, especially in her purity, goodness, and morality. Small wonder that the American suffragist claims for her vote the most miraculous powers. In her exalted conceit she does not see how truly enslaved she is, not so much by man, as by her own silly notions and traditions. Suffrage can not ameliorate that sad fact; it can only accentuate it, as indeed it does.

One of the great American women leaders claims that woman is entitled not only to equal pay, but that she ought to be legally entitled even to the pay of her husband. Failing to support her, he should be put in convict stripes, and his earnings in prison be collected by his equal wife. Does not another brilliant exponent of the cause claim for woman that her vote will abolish the social evil, which has been fought in vain by the collective efforts of the most illustrious minds the world over? It is indeed to be regretted that the alleged creator of the universe has already presented us with his wonderful scheme of things, else woman suffrage would surely enable woman to outdo him completely.

Nothing is so dangerous as the dissection of a fetich. If we have outlived the time when such heresy was punishable by the stake, we have not outlived the narrow spirit of condemnation of those who dare differ with accepted notions. Therefore I shall probably be put down as an opponent of woman. But that can not deter me from looking the question squarely in the face. I repeat what I have said in the beginning: I do not believe that woman will make politics worse; nor can I believe that she could make it better. If, then, she cannot improve on man's mistakes, why perpetrate the latter?

History may be a compilation of lies; nevertheless, it contains a few truths, and they are the only guide we have for the future. The history of the political activities of men proves that they have given him absolutely nothing that he could not have achieved in a more direct, less costly, and more lasting manner. As a matter of fact, every inch of ground he has gained has been through a constant fight, a ceaseless struggle for self-assertion, and not through suffrage. There is no reason whatever to assume that woman, in her climb to emancipation, has been, or will be, helped by the ballot.

In the darkest of all countries, Russia, with her absolute despotism, woman has become man's equal, not through the ballot, but by her will to be and to do. Not only has she conquered for herself every avenue of learning and vocation, but she has won man's esteem, his respect, his comradeship; aye, even more than that: she has gained the admiration, the respect of the whole world. That, too, not through suffrage, but by her wonderful heroism, her fortitude, her ability, willpower, and her endurance in her struggle for liberty. Where are the women in any suffrage country or State that can lay claim to such a victory? When we consider the accomplishments of woman in America, we find also that something deeper and more powerful than suffrage has helped her in the march to emancipation.

It is just sixty-two years ago since a handful of women at the Seneca Falls Convention set forth a few demands for their right to equal education with men, and access to the various professions, trades, etc. What wonderful accomplishments, what wonderful triumphs! Who but the most ignorant dare speak of woman as a mere domestic drudge? Who dare suggest that this or that profession should not be open to her? For over sixty years she has molded a new atmosphere and a new life for herself. She has become a world-power in every domain of human thought and activity. And all that without suffrage, without the right to make laws, without the "privilege" of becoming a judge, a jailer, or an executioner.

Yes, I may be considered an enemy of woman; but if I can help her see the light, I shall not complain.

The misfortune of woman is not that she is unable to do the work of a man, but that she is wasting her life-force to outdo him, with a tradition of centuries which has left her physically incapable of keeping pace with him. Oh, I know some have succeeded, but at what cost, at what terrific cost! The import is not the kind of work woman does, but rather the quality of the work she furnishes. She can give suffrage or the ballot no new quality, nor can she receive anything from it that will enhance her own quality. Her development, her freedom, her independence, must come from and through herself. First, by asserting herself as a personality, and not as a sex commodity. Second, by refusing the right to anyone over her body; by refusing to bear children, unless she wants them; by refusing to be a servant to God, the State, society, the husband, the family, etc., by making her life simpler, but deeper and richer. That is, by trying to learn the meaning and substance of life in all its complexities, by freeing herself from the fear of public opinion and public condemnation. Only that, and not the ballot, will set woman free, will make her a force hitherto unknown in the world, a force for real love, for peace, for harmony; a force of divine fire, of life-giving; a creator of free men and women.

* * *

Marriage and Love

The popular notion about marriage and love is that they are synonymous, that they spring from the same motives, and cover the same human needs. Like most popular notions this also rests not on actual facts, but on superstition.

Marriage and love have nothing in common; they are as far apart as the poles; are, in fact, antagonistic to each other. No doubt some marriages have been the result of love. Not, however, because love could assert itself only in marriage; much rather is it because few people can completely outgrow a convention. There are today large numbers of men and women to whom marriage is naught but a farce, but who submit to it for the sake of public opinion. At any rate, while it is true that some marriages are based on love, and while it is equally true that in some cases love continues in married life, I maintain that it does so regardless of marriage, and not because of it.

On the other hand, it is utterly false that love results from marriage. On rare occasions one does hear of a miraculous case of a married couple falling in love after marriage, but on close examination it will be found that it is a mere adjustment to the inevitable. Certainly the growing-used to each other is far away from the spontaneity, the intensity, and beauty of love, without which the intimacy of marriage must prove degrading to both the woman and the man.

Marriage is primarily an economic arrangement, an insurance pact. It differs from the ordinary life insurance agreement only in that it is more binding, more exacting. Its returns are insignificantly small compared with the investments. In taking out an insurance policy one pays for it in dollars and cents, always at liberty to discontinue payments. If, however, woman's premium is a husband, she pays for it with her name, her privacy, her self-respect, her very life, "until death doth part." Moreover, the marriage insurance condemns her to life-long dependency, to parasitism, to complete uselessness, individual as well as social. Man, too, pays his toll, but as his sphere is wider, marriage does not limit him as much as woman. He feels his chains more in an economic sense.

Thus Dante's motto over Inferno applies with equal force to marriage: "Ye who enter here leave all hope behind."

That marriage is a failure none but the very stupid will deny. One has but to glance over the statistics of divorce to realize how bitter a failure marriage really is. Nor will the stereotyped Philistine argument that the laxity of divorce laws and the growing looseness of woman account for the fact that: first, every twelfth marriage ends in divorce; second, that since 1870 divorces have increased from 28 to 73 for every hundred thousand population; third, that adultery, since 1867, as ground for divorce, has increased 270.8 per cent; fourth, that desertion increased 369.8 per cent.

Added to these startling figures is a vast amount of material, dramatic and literary, further elucidating this subject. Robert Herrick, in *Together;* Pinero, in *Mid-Channel;* Eugene Walter, in *Paid in Full,* and scores of other writers are discussing the barrenness, the monotony, the sordidness, the inadequacy of marriage as a factor for harmony and understanding.

The thoughtful social student will not content himself with the popular superficial excuse for this phenomenon. He will have to dig down deeper into the very life of the sexes to know why marriage proves so disastrous.

Edward Carpenter says that behind every marriage stands the life-long environment of the two sexes; an environment so different from each other that man and woman must remain strangers. Separated by an insurmountable wall of superstition, custom, and habit, marriage has not the potentiality of developing knowledge of, and respect for, each other, without which every union is doomed to failure.

Henrik Ibsen, the hater of all social shams, was probably the first to realize this great truth. Nora [in *A Doll's House*] leaves her husband, not —as the stupid critic would have it—because she is tired of her responsibilities or feels the need of woman's rights, but because she has come to know that for eight years she had lived with a stranger and borne him children. Can there be anything more humiliating, more degrading than a life-long proximity between two strangers? No need for the woman to know anything of the man, save his income. As to the knowledge of the woman—what is there to know except that she has a pleasing appearance? We have not yet outgrown the theologic myth that woman has no soul, that she is a mere appendix to man, made out of his rib just for the convenience of the gentleman who was so strong that he was afraid of his own shadow.

Perchance the poor quality of the material whence woman comes is responsible for her inferiority. At any rate, woman has no soul—what is there to know about her? Besides, the less soul a woman has the greater her asset as a wife, the more readily will she absorb herself in her husband. It is this slavish acquiescence to man's superiority that has kept the marriage institution seemingly intact for so long a period. Now that woman is coming into her own, now that she is actually growing aware of herself as a being outside of the master's grace, the sacred institution of marriage is gradually being undermined, and no amount of sentimental lamentation can stay it.

From infancy, almost, the average girl is told that marriage is her ultimate goal; therefore her training and education must be directed towards that end. Like the mute beast fattened for slaughter, she is prepared for that. Yet, strange to say, she is allowed to know much less about her function as wife and mother than the ordinary artisan of his trade. It is indecent and filthy for a respectable girl to know anything of the marital relation. Oh, for the inconsistency of respectability, that needs the marriage vow to turn something which is filthy into the purest and most sacred arrangement that none dare question or criticize. Yet that is exactly the attitude of the average upholder of marriage. The prospective wife and mother is kept in complete ignorance of her only asset in the competitive field—sex. Thus she enters into life-long relations with a man only to find herself shocked, repelled, outraged beyond measure by the most natural and healthy instinct, sex. It is safe to say that a large percentage of the unhappiness, misery, distress, and physical suffering of matrimony is due to the criminal ignorance in sex matters that is being extolled as a great virtue. Nor is it at all an exaggeration when I say that more than one home has been broken up because of this deplorable fact.

If, however, woman is free and big enough to learn the mystery of sex without the sanction of State or Church, she will stand condemned as utterly unfit to become the wife of a "good" man, his goodness consisting of an empty head and plenty of money. Can there be anything more outrageous than the idea that a healthy, grown woman, full of life and passion, must deny nature's demand, must subdue her most intense craving, undermine her health and break her spirit, must stunt her vision, abstain from the depth and glory of sex experience until a "good" man comes along to take her unto himself as a wife? That is precisely what marriage means. How can such an arrangement end except in failure? This is one, though not the least important, factor of marriage, which differentiates it from love.

Ours is a practical age. The time when Romeo and Juliet risked the wrath of their fathers for love, when Gretchen exposed herself to the gossip of her neighbors for love, is no more. If, on rare occasions, young people allow themselves the luxury of romance, they are taken in care by the elders, drilled and pounded until they become "sensible."

The moral lesson instilled in the girl is not whether the man has aroused her love, but rather is it, "How much?" The important and only God of practical American life: Can the man make a living? Can he support a wife? That is the only thing that justifies marriage. Gradually this saturates every thought of the girl; her dreams are not of moonlight and kisses, of laughter and tears; she dreams of shopping tours and bargain counters. This soul-poverty and sordidness are the elements inherent in the marriage institution. The State and the Church approve of no other ideal, simply because it is the one that necessitates the State and Church control of men and women.

Doubtless there are people who continue to consider love above dollars and cents. Particularly is this true of that class whom economic necessity has forced to become self-supporting. The tremendous change in woman's position, wrought by that mighty factor, is indeed phenomenal when we reflect that it is but a short time since she has entered the industrial arena. Six million women wage-earners; six million women, who have the equal right with men to be exploited, to be robbed, to go on strike; aye, to starve even. Anything more, my lord? Yes, six million wage-workers in every walk of life, from the highest brain work to the mines and railroad tracks; yes, even detectives and policemen. Surely the emancipation is complete.

Yet with all that, but a very small number of the vast army of women wage-workers look upon work as a permanent issue, in the same light as does man. No matter how decrepit the latter, he has been taught to be independent, self-supporting. Oh, I know that no one is really independent in our economic treadmill; still, the poorest specimen of a man hates to be a parasite; to be known as such, at any rate.

The woman considers her position as worker transitory, to be thrown aside for the first bidder. That is why it is infinitely harder to organize women than men. "Why should I join a union? I am going to get married, to have a home." Has she not been taught from infancy to look upon that as her ultimate calling? She learns soon enough that the home, though not so large a prison as the factory, has more solid doors and bars. It has a keeper so faithful that naught can escape him. The most tragic part, however, is that the home no longer frees her from wage-slavery; it only increases her task.

According to the latest statistics submitted before a Committee "on labor and wages, and congestion of population," ten per cent of the [female] wage workers in New York City alone are married, yet they must continue to work at the most poorly paid labor in the world. Add to this horrible aspect the drudgery of housework, and what remains of the protection and glory of the home? As a matter of fact, even the middle-class girl in marriage can not speak of her home, since it is the man who creates her sphere. It is not important whether the husband is a brute or a darling. What I wish to prove is that marriage guarantees woman a home only by the grace of her husband. There she moves about in *his* home, year after year, until her aspect of life and human affairs becomes as flat, narrow, and drab as her surroundings. Small wonder if she becomes a nag, petty, quarrelsome, gossipy, unbearable, thus driving the man from the house. She could not go, if she wanted to; there is no place to go. Besides, a short period of married life, of complete surrender of all faculties, absolutely incapacitates the average woman for the outside world. She becomes reckless in appearance, clumsy in her movements, dependent in her decisions, cowardly in her judgment, a weight and a bore, which most men grow to hate and despise. Wonderfully inspiring atmosphere for the bearing of life, is it not?

But the child, how is it to be protected, if not for marriage? After all, is not that the most important consideration? The sham, the hypocrisy of it! Marriage protecting the child, yet thousands of children destitute and homeless. Marriage protecting the child, yet orphan asylums and reformatories overcrowded, the Society for the Prevention of Cruelty to Children keeping busy in rescuing the little victims from "loving" parents, to place them under more loving care, the Gerry Society. Oh, the mockery of it!

Marriage may have the power to "bring the horse to water," but has it ever made him drink? The law will place the father under arrest, and put him in convict's clothes; but has that ever stilled the hunger of the child? If the parent has no work, or if he hides his identity, what does marriage do then? It invokes the law to bring the man to "justice," to put him safely behind closed doors; his labor, however, goes not to the child, but to the State. The child receives but a blighted memory of its father's stripes.

As to the protection of the woman,—therein lies the curse of marriage. Not that it really protects her, but the very idea is revolting, such an outrage and insult on life, so degrading to human dignity, as to forever condemn this parasitic institution.

It is like that other paternal arrangement—capitalism. It robs man of his birthright, stunts his growth, poisons his body, keeps him in ignorance, in poverty and dependence, and then institutes charities that thrive on the last vestige of man's self-respect.

The institution of marriage makes a parasite of woman, an absolute dependent. It incapacitates her for life's struggle, annihilates her social

133

consciousness, paralyzes her imagination, and then imposes its gracious protection, which is in reality a snare, a travesty on human character.

If motherhood is the highest fulfillment of woman's nature, what other protection does it need save love and freedom? Marriage but defies, outrages, and corrupts her fulfillment. Does it not say to woman, Only when you follow me shall you bring forth life? Does it not condemn her to the block, does it not degrade and shame her if she refuses to buy her right to motherhood by selling herself? Does not marriage only sanction motherhood, even though conceived in hatred, in compulsion? Yet, if motherhood be of free choice, of love, of ecstasy, of defiant passion, does it not place a crown of thorns upon an innocent head and carve in letters of blood the hideous epithet, Bastard? Were marriage to contain all the virtues claimed for it, its crimes against motherhood would exclude it forever from the realm of love.

Love, the strongest and deepest element in all life, the harbinger of hope, of joy, of ecstasy; love, the defier of all laws, of all conventions; love, the freest, the most powerful moulder of human destiny; how can such an all-compelling force be synonymous with that poor little State and Church-begotten weed, marriage?

Free love? As if love is anything but free! Man has bought brains, but all the millions in the world have failed to buy love. Man has subdued bodies, but all his armies could not conquer love. Man has chained and fettered the spirit, but he has been utterly helpless before love. High on a throne, with all the splendor and pomp his gold can command, man is yet poor and desolate, if love passes him by. And if it stays, the poorest hovel is radiant with warmth, with life and color. Thus love has the magic power to make of a beggar a king. Yes, love is free; it can dwell in no other atmosphere. In freedom it gives itself unreservedly, abundantly, completely. All the laws on the statutes, all the courts in the universe, cannot tear it from the soil, once love has taken root. If, however, the soil is sterile, how can marriage make it bear fruit? It is like the last desperate struggle of fleeting life against death.

Love needs no protection; it is its own protection. So long as love begets life no child is deserted, or hungry, or famished for the want of affection. I know this to be true. I know women who became mothers in freedom by the men they loved. Few children in wedlock enjoy the care, the protection, the devotion free motherhood is capable of bestowing.

The defenders of authority dread the advent of a free motherhood, lest it will rob them of their prey. Who would fight wars? Who would create wealth? Who would make the policeman, the jailer, if woman were to refuse the indiscriminate breeding of children? The race, the race! shouts the king, the president, the capitalist, the priest. The race must be preserved, though woman be degraded to a mere machine,—and the marriage institution is our only safety valve against the pernicious sex-awakening of woman. But in vain these frantic efforts to maintain a state of bondage. In vain, too, the edicts of the Church, the mad attacks of rulers, in vain even the arm of the law. Woman no longer wants to be a party to the production of a race of sickly, feeble, decrepit, wretched human beings, who have neither the strength nor moral courage to throw off the yoke of poverty and slavery. Instead she desires fewer and better children, begotten and reared in love and through free choice; not by compulsion, as marriage imposes. Our pseudo-moralists have yet to learn the deep sense of responsibility toward the child, that love in freedom has awakened in the breast of woman. Rather would she forego forever the glory of motherhood than bring forth life in an atmosphere that breathes only destruction and death. And if she does become a mother, it is to give to the child the deepest and best her being can yield. To grow with the child is her motto; she knows that in that manner alone can she help build true manhood and womanhood.

Ibsen must have had a vision of a free mother, when, with a master stroke, he portrayed Mrs. Alving. [*Ghosts.*] She was the ideal mother because she had outgrown marriage and all its horrors, because she had broken her chains, and set her spirit free to soar until it returned a personality, regenerated and strong. Alas, it was too late to rescue her life's joy, her Oswald; but not too late to realize that love in freedom is the only condition of a beautiful life. Those who, like Mrs. Alving, have paid with blood and tears for their spiritual awakening, repudiate marriage as an imposition, a shallow, empty mockery. They know, whether love last but one brief span of time or for eternity, it is the only creative, inspiring, elevating basis for a new race, a new world.

In our present pygmy state love is indeed a stranger to most people. Misunderstood and shunned, it rarely takes root; or if it does, it soon withers and dies. Its delicate fiber can not endure the stress and strain of the daily grind. Its soul is too complex to adjust itself to the slimy woof of our social fabric. It weeps and moans and suffers with those who have need of it, yet lack the capacity to rise to love's summit.

Some day, some day men and women will rise, they will reach the mountain peak, they will meet big and strong and free, ready to receive, to partake, and to bask in the golden rays of love. What fancy, what imagination, what poetic genius can foresee even approximately the potentialities of such a force in the life of men and women. If the world is ever to give birth to true companionship and oneness, not marriage, but love will be the parent.

WE ARE MANY

Ella Reeve Bloor

Ella Reeve Bloor was born in 1862 on Staten Island into a middle class, somewhat distinguished old American family and died on August 10, 1951, in Quaker-
town, Pennsylvania, after seventy years of political activity that spanned the
American Left. Her autobiography, *We Are Many*, published in 1940, is an
important view of American labor history. It includes her analysis of the relationship among the conservative American Federation of Labor (AFL) which
aimed at unionizing *skilled* workers into many separate "craft" unions, the
International Workers of the World (Wobblies, IWW) who sought revolutionary
social changes by organizing *unskilled* workers (a large percentage of whom
were immigrants and women) into one industrial union that would unify the
entire working class, regardless of race, sex, or national origin,[1] and the
woman's rights movement.

The first half of *We Are Many* is a record of Bloor's life before she joined
the Communist Party in 1919. She writes of joining the Prohibition Party[2] in
the 1880s, the Knights of Labor,[3] and the reform section of the Ethical Culture
Society, which dealt with problems of labor. She then recounts her discouragement after a brief membership in "The Social Democracy of America," organized by Eugene Debs in 1897 and the reasons that lead her to join the Socialist

Ella Reeve Bloor, *We are Many* (New York: International Publishers, 1940), pp. 26, 36–37,
77–81, 92–94, 99–101, 113, 116–117, 176–177. Reprinted by permission. Heads within text
are chapter titles in the original.

[1] The Wobblies believed working class unity was impossible as long as craft was
separated from craft because this caused workers to scab upon each other and caused
some workers to hate their fellow workers.
[2] Formed to fight use of alcohol as a beverage, it also supported woman suffrage and
direct election of U.S. Senators.
[3] The "Noble Order of the Knights of Labor" began as a secret order in 1869 and
became a public organization in 1881 when it started to have, in the words of Philip S.
Foner, "a meteoric career... [with] few if any parallels in the history of the labor
movement of the world," *History of the Labor Movement in the United States* (New
York: International Publishers, 1955), Vol. II, p. 47. Its purpose, briefly stated, was to
unite isolated craft unions and labor sympathizers into one big union with "solidarity"
as its watchword. By 1886, however, the anti-trade-union faction of the order had taken
over. They believed trade unions were outmoded by widespread use of machinery; the
industrial revolution had diminished the number of skilled workers so there was no
longer any need for craft unions: "Trade unions isolated from other trades are failures,
and it is the duty and aim of the K. of L. to wipe out this trade union feeling and make
one common brotherhood of man," said the General Secretary. The General Secretary
was mistaken in believing that a utopian, classless society—his "brotherhood of man"—
was possible in a capitalist economy.

Labor Party (SLP) in 1898.[4] Four years later, in 1902, she left the SLP, when the Socialist Party was founded:[5]

Gradually the defects of the SLP were brought home to me. I found many workers antagonistic because I was organizing a rival union. The Socialist Trade and Labor Alliance was weakening the AF of L by drawing off its more radical elements and leaving the reactionaries in control, and was itself organized on too narrow and sectarian a basis to accomplish anything.[6]

Ella Bloor organized for the Socialist Party for over fifteen years. Her sympathies were with the left wing of the party. She also thought the IWW "carried on some grand fights," but did not agree with the Wobblies that a first step to revolutionary change was worker control: "I believed strongly in industrial unionism. But I also believed that even if the workers won control in the shops, they could not hold the shops or the means of production without a workers' state to back up their ownership."[7] In 1912 she, along with others, was dismayed with the Socialist Party's split with the Wobblies; by 1917, the year of America's entrance into World War I, the differences between the right and left factions of the Socialist Party were greatly acerbated: "Debs and other left wingers went to prison for their stand against war. But the right wing leaders became more and more passive and in many cases came out for the war. It became clearer every day that the leaders of the American Socialist Party were deserting the interests of the workers, following the example of the Social-Democrats abroad who had turned against the working class, voted for military appropriations. . . ."[8]

The second half of *We Are Many* is an account of Bloor's life and political activities in the Communist Party, which she helped to found in 1919. In 1921 she was a delegate to the Red International of Labor Unions, a congress "of all progressive and radical unions of the world," which was held in Moscow. According to Bloor, "The issue at the congress which most affected the American delegates was that of dual unionism. Our policy of working within the AF of L . . . won over the I.W.W. policy."[9] In the following selection (pp. 146–47) she

[4] The Socialist Labor Party was largely composed of German immigrants and it operated among the foreign-born with organizers who spoke Yiddish, Polish, Russian, Italian and a scattering of other tongues—the mass immigrations of the 1880s had radically changed the ethnic composition of labor. The party declared itself an enemy of anarchism, and in 1895 was identified with the concept of "dual unionism" (the belief that it was better to organize workers into a separate rival union than organize as a radical faction *within* an already existing union). Daniel DeLeon, its leader, seeing the conservatism of Samuel Gompers and the AFL and the failure of the Socialists to make inroads into the Knights of Labor, set up a new, rival (dual) union, The Socialist Trade and Labor Alliance (STLA), which stood for industrial unionism, and called for all radicals to leave the AFL and build another national socialist organization.
[5] The Socialist Party differed from the SLP mainly in that it repudiated the policy of dual unionism, and the actual rival or dual union, the Socialist Trade and Labor Alliance. In 1900, it adopted a position in favor of all trade unions regardless of their political affiliation. Such an unwillingness to make a political commitment is, at best, difficult to maintain and it is a rather contradictory position for a radical political organization to take.
[6] Ella Reeve Bloor, *We Are Many* (New York: International Publishers, 1940), p. 57.
[7] *Ibid.*, pp. 94–95.
[8] *Ibid.*, p. 140.
[9] *Ibid.*, p. 173.

describes the Women's Conference held at the congress.

In 1925 (when she was 63), she hitchhiked from California to New York to distribute the party paper, the *Daily Worker*. In 1927 she campaigned throughout the country to free Sacco and Vanzetti. A year later Ella Bloor began organizing with miners and textile workers—an experience that led her to reverse her former position of working within the AFL and instead to advocate the formation of new, more militant unions. She explained that the AFL United Textile Workers Union was so passive that a "dual" independent National Textile Workers Union had to be formed.

Ella Bloor's feminism was a result of a middle-class education and her subsequent strong identification with the working class. In her youth she was inspired by the writings and activities of Lucretia Mott, Elizabeth Cady Stanton, Susan B. Anthony, and Frances Willard. Later she tells of her admiration for Mother Jones, an Irish-born labor organizer, Elizabeth Gurley Flynn, who became chairwoman of the Communist Party, the American socialist Florence Kelley, and Clara Zetkin and Alexandra Kollontai, who were European revolutionaries. Around 1908 she wrote an article entitled "Rational Housekeeping," which urged cooperative family living. Her arguments in this article are similar in many ways to those of Charlotte Perkins Gilman. However, Ella Bloor consistently opposed what she called "the narrow feminist idea, which I never accepted, of working for women alone."[10] Today many members of the women's liberation movement would do what Bloor states English feminist Emmeline Pankhurst did in 1910, "Scold me soundly for lending my name, energy and work to a 'man's party.' "[11]

My Pioneer Forefathers

. . .

When the time came for me to go to high school, my father insisted on my going to the Ivy Hall Seminary, a "finishing school" where I could associate with young ladies of good family, although I wanted to continue in the public schools. I hated Ivy Hall, except for one teacher, Miss Miriam Shephard, who made history very exciting because she told about events other than the dreary succession of births and deaths of kings that made up the text-books of those days. She told us about the real makers of history, the people, and history became my favorite study.

My mother took me out of Ivy Hall when I was fourteen. I stayed at home with her after that, and helped her with the children. My mother was an excellent mathematician and she taught me. Since I read so much at home, I really had a better education than most of the children around me.

[10] *Ibid.*, p. 93.
[11] *Ibid.*, p. 93.

At this period I became interested in biographies of great women. I had always loved George Eliot's novels, and was enthralled with the story of her life written by George Henry Lewes. The life of James and Lucretia Mott gave me my first glimpse of the great struggle for woman suffrage. The story of Harriet Beecher Stowe's life was also an inspiration to me. I was very much impressed, too, with the essays of Lydia Maria Child, an American writer about whom little is written these days. She had to write in the kitchen. "Neither God nor man" she wrote "can keep my soul here among the pots and pans if I choose to soar among the lovely fields and woods and enjoy the beautiful things of life. . . ." Like all girls of that period, I loved Louisa May Alcott. As I grew a little older I was greatly drawn to Emerson and read his essays on *Self-Reliance, Compensation, Friendship.*

. . .

Through the Quakers, who believed in equality for women, I first came into touch with the woman suffrage movement. I began to be very much interested in the question, especially after reading about Lucy Stone, one of the earliest fighters against Negro slavery, and a leader for many years in the struggle for woman's suffrage. When she married the Abolitionist, Henry Brown Blackwell, she continued as a matter of principle to use her own name. His championship of higher education for women opened the way for women in the professions and his sister Elizabeth Blackwell was the first woman in this country to get a medical degree.

Lucy Stone had founded in 1870 the *Woman's Journal,* for nearly 50 years official organ of the American Woman Suffrage Association. After her death in 1893 it was edited by her daughter, Alice Stone Blackwell, who naturally became a champion for woman's political and legal freedom and for the equality of the Negro people. These interests led her to an understanding of socialism. Today, at eighty-three, she is still a vigorous champion of human rights. Just last year I had a wonderful visit with her at her home in Boston, discussing our precious heritage of great American women.

While visiting Uncle Dan at Woodstown, I tried my hand at an article on suffrage. Uncle Dan looked it over and approved. This encouraged me to send it to the Woodstown *Register,* and it was printed.

I then discovered that women could vote in New Jersey for school trustees, although they had never availed themselves of the right. So at the next election, I attempted to get the women to come with me to vote. Only one Quaker lady, whose husband was very critical, came. As we stood in line at the polls with people staring and jeering at us, her husband came up and said sarcastically, "I hope you are enjoying this." "Not exactly enjoying this," I told him, nodding toward the jeering crowd, "but enjoying the right to vote."

At the next elections I was able to marshal a large group of women and after that the politicians of the town began to show an interest in the women, and around election time the candidates all told us how wonderful we were.

In the 1880's and '90's Susan B. Anthony's influence on the women of the country—and on the men, too—was still strong. She was over sixty, but still fighting for women's right to vote as earlier she had fought against slavery. Ridiculed and denounced as a "revolutionary firebrand" she kept right on. She and other women pioneers such as Lucretia Mott and Elizabeth Cady Stanton traveled and lectured throughout the United States making woman suffrage a national issue.

. . .

Two years later, in 1908, I had the gratification of being elected state organizer of Connecticut by a large majority. I was also nominated for secretary of state on the Socialist ticket—the first time any woman was nominated for public office in Connecticut.

The opposing parties contested my right to run for office, since women did not even have the vote, and the idea of a woman running for office was indeed a shock to the conservative politicians. The Attorney General ruled that if the voters of the state wanted to vote for me at the ballot box, they had a right to do so—there was nothing in the law to prevent them.

One day I made a speech near our newspaper office on "The Cause and Cure of Child Labor." The editor of the *Waterbury American* sent for me soon after. "I am very sorry but we shall have to let you go," he said. "You are one of our best workers. I want to tell you that there will always be a place open on the editorial staff for you—on condition that you renounce your political faith."

Hearing I had lost my newspaper job, Mr. Saro, the local orchestra conductor and others offered me the editorship of a monthly magazine, *Musical Waterbury*, which I gladly accepted. Saro was a fine musician and considered my daughter, Helen, for whom he arranged an extremely successful recital in Waterbury, a great violinist.

There was at that time a group in Connecticut called the Unitarian Universalist Congress, which tried to unite all the more progressive religions into a single body. Through one of our Socialist members active in this group I was frequently asked to speak at their large church in Meriden. I used to take such texts as "Suffer the little children to come unto me" in order to talk about child labor, and used the story of driving the money changers from the temple to attack capitalism. The suggestion was made that I obtain a license to preach, which I did at one of the church conferences, although of course I was not ordained. Thus I was able to carry the campaign against child labor and other socialist issues right into the churches, speaking not as an outsider, but as a preacher.

At this point I want to speak of Florence Kelley, whom I knew in this period and who was one of the first American women Socialists who influenced me greatly. Florence Kelley made an important contribution to the literature of socialism in this country by her translation of Engels' *Conditions of the Working Class in England in 1844,* and her own writings. She was for many years secretary of the National Consumers' League of America and a leading member of the National Child Labor Committee. Her influence was great among working class women and her death in 1932 was a terrible loss.

In those days the Intercollegiate Socialist was a vigorous organization. I remember one occasion when the I.S.S. was giving a dinner in New Haven at which Florence Kelley was the main speaker. The chairman, Graham Phelps Stokes, was called away at the last moment, and Upton Sinclair, one of the vice-presidents, was called upon to preside. In introducing Mrs. Kelley he explained the purposes of the I.S.S. and how people were drawn into the socialist movement through its activities, attracting even such nationally known persons as Mrs. Kelley. Mrs. Kelley got up and told him that she had been a Socialist before he was dry behind the ears.

•   •   •

I remember writing one article for *Wilshire's* called "Rational Housekeeping," a subject very close to my heart. Women had to fight hard to have careers in those days, and many of the women comrades felt that they had to sacrifice their family life for the movement. I had always contended that it was possible to do both. But I had the help of my family and friends who in themselves constituted a sort of cooperative group, with a home base in Arden. So many struggling young people who had not these facilities came to me with their problems that I proposed a plan for groups of families to live together cooperatively, pooling their basic housekeeping expenses so that they could have a common dining room, a well run household, and a great sunny play room on the top floor for the children and expert care for them. I worked out detailed budgets for families with an average income of $30 a week, or less.

When I discussed this plan the objection was always raised that it did not allow for sufficient privacy, so I ended my article:

". . . We know that the struggle of motherly, good women to maintain a good spirit in the home is growing harder every year. The energy expended to keep up the outward form of the household, just the necessary details of living, uses up the vital force to such a degree that there is none left for the cultivation of the true spirt of home life—helpfulness, comradeship and congenial work. Given the leisure that comes even to a business woman, if free from domestic cares, the mother will then bring to her children the best of her intellect—the vigor of a fully developed individuality. Privacy becomes, in the light of this new development, only a secondary consideration, and enough of it will always be secure where an intelligent, well-balanced woman reigns supreme.

"Is it worth while, then, for those of us who desire to preserve a true and highly developed motherhood and the perpetuation of the race, to endeavor to work out some of these problems?

"While the greater problems still clamor for solution, and the class war that may be more than a 'thirty years' war' rages around us, may we not, in all good faith, make our tents on the battlefield a little more comfortable and spend more time on the physical development of our soldiers?

"Surely our campaign will be more effective if we have better rations, more music, and occasional resting places along the weary march."

Naturally I had offered this co-operative scheme as no fundamental solution. However, small groups here and there tried out such plans as a temporary solution to their problems.

I was supporting myself by these articles and by research and newspaper work, when Upton Sinclair asked me to help in the stockyards investigation that followed the publication of *The Jungle*.

. . .

Organizing for the Socialist Party

After my investigations of 1906, 1907 and 1908, I returned again to Connecticut. While I continued my work in the Socialist Party there, I was now drawn into more active participation in the suffrage movement. I worked closely with Mrs. Hepburn, mother of Katherine, the actress. She was state president of the Woman's Suffrage Association and one of the most brilliant women I ever met. Her husband was the eminent social hygienist, Dr. Thomas Hepburn. They shared each other's interests, and I enjoyed my visits to their beautiful home in the Connecticut hills, full of pictures and books and good talk and warm companionship. Mrs. Hepburn spent a great deal of time with her children in spite of her varied interests, and they adored her, as we all did. Little Katherine was a gay and vivacious child, who always displayed deep interest in our conversations.

For many of the secure middle class ladies the suffrage movement was a mere feminist fad. I tried to make them see the really vital importance of suffrage to the working women, as a weapon against economic inequality. And I tried to make them see that not the vote alone was important, but its proper use in building a better society. Mrs. Hepburn understood these things better than the others, and it was through her insistence that the Department of Working Women, of which I became chairman, was established.

It was only through the participation of our Socialist women that the suffrage movement in general became awakened to the problems of working women. In 1908 the Socialist women in New York organized a mass demonstration of proletarian women for suffrage which inaugurated the establishment of March 8 as Women's Day on a national scale.

In 1910, on a motion of the great German Socialist leader, Clara Zetkin, the International Conference of Women Socialists in Copenhagen, made March 8 international. Thus International Women's Day is a contribution of the American workers to the world labor movement, as is May Day, which was originated in 1886 when the Knights of Labor, the Socialists and the A. F. of L. organized a great united walk-out on behalf of the eight hour day.

I helped Mrs. Hepburn get rid of the old-fashioned suffragists who had been in the office for forty years and were a dead weight on the movement. Together we brought in new elements. Mrs. Hepburn helped organize the National Woman's Party in Connecticut, and drew into it many of the more progressive suffragettes. This organization, which was quite militant and believed in the use of parades, demonstrations, and other active methods of agitation, was frowned on by the more conservative group.

The militant English suffrage leader, Emmeline Pankhurst, came to see me in Connecticut and scolded me soundly for lending my name, energy and work to a "man's party." She had the narrow feminist idea, which I never accepted, of working for women alone. She felt that women should not work for any political party until they got the vote.

Unfortunately the National Woman's Party[1] which at one time carried on a splendidly militant fight has today degenerated into a narrow, anti-labor sect. Not long ago I had a stiff argument with one of my old Connecticut co-workers, the daughter of Ebenezer Hill, a Republican Congressman, who used to be mightily shocked by his daughter's socialistic views. She was attending the hearing on the equal rights bill backed by the Woman's Party, a bill that doesn't mean equal rights at all. If passed it would repeal all the protective laws for women in industry won by years of struggle to limit the exploitation of women—just because they

[1] Bloor mentions the National Woman's Party twice on this page. The first time ("Mrs. Hepburn helped organize the National Woman's Party") she is referring to the organizational effort begun in 1907 by Harriet Stanton Blatch, a daughter of Elizabeth Cady Stanton. Blatch learned militant tactics and the need to unite with working class women from years of collaboration in England with the Pankhursts. When she returned to the States in 1907 she broke with the conservative NAWSA, but her efforts to build a more radical woman's organization—one that advocated militant actions: parades, pickets, hunger strikes—were not successful until 1913 when Alice Paul and Lucy Burns—Americans who had also worked with English feminists—formed the Congressional Union (CU). The CU and its successor, the Women's Party, are credited with giving the impetus for the final fight that was successful in winning the vote.

The second time Ella Bloor mentions the National Woman's Party she again refers to Alice Paul and her party, but to a struggle taking place in 1940: the fight for a constitutional amendment prohibiting any discrimination in salary and employment practices on account of sex. Today this struggle goes under the name of the *Equal Rights Amendment* (ERA) and simply states, "Equality of rights under the law shall not be denied on account of sex." It is opposed by many working class women and radicals in the Women's Liberation Movement today for much the same reason as Ella Reeve Bloor opposed it thirty years ago—because it would tend to repeal protective laws for women instead of extending and improving them for female and male workers. Interestingly enough, in 1970 the Communist Party is still opposed to the ERA and the Socialist Workers Party and its affiliate, the Young Socialist Alliance (YSA), urge its adoption, as does the National Organization for Women (NOW). [Ed.]

are women. I was sorry to find old Ebenezer's daughter no longer on the side of progress.

. . .

In [my] tours of the Ohio minefields [in 1912, to learn the conditions under which miners lived and worked and to help them organize unions] I often met Mother Jones.[2] Our paths had crossed many times before, especially in the early 1900's in the Pennsylvania mining fields, and we were good friends. Mother Jones became interested in the labor movement after the death of her husband, who had been a soldier in the Civil War. She herself was born in Cork, Ireland, in 1830. She was an instinctive fighter against the capitalist class and spent her time organizing the miners into the U.M.W.A.

During the 1912 campaign for Debs, we were trying to get out a large vote in New York and flooded the city with speakers. One day the comrades informed me that Mother Jones, who had come to New York to speak, was lying sick in a furnished room, but would not let them help her. I went down to see her and found her in bed in a fever and wearing a coarse woolen undershirt. I got a new nightdress for her, made up the bed and got her something to eat.

"Don't fuss over me!" she expostulated. "I want you to write some letters for me while you are here. Do you suppose I'd want any Tom, Dick or Harry to write my letters?"

I told her I could do both. I fixed her all up and then wrote to her miners for her, letters that revealed how close she was to them. She wrote about their union problems, and their sick children. She told them they mustn't give in to wage reductions. She knew every petty mine boss by name.

. . .

In later years Mother Jones came under the wrong influences, and was sometimes made use of to play a reactionary role. She always retained great prestige among the miners, who would do almost anything she asked. I can remember time after time when a caucus in the A. F. of L. prepared to make a demonstration of strength against Gompers, she would come in at the last moment and say, "Stick to your old Sammy, boys, stick to your old Sammy!" and they would vote for him again. But just the same Mother Jones was an historical figure, a fine woman and a fine courageous fighter.

I met this remarkable woman many more times, since a great deal of my work in the Socialist Party was spent among the miners, and we often held meetings together. Mother Jones died in December, 1930, at the age of 100. The last major strike in which she participated was the great steel strike of 1919, but she was in touch with things and spoke at meetings until 1923, when she was in her nineties. After that she went to stay with a Socialist family who took care of her until the end.

[2] For details on her life, see Autobiography of Mother Jones. Chicago: 1925. [Ed.]

. . .

Europe's Social Democrats

I came to Ohio . . . [in 1927] in the midst of a heated campaign for a referendum in that state on the women's suffrage amendment. I plunged in. At the same time there was a campaign for a new bill providing for a nine-hour day for women in industry. Women were then working ten hours a day and the bill was considered very radical. I attended a hearing on that bill during which a corporation lawyer struck a dramatic pose, and delivered himself of the following: "When I left home tonight, my dear old mother, 92 years old, said to me, 'Where are you going, my son?' and I answered, 'I am going to Columbus to fight against a nine-hour law for women.' And my mother said to me, 'That's right, my son. Women ought to work ten hours a day. Ten hours of useful work each day is what brought me to the ripe old age of 92!' "

In the audience was a fine woman who had dedicated her life to helping the working women—Mary McDowell. She arose and said, "Gentlemen, it is a far cry from the dear old mother of 92 who sits safely at home doing her sewing when she pleases, to the drudging girls in the sweatshops of America. It is a far cry from that dear old mother in her comfortable home, to the girls in the laundries, walking back and forth in the heat, running a mangle. . . ." In spite of Mary McDowell's moving speech, the nine-hour law for women was not passed until a year later.

. . .

All my suffrage speeches were class struggle speeches. I did not mention the word "socialism" but I handed out good, strong socialist doses. I always tried to make clear that the object of our campaign was not alone to get the vote but to prepare women to use the power of the ballot to get decent pay and decent working conditions for women and so to strengthen the position of the whole working class.

Our meetings and demonstrations for the suffrage amendment culminated in a great national parade in Washington, in 1913.[3] Woodrow Wilson had just been inaugurated and the city was still crowded with visitors.

We had a tremendous parade with the thousands of women in line—working women, middle class women, society women, wives of congressmen, women of all kinds—and a few brave men. Marshals on horseback pranced up and down. Beautiful Inez Milholland, the well known suffragette leader, was grand marshal, riding a white horse.

As we started marching, we were set upon by hundreds of thugs and

[3] The reference is to the first militant parade for woman's suffrage organized by Alice Paul and the Congressional Union. Five thousand women marched up Pennsylvania Ave. the day before Woodrow Wilson's Presidential inauguration to dramatize the suffragists' cause. It did. Among other things, the Washington Chief of Police lost his job for having issued a permit for the parade. [Ed.]

ignorant men (and some women). People had come across the Potomac from Virginia and from other nearby places to break up our parade. The chief of police gave us no protection whatsoever and not a policeman was on duty along the line of parade. It was a cold day in March and the thugs tore off women's furs and coats and struck the women brutally, knocking some of them down.

That night on my way by street car to a protest mass meeting a few hoodlums, seeing my "Votes for Women" button, began to get ugly. I stood up in the middle of the crowded car and made a grandstand play. I said, "I have heard a great deal about the chivalry of Southern gentlemen and I appeal now to that chivalry. I have had enough of these insults—after what we have gone through today on the streets of Washington—just because the women want to take equal part with the men in their government. I am a mother with six sons and daughters and I protest against this treatment. Is there any Southern gentleman who will protect me in this public conveyance?"

An old gentleman, sitting with his wife and daughter, stood up, tipped his hat, and said, "Come sit with us. We will protect you." (As though I really needed "protection!") So I went over and sat with them and the hoodlums did not say another word.

•　•　•

My First Visit to Socialism

The women at the Congress,[4] including Clara Zetkin and Alexandra Kollontai, organized a Communist Women's Conference. As the only woman from America, I represented America on the presidium. We held our conference in Sverdlov Hall, a smaller building in the Kremlin in an upper floor of which Lenin, his wife, and his sister had a simple little apartment. Tremendous emotion swept the hall when a group of Mohammedan women delegates took off their veils for the first time there before us, and faced the world as free human beings. I reported on the condition of the 8,000,000 women at work in American industry, and I can remember how shocked the delegates were to learn of the extent of child labor in a developed country like ours.

It was a great privilege to work so closely with these wonderful women of our movement. Clara Zetkin, one of the outstanding members of the German Party, all her life long devoted herself especially to work among women. She was known throughout the world for her great fight against the World War. She had been a friend of Engels, and Lenin was very fond of her, and loved to talk with her. She was a fine orator, and spoke with a strong resonant voice. Though she suffered from a heart ailment, she never spared herself. I have seen her talk until she dropped unconscious. At such times her son, who was always with her, would

---

[4] Refers to the Red International of Labor Unions, a congress held in Moscow in 1921. See p. 137 for description. [Ed.]

revive her, and then she would continue. The last time I saw her was in 1929. She was already beginning to fail. She was sitting outside the door of a committee meeting, resting, and I can remember her telling me she wished that she still had the strength I had. In the last popular election in Germany before Hitler became dictator, she was elected to the Reichstag on the Communist ticket, and, as the oldest member, opened the session. Weak and frail as she was at that time, she made a powerful attack on Nazi brutality, appealing to the German people to unite against fascism. The year I was seventy, she was seventy-five, and she sent me birthday greetings. She spent her last months in the Soviet Union, where she died in June 1933.

I was very much impressed too with the brilliant and handsome Alexandra Kollontai, who had been active in the woman's movement even in pre-revolutionary days. She had been for a time People's Commissar of Social Welfare. When I first met her, she was one of the leaders of the Workers' Opposition, taking the line that the interests of the trade unions were opposed to those of the Soviet state and the Party. Lenin, to whom she was deeply devoted, convinced her of the fallacy of her position, and she abandoned her oppositionist stand, becoming a loyal supporter of the Party's position. She became Minister Plenipotentiary to Norway, the first woman ambassador in the world, was for a time ambassador to Mexico and is today Soviet Ambassador to Sweden.

One of the greatest privileges of all was meeting Nadezhda Krupskaya, Lenin's wife, one of the most selflessly devoted human beings I have ever known. She always worked closely with Lenin, helping him in all his problems, and was technical secretary of the Party's Central Committee during their days of exile, a task which involved the handling of voluminous correspondence under conspiratorial conditions, and the most exacting labor with codes. Originally a teacher, her greatest interest was always in education, and her early work in the revolutionary movement had been organizing workers' study circles. As Vice Commissar of Education, she was in charge of adult education in the U.S.S.R. She told me of the immense problem of overcoming the illiteracy inherited from the tsarist regime. On my later visits she always sent for me to ask me for ideas from America which might be useful to the Soviet educational system.

· · ·

DIVORCE
INSURANCE
FOR
HOUSEWIVES!
KNOCKOUT:
POVERTY
&
DEPENDENCY

The New Feminism

I Give a damn

The restrictions that education and custom impose on woman now limit her grasp on the universe; when the struggle to find one's place in this world is too arduous, there can be no question of getting away from it. Now, one must first emerge from it into a sovereign solitude if one wants to try to regain a grasp upon it: what woman needs first of all is to undertake, in anguish and pride, her apprenticeship in abandonment and transcendence: that is, in liberty

Simone de Beauvoir, *The Second Sex*

Part 1 dealt with the theoretical bases of the woman's rights movement as well as the social issues relevant to it. Part 1 also showed that one of the reasons the movement fell apart was its inability to integrate the goals of white middle-class women with those of the working class. Another shortcoming of nineteenth-century feminism was that it did not recognize that both personal and political oppression must be fought if one is striving to make radical changes in both economic structures and human beings.

Simone de Beauvoir explained the relation between a woman's specific and general oppression over twenty years ago in *The Second Sex,* and in this sense the book is a classic. It articulates the female's struggle to reject the social and psychological conditioning that keeps her passive and reactive by tying her to an inferior self-concept. De Beauvoir explains the relationship between a woman's "public" inferior political, economic, and social status and her "personal" self-deprecation, and how, in turn, her negative personal image is a powerful deterrent to recognizing and casting off her inferior public role. *The Second Sex* thus bridges the past and present movements, testifying to what nineteenth-century feminism left undone; prophesying much of what is taking place today.

Today's feminist movement recognizes that understanding why one has a mutilated self-concept can be a highly politicizing experience. For example, the small "rap group" where each woman shares her life experience with other women—what the Chinese now call "speaking pain to recall pain"—often leads to political action groups. And the movement seeks to incorporate personal oppression into ideology and organizational structure. The articles in this section reflect and analyze the new feminism, showing, among other things, the different ways of relating subjective and objective, personal and political experiences found within the women's liberation movement.

Of the nine articles included in "The New Feminism" three are published here for the first time: Marlene Dixon's "Why Women's Liberation—2,"[1] my "The Development of the American Women's Liberation Movement, 1967–71," and Kate Ellis' "The Politics of Day Care." Dixon's introductory article surveys the conditions which gave rise to the Women's Liberation Movement in the past several years. "The Development of the American Woman's Liberation Movement" summarizes important works and trends in the movement since 1967, with particular emphasis on manifestos, documents, articles, I could not include in this section due to lack of space. The Ellis article on day care is valuable for its analysis of how child care should *not* be established; of the dangers ensuing from institutionalized day care that is not client-controlled.

"Bread & Roses," written in 1969, was one of the first important analyses of why a woman's liberation movement is needed, and of the relationship of a woman's movement to mixed radical organizations. It also attempts to define the politics of such a movement: "We maintain that the oppression of women is based on class division; these in turn are derived from the division of labor which developed between the stronger and weaker, the owner and the owned."

[1] A major revision of the article that appeared with the same title in *Ramparts,* December 1969.

Frances Beal's "Double Jeopardy: To Be Black and Female" is one of the most cogent statements on black women's liberation. She asserts that black women are doubly oppressed: by the sexism of black and white men and by the racism of the society as a whole. She also discusses the difficulties in relating to the white women's movement.

A portion of Meredith Tax's article first appeared in the 1970 collection *Notes from the Second Year of Women's Liberation*, and the complete article was published in 1971. It is a lucid analysis of the female condition integrating a Marxist analysis with politics of personal oppression. The Fourth World Manifesto was published early in 1971. It was widely read immediately because it argues for the legitimatization of the concept of a female culture, a "Fourth World"—a topic which is one of the current sources of tension and debate in the women's movement.

I have also included works by Roxanne Dunbar and Dana Densmore who helped found *No More Fun and Games: A Journal of Female Liberation*, one of the first serious and reflective publications to combine "personal" and "political" issues. The growth of this Boston-based journal in the course of its first three issues (October 1968, February 1969, November 1969) shows the development of this dual concern of new feminism. In a December 1969 reedition of the first issue, the editors wrote:

The writing in this issue of the journal reflects our intense rage, isolation, and fear. We were not certain that a movement would develop, much less a social revolution. We did not know that we were determined to stand and fight, even if we were alone. Soon we discovered that we were not alone. Parallel, but unconnected with our own formation, hundreds of women's groups, just as isolated and enraged, had formed throughout the country and in Canada and Europe.
This journal represents our first thoughts . . .[2]

In the second and third numbers of the journal concern for the condition of working class women becomes apparent.[3] (Approximately a year later, Dunbar and others went to New Orleans to found the Southern Female Rights Union, an organization of and about poor southern women.)

This dialectic between the personal and the political, the integration of the expression of individual rage with collective anger and class concerns is at the heart of the most positive aspects of new feminism. Dunbar's "The Trip" and Densmore's "On the Temptation to Be a Beautiful Object" are examples of the kind of personal anger that can and have become a catalyst working for radical changes in society.

The New University Conference (NUC) is a national organization of the "New Left," consisting of students, faculty, and staff committed to achieving a socialist America. Its membership consists of males and females, predom-

---

[2] *No More Fun and Games: A Journal of Female Liberation.* Somerville, Mass. December 1969 reissue of October 1968 issue. Last page.
[3] Dunbar's "The Trip" is from the first number; Densmore's article from the second. Dunbar's theoretical analysis, "Female Liberation as the Basis for Social Revolution" is a reworking of an article from the third number (see my article "The Development of the American Women's Liberation Movement," 1967–1971). Dunbar also wrote about working class women: "Poor White Women" (February 1969); "Country Women" (November 1969).

inantly of white middle-class background, and connected in some way to institutions of higher education. NUC is one organizational model for developing a theory and practice of women's liberation: a radical "coed" organization with an active Woman's Caucus and "deliberate sexual parity" in the governing structure. However, like male-dominated movement organizations, feminism is not given priority in the organization as a whole. "Politics, Practice and Small Groups" was written by members of the Woman's Caucus in the summer of 1970. I recommend that students obtain this and other NUC articles. (I could not include them for lack of space.)

BREAD & ROSES

Kathy McAfee and Myrna Wood

"Bread & Roses"[1] was one of the early published responses to the 1968 SDS Resolution on Women. In June 1969, Kathy McAfee and Myrna Wood entered the debate between radical feminists and radical socialist women (some of whom were working with mixed left organizations), about whether the main problem was sexism or capitalism. The discussion also attempted to identify the most urgent feminist demands and what kind of social structure was needed to meet them. McAfee and Wood believe a radical women's liberation movement should become a movement dominated by the interests of working class women, one that has a structure and program independent of mixed radical organizations like SDS,[2] but that the women's movement should work closely with such male-female groups. They disagree with "women who advocate a radical feminist movement totally separate from any other political movement."

According to Wood and McAfee, all women, even those in the ruling class, "are oppressed as women in the sense that their real fulfillment is linked to their role as girlfriend, wife, or mother." They contend that women must struggle on a double front because the cultural conditions under which people live are as important as the economic basis of their oppression in determining conscious- ness. A purely economic revolution is not enough; neither is a movement based on a politic of personal liberation. "Bread & Roses" emphasizes that the basically white middle class woman's movement must realize that it is the working class women—whose material and psychological oppressions reinforce each other—who will lead a revolutionary woman's liberation movement.

Kathy McAfee and Myrna Wood, "Bread & Roses," *Leviathan*, Vol. 1, No. 3 (June 1969). Reprinted by permission.

[1] Originally published in *Leviathan magazine* (Berkeley).
[2] When "Bread & Roses" was written, the Students for a Democratic Society still existed; however, its last convention was held in June, 1969, at which time the splits that had been developing over the previous two or three years finally divided the organization and signaled its demise as a national student organization.

A great deal of confusion exists today about the role of women's liberation in a revolutionary movement. Hundreds of women's groups have sprung up within the past year or two, but among them, a number of very different and often conflicting ideologies have developed. The growth of these movements has demonstrated the desperate need that many women feel to escape their own oppression, but it has also shown that organization around women's issues need not lead to revolutionary consciousness, or even to an identification with the left. (Some groups mobilize middle class women to fight for equal privileges as businesswomen and academics; others maintain that the overthrow of capitalism is irrelevant for women.)

Many movement women have experienced the initial exhilaration of discovering women's liberation as an issue, of realizing that the frustration, anger, and fear we feel are not a result of individual failure but are shared by all our sisters, and of sensing—if not fully understanding—that these feelings stem from the same oppressive conditions that give rise to racism, chauvinism and the barbarity of American culture. But many movement women, too, have become disillusioned after a time by their experiences with women's liberation groups. More often than not these groups never get beyond the level of therapy sessions; rather than aiding the political development of women and building a revolutionary women's movement, they often encourage escape from political struggle.

The existence of this tendency among women's liberation groups is one reason why many movement activists (including some women) have come out against a women's liberation movement that distinguishes itself from the general movement, even if it considers itself part of the left. A movement organized by women around the oppression of women, they say, is bound to emphasize the bourgeois and personal aspects of oppression and to obscure the material oppression of working class women *and men.* At best, such a movement "lacks revolutionary potential" (Bernadine Dohrn, N.L.N., V.4, No. 9). In SDS, where this attitude is very strong, questions about the oppression and liberation of women are raised only within the context of current SDS ideology and strategy; the question of women's liberation is raised only as an incidental, subordinate aspect of programs around "*the* primary struggle," anti-racism. (Although most people in SDS now understand the extent of black people's oppression, they are not aware of the fact that the median wage of working women (black and white) is lower than that of black males.) The male domination of the organization has not been affected by occasional rhetorical attacks on male chauvinism and most important, very little organizing of women is being done.

Although the reason behind it can be understood, this attitude toward women's liberation is mistaken and dangerous. By discouraging the development of a revolutionary women's liberation movement, it avoids a serious challenge to what, along with racism, is the deepest source of division and false consciousness among workers. By setting up (in the name of Marxist class analysis) a dichotomy between the "bourgeois," personal and psychological forms of oppression on the one hand, and the "real" material forms on the other, it substitutes a mechanistic model of class relations for a more profound understanding of how these two aspects of oppression depend upon and reinforce each other. Finally, this anti-women's liberationist attitude makes it easier for us to bypass a confrontation of male chauvinism and the closely related values of elitism and authoritarianism which are weakening our movement.

I

Before we can discuss the potential of a women's liberation movement, we need a more precise description of the way the oppression of women functions in a capitalist society. This will also help us understand the relation of psychological material oppression.

(1) *Male Chauvinism—the attitude that women are the passive and inferior servants of society and of men—sets women apart from the rest of the working class.* Even when they do the same work as men, women are not considered workers in the same sense, with the need and right to work to provide for their families or to support themselves independently. They are expected to accept work at lower wages and without job security. Thus they can be used as a marginal or reserve labor force when profits depend on extra low costs or when men are needed for war.

Women are not supposed to be independent, so they are not supposed to have any "right to work." This means, in effect, that although they do work, they are denied the right to organize and fight for better wages and conditions. Thus the role of women in the labor force undermines the struggles of male workers as well. The boss can break a union drive by threatening to hire lower paid women or blacks. In many cases, where women are organized, the union contract reinforces their inferior position, making women the least loyal and militant union members. (Standard Oil workers in San Francisco recently paid the price of male supremacy. Women at Standard Oil have the least chance for advancement and decent pay, and the union has done little to fight this. Not surprisingly, women formed the core of the back to work move that eventually broke the strike.[1])

In general, because women are defined as docile, helpless, and inferior, they are forced into the most demanding and mind-rotting jobs —from scrubbing floors to filing cards—under the most oppressive conditions where they are treated like children or slaves. Their very position reinforces the idea, even among the women themselves, that they are fit for and should be satisfied with this kind of work.

(2) *Apart from the direct, material exploitation of women, male supremacy acts in more subtle ways to undermine class consciousness.* The tendency of male workers to think of themselves primarily as men

[1] See *Movement*, May 1969, p. 6–7.

(i.e., powerful) rather than as workers (i.e., members of an oppressed group) promotes a false sense of privilege and power, and an identification with the world of men, including the boss. The petty dictatorship which most men exercise over their wives and families enables them to vent their anger and frustration in a way which poses no challenge to the system. The role of the man in the family reinforces aggressive individualism, authoritarianism, and a hierarchical view of social relations—values which are fundamental to the perpetuation of capitalism. In this system we are taught to relieve our fears and frustrations by brutalizing those weaker than we are: a man in uniform turns into a pig; the foreman intimidates the man on the line; the husband beats his wife, child, and dog.

(3) *Women are further exploited in their roles as housewives and mothers, through which they reduce the costs (social and economic) of maintaining the labor force.* All of us will admit that inadequate as it may be American workers have a relatively decent standard of living, in a strictly material sense, when compared to workers of other countries or periods of history. But American workers are exploited and harassed in other ways than through the size of the weekly paycheck. They are made into robots on the job; they are denied security; they are forced to pay for expensive insurance and can rarely save enough to protect them from sudden loss of job or emergency. They are denied decent medical care and a livable environment. They are cheated by inflation. They are "given" a regimented education that prepares them for a narrow slot or for nothing. And they are taxed heavily to pay for these "benefits."

In all these areas, it is a woman's responsibility to make up for the failures of the system. In countless working class families, it is mother's job that bridges the gap between week to week subsistence and relative security. It is her wages that enable the family to eat better food, to escape their oppressive surroundings through a trip, an occasional movie, or new clothes. It is her responsibility to keep her family healthy despite the cost of decent medical care; to make a comfortable home in an unsafe and unlivable neighborhood; to provide a refuge from the alienation of work and to keep the male ego in good repair. It is she who must struggle daily to make ends meet despite inflation. She must make up for the fact that her children do not receive a decent education and she must salvage their damaged personalities.

A woman is judged as a wife and mother—the only role she is allowed—according to her ability to maintain stability in her family and to help her family "adjust" to harsh realities. She therefore transmits the values of hard work and conformity to each generation of workers. It is she who forces her children to stay in school and "behave" or who urges her husband not to risk his job by standing up to the boss or going on strike.

Thus the role of wife and mother is one of social mediator and pacifier. She shields her family from the direct impact of class oppression. She is the true opiate of the masses.

156

(4) *Working class women and other women as well are exploited as consumers.* They are forced to buy products which are necessities, but which have waste built into them, like the soap powder the price of which includes fancy packaging and advertising. They also buy products which are wasteful in themselves because they are told that a new car or TV will add to their families' status and satisfaction, or that cosmetics will increase their desirability as sex objects. Among "middle class" women, of course, the second type of wasteful consumption is more important than it is among working class women, but all women are victims of both types to a greater or lesser extent, and the values which support wasteful consumption are part of our general culture.

(5) *All women, too, are oppressed and exploited sexually.* For working class women this oppression is more direct and brutal. They are denied control of their own bodies, when as girls they are refused information about sex and birth control, and when as women they are denied any right to decide whether and when to have children. Their confinement to the role of sex partner and mother, and their passive submission to a single man are often maintained by physical force. The relative sexual freedom of "middle class" or college educated women, however, does not bring *them* real independence. Their sexual role is still primarily a passive one; their value as individuals still determined by their ability to attract, please, and hold onto a man. The definition of women as docile and dependent, inferior in intellect and weak in character cuts across class lines.

A woman of any class is expected to sell herself—not just her body but her entire life, her talents, interests, and dreams—to a man. She is expected to give up friendships, ambitions, pleasures, and moments of time to herself in order to serve his career or his family. In return, she receives not only her livelihood but her identity, her very right to existence, for unless she is the wife of someone or the mother of someone, a woman is nothing.

In this summary of the forms of oppression of women in this society, the rigid dichotomy between material oppression and psychological oppression fails to hold, for it can be seen that these two aspects of oppression reinforce each other at every level. A woman may seek a job out of absolute necessity, or in order to escape repression and dependence at home. In either case, on the job she will be persuaded or forced to accept low pay, indignity and a prison-like atmosphere because a woman isn't supposed to need money or respect. Then, after working all week turning tiny wires, or typing endless forms, she finds that cooking and cleaning, dressing up and making up, becoming submissive and childlike in order to please a man is her only relief, so she gladly falls back into her "proper" role.

All women, even including those of the ruling class, are oppressed as women in the sense that their real fulfillment is linked to their role as girlfriend, wife or mother. This definition of women is part of bourgeois culture—the whole superstructure of ideas that serves to explain and reinforce the social relations of capitalism. It is applied to all women, but it has very different consequences for women of different classes. For a ruling class woman, it means she is denied real independence, dignity, and sexual freedom. For a working class woman it means this too, but it also justifies her material super-exploitation and physical coercion. Her oppression is a total one.[2]

II

It is true, as the movement critics assert, that the present women's liberation groups are almost entirely based among "middle class" women, that is, college and career women; and the issues of psychological and sexual exploitation and, to a lesser extent, exploitation through consumption, have been the most prominent ones.

It is not surprising that the women's liberation movement should begin among bourgeois women, and should be dominated in the beginning by their consciousness and their particular concerns. Radical women are generally the post war middle class generation that grew up with the right to vote, the chance at higher education and training for supportive roles in the professions and business. Most of them are young and sophisticated enough to have not yet had children and do not have to marry to support themselves. In comparison with most women, they are capable of a certain amount of control over their lives.

The higher development of bourgeois democratic society allows the women who benefit from education and relative equality to see the contradictions between its rhetoric (every boy can become president) and their actual place in that society. The working class woman might believe that education could have made her financially independent but the educated career woman finds that money has not made her independent. In fact, because she has been allowed to progress halfway on the upward-mobility ladder she can see the rest of the distance that is denied her only because she is a woman. She can see the similarity between her oppression and that of other sections of the population. Thus, from their own experience, radical women in the movement are

[2] We referred above to "middle class" forms of oppression, contrasting the opportunity for wasteful consumption among relatively affluent women, and superficial sexual freedom of college women to the conditions of poor and uneducated working women. Here "middle class" refers more to a life style, a bourgeois cultural ideal, than to a social category. Strictly speaking, a middle class person is one who does not employ other people but also does not have to sell his labor to live, e.g., a doctor or owner of a small family business. Many people who think of themselves as "middle class," and who can afford more than they need to live on are, strictly speaking, working class people because they must sell their labor, e.g., high school teachers and most white collar workers. There is, of course, a real difference in living conditions as well as consciousness between these people and most industrial workers. But because of the middle class myth, a tremendous gap in consciousness can exist even where conditions are essentially the same. There are literally millions of female clerical workers, telephone operators, etc., who work under the most proletarianized conditions, doing the most tedious female-type labor, and making the same wages, or even less, as sewing-machine factory workers, who nevertheless think of themselves as in a very different "class" from those factory women.

aware of more faults in the society than racism and imperialism. Because they have pushed the democratic myth to its limits, they know concretely how it limits them.

At the same time that radical women were learning about American society they were also becoming aware of the male chauvinism in the movement. In fact, that is usually the cause of their first conscious verbalization of the prejudice they feel; it is more disillusioning to know that the same contradiction exists between the movement's rhetoric of equality and its reality, for we expect more of our comrades.

This realization of the deep-seated prejudice against themselves in the movement produces two common reactions among its women: (1) a preoccupation with this immediate barrier (and perhaps a resultant hopelessness), and (2) a tendency to retreat inward, to buy the fool's gold of creating a personally liberated life style.

However, our concept of liberation represents a consciousness that conditions have forced on us while most of our sisters are chained by other conditions, biological and economic, that overwhelm their humanity and desires for self fulfillment. Our background accounts for our ignorance about the stark oppression of women's daily lives.

Few radical women really know the worst of women's condition. They do not understand the anxious struggle of an uneducated girl to find the best available man for financial security and escape from a crowded and repressive home. They have not suffered years of fear from ignorance and helplessness about pregnancies. Few have experienced constant violence and drunkenness of a brutalized husband or father. They do not know the day to day reality of being chained to a house and family, with little money and lots of bills, and no diversions but TV.

Not many radical women have experienced 9-11 hours a day of hard labor, carrying trays on aching legs for rude customers who may leave no tip, but leave a feeling of degradation from their sexual or racist remarks—and all of this for $80–$90 a week. Most movement women have not learned to blank out their thoughts for 7 hours in order to type faster or file endless numbers. They have not felt their own creativity deadened by this work, while watching men who were not trained to be typists move on to higher level jobs requiring "brain-work."

In summary: because male supremacy (assumption of female inferiority, regulation of women to service roles, and sexual objectification) crosses class lines, radical women are conscious of women's oppression, but because of their background, they lack consciousness of most women's class oppression.

III

The development of the movement has produced different trends within the broad women's liberation movement. Most existing women's groups fall into one of the four following categories:

(1) *Personal Liberation Groups.* This type of group has been the first

manifestation of consciousness of their own oppression among movement women. By talking about their frustrations with their role in the movement, they have moved from feelings of personal inadequacy to the realization that male supremacy is one of the foundations of the society that must be destroyed. Because it is at the level of the direct oppression in our daily lives that most people become conscious, it is not surprising that this is true of women in the movement. Lenin once complained about this phenomenon to Clara Zetkin, leader of the German women's socialist movement: "I have been told that at the evening meetings arranged for reading and discussion with working women, sex and marriage problems come first."

But once women have discovered the full extent of the prejudice against them they cannot ignore it, whether Lenin approves or not, and they have found women's discussions helpful in dealing with their problems. These groups have continued to grow and split into smaller, more viable groups, showing just how widespread is women's dissatisfaction.

However, the level of politicization of these groups has been kept low by the very conditions that keep women underdeveloped in this society; and alienation from the male dominated movement has prolonged the politicization process. These groups still see the source of their oppression in "chauvinist attitudes," rather than in the social relations of capitalism that produce those attitudes. Therefore, they don't confront male chauvinism collectively or politically. They become involved solely in "personal liberation"—attempts to create free life styles and define new criteria for personal relations in the hoped for system of the future. Bernadine Dohrn's criticism of these groups was a just one: "Their program is only a cycle that produces more women's groups, mostly devoted to a personal liberation/therapy function and promises of study which are an evasion of practice" (*N.L.N.*, V.4, No.9).

(2) *Anti-Left Groups.* Many women have separated from the movement out of bitterness and disillusionment with the left's ability to alter its built-in chauvinism. Some are now vociferously anti-left; others simply see the movement as irrelevant. In view of the fate of the ideal of women's equality in most socialist countries, their skepticism is not surprising. Nor is it surprising that individuals with leadership abilities who are constantly thwarted in the movement turn to new avenues.

These women advocate a radical feminist movement totally separate from any other political movement. Their program involves female counter-institutions, such as communes and political parties, and attacks upon those aspects of women's oppression that affect all classes (abortion laws, marriage, lack of child care facilities, job discrimination, images of women in the media).

The first premise of the theory with which these radical feminists justify their movement is that women have always been exploited. They admit that women's oppression has a social basis—*men as a group oppress women as a group*—therefore, women must organize to confront male supremacy collectively. But they say that since women were exploited before capitalism, as well as in capitalist and "socialist" societies, the overthrow of capitalism is irrelevant to the equality of women. Male supremacy is a phenomenon outside the left-right political spectrum and must be fought separately.

But if one admits that female oppression has a social basis, it is necessary to specify the social relations on which this condition is based, and then to change those relations. (We maintain that the oppression of women is based on class divisions; these in turn are derived from the division of labor which developed between the stronger and weaker, the owner and the owned; e.g., women, under conditions of scarcity in primitive society.) Defining those relations as "men as a group *vs.* women as a group," as the anti-left groups seem to do, is ultimately reducible only to some form of biological determinism (women are inherently oppress-able) and leads to no solution in practice other than the elimination of one group or the other.

(3) *Movement Activists.* Many radical women who have become full time activists accept the attitude of most men in the movement that women's liberation is bourgeois and "personalist." They look at most of the present women's liberation groups and conclude that a movement based on women's issues is bound to emphasize the relatively mild forms of oppression experienced by students and "middle class" women while obscuring the fundamental importance of class oppression. "Sure middle class women are oppressed," they say, "but how can we concentrate on making our own lives more comfortable when working class women and men are so much more oppressed." Others point out that "women cannot be free in an unfree society; their liberation will come

with that of the rest of us." These people maintain that organizing around women's issues is reformist because it is an attempt to ameliorate conditions within bourgeois society. Most movement activists agree that we should talk about women's oppression, but say we should do so only in terms of the super-exploitation of working women, especially black and brown working women, and not in terms of personal, psychological, and sexual oppression, which they see as a very different (and bourgeois) thing. They also say we should organize around women's oppression, but only as an aspect of our struggles against racism and imperialism. In other words, there should not be a separate revolutionary women's organization.

Yet strangely enough, demands for the liberation of women seldom find their way into movement programs, and very little organizing of women, within or apart from other struggles, is actually going on:

—In student organizing, no agitation for birth control for high school and college girls; no recognition of the other special restrictions that keep them from controlling their own lives; no propaganda about how women are still barred from many courses, especially those that would enable them to demand equality in employment.

—In open admissions fights, no propaganda about the channeling of girls into low-paying, deadend service occupations.

—In struggles against racism, talk about the black man's loss of manhood, but none about the sexual objectification and astounding exploitation of black women.

—In anti-repression campaigns, no fights against abortion laws; no defense of those "guilty" of abortion.

—In analysis of unions, no realization that women make less than black men and that most women aren't even organized yet. The demands for equal wages were recently raised in the Women's Resolution (at the December SDS, NC), but there are as yet no demands for free child care and equal work by husbands that would make the demand for equal wages more than an empty gesture.

It is clear that radical women activists have not been able to educate the movement about its own chauvinism or bring the issue of male supremacy to an active presence in the movement's program any more than have the personal liberation groups.

The failure of the movement to deal with male supremacy is less the result of a conscious evaluation of the issue's impact than a product of the male chauvinism that remains deeply rooted in the movement itself. Most full-time women organizers work in an atmosphere dominated by aggressive "guerilla" street fighters and organizers (who usually have a silent female appendage), of charismatic theoreticians (whose ability to lay out an analysis is not hampered by the casual stroking of their girl's hair while everyone listens raptly), of decision-making meetings in which the strong voices of men in "ideological struggle" are only rarely punctuated by the voice of one of the girls more skilled in debate, and of movement offices in which the women are still the most reliable (after all, the men are busy speaking and organizing).

"Bad politics" and "sloppy thinking" baiting is particularly effective against women who have been socialized to fear aggressiveness, who tend to lack experience in articulating abstract concepts. And at the same time, a woman's acceptance in the movement still depends on her attractiveness, and men do not find women attractive when they are strong-minded and argue like men.

Many of the characteristics which one needs in order to become respected in the movement—like the ability to argue loud and fast and aggressively and to excel in the "I'm more revolutionary than you" style of debate—are traits which our society consistently cultivates in men and discourages in women from childhood. But these traits are neither inherently male nor universally human; rather they are particularly appropriate to a brutally competitive capitalist society.

That most movement women fail to realize this, that their ideal is still the arrogant and coercive leader-organizer, that they continue to work at all in an atmosphere where women are consistently scorned, and where chauvinism and elitism are attacked in rhetoric only—all this suggests that most movement women are not really aware of their *own* oppression. They continue to assume that the reason they haven't "made it" in the movement is that they are not dedicated enough or that their politics are not developed enough. At the same time, most of these women are becoming acutely aware, along with the rest of the movement, of their own comfortable and privileged backgrounds compared with those of workers (and feel guilty about them). It is this situation that causes them to regard women's liberation as a sort of counter-revolutionary self-indulgence.

There is a further reason for this; in the movement we have all become aware of the central importance of working people in a revolutionary movement and of the gap between their lives and most of our own. But at this point our understanding is largely an abstract one; we remain distant from and grossly ignorant of the real conditions working people face day to day. Thus our concept of working class oppression tends to be a one-sided and mechanistic one, contrasting "real" economic oppression to our "bourgeois hang-ups" with cultural and psychological oppression. We don't understand that the oppression of working people is a total one, in which the "psychological" aspects—the humiliation of being poor, uneducated, and powerless, the alienation of work, and the brutalization of family life—are not only real forms of oppression in themselves, but reinforce material oppression by draining people of their energy and will to fight. Similarly, the "psychological" forms of oppression that affect all women—sexual objectification and the definition of women as docile and serving—work to keep working class women in a position where they are super-exploited as workers and as housewives.

But because of our one-sided view of class oppression, most movement women do not see the relationship of their own oppression to that of working class women. This is why they conclude that a women's liberation movement cannot lead to class consciousness and does not have revolutionary potential.

(4) *Advocates of a Women's Liberation Movement.* A growing number of radical women see the need for an organized women's movement because: (1) they see revolutionary potential in women organizing against their direct oppression, that is, against male supremacy as well as their exploitation as workers; and (2) they believe that a significant movement for women's equality will develop within any socialist movement only through the conscious efforts of organized women, and they have seen that such consciousness does not develop in a male chauvinist movement born of a male supremacist society.

These women believe that radical women must agitate among young working class girls, rank and file women workers, and workers' wives, around a double front; against their direct oppression by male supremacist institutions, and against their exploitation as workers. They maintain that the cultural conditions of people's lives is as important as the economic basis of their oppression in determining consciousness. If the movement cannot incorporate such a program, these women say, then an organized women's liberation movement distinguished from the general movement must be formed, for only through such a movement will radical women gain the consciousness to develop and carry through this program.

The question of "separation" from the movement is a thorny one, particularly if it is discussed only in the abstract. Concretely, the problem at the present time is simply: should a women's liberation movement be a caucus within SDS, or should it be more than that? The radical women's liberationists say the latter; their movement should have its own structure and program, although it should work closely with SDS, and most of its members would probably be active in SDS (or other movement projects and organizations) as individuals. It would be "separate" *within* the movement in the same sense that say, NOC is separate, or in the way that the organized women who call themselves "half of China" are separate within the Chinese revolution.

The reason for this is not simply that women need a separate organization in order to develop themselves. The radical women's liberationists believe that the true extent of women's oppression can be revealed and fought only if the women's liberation movement is dominated by working class women. This puts the question of "separation" from SDS in a different light. Most of us in the movement would agree that a revolutionary working class movement cannot be built within the present structure of the student movement, so that if we are serious about our own rhetoric, SDS itself will have to be totally transformed, or we will have to move beyond it, within the coming years.

The radical women's liberationists further believe that the American liberation movement will fail before it has barely begun if it does not recognize and deal with the elitism, coerciveness, aggressive individualism, and class chauvinism it has inherited from capitalist society. Since it is women who always bear the brunt of these forms of oppression, it is they who are most aware of them. Elitism, for example, affects many people in the movement to the detriment of the movement as a whole, but women are always on the very bottom rung of participation in decision-making. The more they are shut out, the less they develop the necessary skills, and elitism in the movement mirrors the vicious circle of bourgeois society.

The same characteristics in the movement that produce male chauvinism also lead to class chauvinism. Because women are politically underdeveloped—their education and socialization have not given them analytic and organizational skills—they are assumed to be politically inferior. But as long as we continue to evaluate people according to this criterion, our movement will automatically consider itself superior to working class people, who suffer a similar kind of oppression.

We cannot develop a truly liberating form of socialism unless we are consciously fighting these tendencies in our movement. This consciousness can come from the organized efforts of those who are most aware of these faults because they are most oppressed by them, i.e. women. But in order to politicize their consciousness of their own oppression, and to make effective their criticisms of the movement, women need the solidarity and self-value they could gain from a revolutionary women's liberation movement involved in meaningful struggle.

What Is the Revolutionary Potential of Women's Liberation?

The potential for revolutionary thought and action lies in the masses of super-oppressed and super-exploited working class women. We have seen the stagnation in New Left women's groups caused by the lack of the *need to fight* that class oppression produces. Unlike most radical women, working class women have no freedom of alternatives, no chance of achieving some slight degree of individual liberation. It is these women, through their struggle, who will develop a revolutionary women's liberation movement.

A women's liberation movement will be necessary if unity of the working class is ever to be achieved. Until working men see their female co-workers and their own wives as equal in their movement, and until those women see that it is in their own interests and that of their families to "dare to win," the position of women will continue to undermine every working class struggle.

The attitude of unions, and of the workers themselves, that women should not work, and that they do not do difficult or necessary work, helps to maintain a situation in which (1) many women who need income or independence cannot work, (2) women who do work are usually not organized, (3) union contracts reinforce the inferior position of women who are organized, and (4) women are further penalized with the costs of child care. As a result, most women workers do not see much value in organizing. They have little to gain from militant fights for better wages and conditions, and they have the most to risk in organizing in the first place.

The position of workers' wives outside their husbands' union often places them in antagonism to it. They know how little it does about safety and working conditions, grievances, and layoffs. The unions demand complete loyalty to strikes—which means weeks without income—and then sign contracts which bring little improvement in wages or conditions.

Thus on the simple trade union level, the oppression of women weakens the position of the workers as a whole. But any working class movement that does not deal with the vulnerable position of totally powerless women will have to deal with the false consciousness of those women.

The importance of a working class women's liberation movement goes beyond the need for unity. A liberation movement of the "slaves of the slave" tends to raise broader issues of peoples' oppression in all its forms, so that it is inherently wider than the economism of most trade union movements. For example, last year 187 women struck British Ford demanding equal wages (and shutting down 40,000 other jobs in the process). They won their specific demand, but Ford insisted that the women work all three rotating shifts, as the men do. The women objected that this would create great difficulty for them in their work as housekeepers and mothers, and that their husbands would not like it.

A militant women's liberation movement must go on from this point to demand (1) that mothers must also be free in the home, (2) that management must pay for child care facilities so that women can do equal work with men, and that (3) equal work *with* men must mean equal work *by* men. In this way, the winning of a simple demand for equality on the job raises much broader issues of the extent of inequality, the degree of exploitation, and the totality of the oppression of all the workers. It can show how women workers are forced to hold an extra full time job without pay or recognition that this is necessary work, how male chauvinism allows the capitalist class to exploit workers in this way, how people are treated like machines owned by the boss, and how the most basic conditions of workers' lives are controlled in the interests of capitalism.

The workplace is not the only area in which the fight against women's oppression can raise the consciousness of everybody about the real functions of bourgeois institutions. Propaganda against sexual objectification and the demeaning of women in the media can help make people understand how advertising manipulates our desires and frustrations, and how the media sets up models of human relationships and values which we all unconsciously accept. A fight against the tracking of girls in school into low-level, deadend service jobs helps show how the education system channels and divides us all, playing upon the false self-images we have been given in school and by the media (women are best as secretaries and nurses; blacks aren't cut out for responsible positions; workers' sons aren't smart enough for college).

Struggles to free women from domestic slavery which may begin around demands for a neighborhood or factory child care center can lead to consciousness of the crippling effects of relations of domination and exploitation in the home, and to an understanding of how the institutions of marriage and the family embody those relations and destroy human potential.

In short, because the material oppression of women is integrally related to their psychological and sexual oppression, the women's liberation movement must necessarily raise these issues. In doing so it can make us all aware of how capitalism oppresses us, not only by drafting us, taxing us, and exploiting us on the job, but by determining the way we think, feel, and relate to each other.

IV

In order to form a women's liberation movement based on the oppression of working class women we must begin to agitate on issues of "equal rights" and specific rights. Equal rights means all those "rights" that men are supposed to have: the right to work, to organize for equal pay, promotions, better conditions, equal (and *not* separate) education. Specific rights means those rights women must have if they are to be equal in the other areas: free, adequate child care, abortions, birth control for young women from puberty, self defense, desegregation of all institutions (schools, unions, jobs). It is not so much an academic question of what is correct theory as an inescapable empirical fact; women must fight their conditions just to participate in the movement.

The first reason why we need to fight on these issues is that we must serve the people. That slogan is not just rhetoric with the Black Panthers but reflects their determination to end the exploitation of their people. Similarly, the women's liberation movement will grow and be effective only to the extent that it abominates and fights the conditions of misery that so many women suffer every day. It will gain support only if it speaks to the immediate needs of women. For instance:

(1) We must begin to disseminate birth control information in high schools and fight the tracking of girls into inferior education. We must do this not only to raise the consciousness of these girls to their condition but because control of their bodies is the key to their participation in the future. Otherwise, their natural sexuality will be indirectly used to repress them from struggles for better jobs and organizing, because they will be encumbered with children and economically tied to the family structure for basic security.

(2) We must raise demands for maternity leave and child-care facilities provided (paid for, but not controlled) by management as a rightful side benefit of women workers. This is important not only for what those issues say about women's right to work but so that women who choose to have children have more freedom to participate in the movement.

(3) We must agitate for rank and file revolt against the male supremacist hierarchy of the unions and for demands for equal wages. Only through winning such struggles for equality can the rank and file *be* united and see their common enemies—management and union hierarchy. Wives of workers must fight the chauvinist attitudes of their husbands simply to be able to attend meetings.

(4) We must organize among store clerks, waitresses, office workers, and hospitals where vast numbers of women have no bargaining rights or security. In doing so we will have to confront the question of a radical strategy towards established unions and the viability of independent unions.

(5) We must add to the liberal demands for abortion reform by fighting against the hospital and doctors' boards that such reforms consist of. They will in no way make abortions more available for the majority of non-middle class women or young girls who will still be forced to home remedies and butchers. We must insist at all times on the right of every woman to control her own body.

(6) We must demand the right of women to protect themselves. Because the pigs protect property and not people, because the violence created by the brutalization of many men in our society is often directed at women, and because not all women are willing or able to sell themselves (or to limit their lives) for the protection of a male, women have a right to self-protection.

This is where the struggle must begin, although it cannot end here. In the course of the fight we will have to raise the issues of the human relationships in which the special oppression of women is rooted: sexual objectification, the division of labor in the home, and the institutions of marriage and the nuclear family. But organizing "against the family" cannot be the basis of a program. An uneducated working class wife with five kids is perfectly capable of understanding that marriage has destroyed most of her potential as a human being—probably she already understands this—but she is hardly in a position to repudiate her source of livelihood and free herself of those children. If we expect that of her, we will never build a movement.

As the women's liberation movement gains strength, the development of cooperative child care centers and living arrangements, and the provision of birth control may allow more working class women to free themselves from slavery as sex objects and housewives. But at the present time, the insistence by some women's liberation groups that we must "organize against sexual objectification," and that only women who repudiate the family can really be part of the movement, reflects the class chauvinism and lack of seriousness of women who were privileged enough to avoid economic dependence and sexual slavery in the first place.

In no socialist country have women yet achieved equality or full liberation, but in the most recent revolutions (Vietnam, Cuba, and China's cultural revolution) the women's struggle has intensified. It may be that in an advanced society such as our own, where women have had relatively more freedom, a revolutionary movement may not be able to avoid a militant women's movement developing within it. But the examples of previous attempts at socialist revolutions prove that the struggle must be instigated *by* militant women; liberation is not handed down from above.

THE DEVELOPMENT OF THE AMERICAN WOMEN'S LIBERATION MOVEMENT, 1967–1971

Roberta Salper

I have been active in the women's liberation movement since 1968 when I helped organize Pittsburgh Women's Liberation. In 1969 I taught a course on "The History and Social Role of Women in America" at the University of Pittsburgh. I have also been active in the Women's Caucus of the New University Conference for several years and in 1970–1971 taught in the country's first Women's Studies Program at San Diego State College. Currently I am at work on a study of women's role in Cuba since 1959.

The following article attempts to summarize highlights in the writings and activities of the women's liberation movement which are not covered elsewhere in this anthology. It is also intended to complement the following article by Marlene Dixon so that together they will present a complete panorama of today's women's movement and will suggest future directions and activities.

The development of the women's liberation movement in the last four years has been marked by a number of central ideological problems. The following pages outline the main theories and events that have influenced or reflected significant organizational developments.

The First Theory

Juliet Mitchell's "Women: The Longest Revolution" appeared in England in 1966[1]—before a movement had developed. The article is an important analysis of how women's liberation is not structurally integrated into classic socialist theory; of its ideological limitations regarding specific aspects of women's oppression (for example, the many forms of sexual repression, woman's "biologically destined" role as socializer of children, and the real socioeconomic powerlessness of the mother masked by a social cult of maternity). Mitchell's piece has been widely read and praised by American feminists, and much of what she says is correct

This article was written especially for this book.

[1] In the *New Left Review* (November-December 1966). Reprinted by the Radical Education Project. All quotes are from the REP pamphlet.

and incisive. However, the assumptions implicit in her methodological perspective are misleading.

Mitchell says women's liberation depends on four separate structures common to women in all societies: production, reproduction, socialization, sexuality. Only if *all four* structures are transformed will women be freed: "A modification of any one of them can be offset by a reinforcement of another, so that mere permutation of the form of exploitation is achieved." As an example of incomplete transformation she cites China, where all the emphasis is being placed on liberating women in production to the exclusion of the other three structural categories. According to Mitchell, however, "Only in the highly developed societies of the West can an authentic liberation of women be envisaged today." This is because, for Mitchell, only superdevelopment of the technological and industrial base can effectively transform all four structural determinants of woman's inequality. Where and how does one start? "A revolutionary movement must base its analysis on the uneven development of each [of these four categories], and attack the weakest link in the combination." Mitchell continues:

Production, reproduction, and socialization are all more or less stationary in the West today, in the sense that they have not changed for three or more decades. There is, moreover, no widespread *demand* for changes in them on the part of women themselves—the governing ideology has effectively prevented critical consciousness. By contrast, the dominant sexual ideology is proving less and less successful in regulating spontaneous behavior. Marriage in its classical form is increasingly threatened by the liberalization of relationships before and after it which affects all classes today. In this sense, it is evidently the weak link in the chain—the particular structure that is the site of the most contradictions.[2]

Drawing heavily on structuralist methods and vocabulary,[3] Mitchell says that each of these four structures is the result of interaction between nature and culture—that is, socialization is what happens when people (nature) are in society (culture). At first glance it seems that she is talking about a process of change, of becoming, a humanist concept of historical progress. In fact, however, the belief that woman's condition has its own structure composed of four elements—elements

[2] "Women: The Longest Revolution," p. 22.
[3] For example: Mitchell says one must reject "the idea that woman's condition can be deduced derivatively from the economy or equated symbolically with society. Rather, it must be seen as a *specific structure*, which is a unity of different elements. The variations of woman's condition throughout history will be the result of different combinations of these elements. . . . Because the unity of woman's condition at any one time is the product of several structures, it is always 'overdetermined!' " *Ibid.*, p. 6. Another explicit example of structuralist methodology and lexicon is found in Mitchell's reference to French theoretician Louis Althusser: "Althusser advocates [in *Pour Marx* (1965)] the notion of a complex totality in which each independent sector has its own autonomous reality but each of which is ultimately, but only ultimately, determined by the economic. As each sector can move at a different pace . . . in the total social structure . . . sometimes contradictions cancel each other out and sometimes they reinforce one another. To describe this complexity, Althusser uses the Freudian term 'overdetermination.' " *Ibid.*, pp. 6–7, footnote 13.

that are constants throughout history (although the *substance* of these constant forms may differ) *negates* the idea of historical progress; indeed, it is ahistorical.

The belief that "production, reproduction, and socialization are all more or less stationary in the West today," and that "sexuality" is moving, implies that we can clearly divide and proportion everything in a woman's life neatly into one of these categories, and secondly, that three structures might stand still while one marches forward. How can the "dominant sexual ideology" be a complete entity, separate from the dominant ideologies regarding production, reproduction, and socialization? Does the "liberalization of relationships before and after [marriage] which affects all classes today" mean that the conflict between structures, that is, between *concepts,* is more primary than the conflicts between classes, that is, between *people?* Can the principal, most basic differences between, say, Jackie Onassis and Fannie Lou Hamer be explained in terms of these four structures? (Although they are both women, definite blocks to sisterhood certainly exist.) Should not the myriad of factors that separate the two women be explained fundamentally by comparing the *work* the two do and the conditions in which they live?

The division of woman's situation into four structures is an abstract relationship; these structures float over one's head like clouds in a comic strip, always there, with a fixed shape, never changing and never subject to change from below. These categories, although couched in Marxist terminology, lend themselves to a subtle variation of idealism: the abstract form (idea) comes first and determines how people will act and react with the material conditions that surround them in a particular time and place in history, instead of vice versa.

"Women: The Longest Revolution" is an isolated theoretical study that does not articulate the desires, needs, of any concrete group of women. Nevertheless, it was important at the outset of the women's liberation movement in America because the central issue—the deficiencies in socialist theory for dealing with women's liberation: its emphasis on economic determination to the exclusion of other factors —has become a focal point of important debates in our movement since 1968.

The Origins of the American Movement

From the beginning of the women's liberation movement tension has existed between women who advocate a radical feminist movement totally separate from any other political movement and women who are in favor of working within or with mixed or "co-ed" radical organizations. This tension is a result of the way in which the movement began.

By now the incident at the 1968 Students for a Democratic Society (SDS) June convention—where women were hissed and thrown out of the convention for demanding that women's liberation become part of the national platform—is well-known. In 1966 Betty Friedan had founded the National Organization for Women (NOW). However, a more decisive event in the creation of the radical women's movement took place in the summer of 1967 when the black members of the Student Non-violent Coordinating Council (SNCC) asked white men and women to leave the organization. This forced white radicals to create their own political movement instead of continuing to "help" in the Civil Rights Movement. Whites were compelled to work elsewhere and leave the leadership of the black liberation movement to black people. This was an important factor in the emergence of the women's liberation movement. Two more specific events were also instrumental: the Chicago Convention for New Politics in 1967 and the Resolution on Women adopted by the SDS National Council in December 1968.

The 1967 Chicago convention generated women's groups in Chicago and New York, the two cities that were the first centers of new feminism. In Chicago, Marlene Dixon, who was then teaching at the University of Chicago, and Naomi Weisstein (teaching at Loyola) shaped the women's caucus of the New University Conference. Joreen Freeman and Heather Booth began to organize women in Chicago; they were particularly involved with the organization of the Women's Radical Action Project (WRAP), a collective of women who had formerly belonged to SDS. At the 1967 convention Joreen started the first women's liberation newsletter, *Voice of the Women's Liberation Movement,* which announced the political legitimacy of women's struggle. Shulamith Firestone and Pamela Allen met in Chicago and decided to return to New York and help build a movement on the East coast.

Within a year the group known as the New York Radical Women

(NYRW) had come into being:[4] "We ask not if something is 'reformist,' 'radical,' 'revolutionary,' or 'normal.' We ask: is it good for women or bad for women? . . . We are critical of all past ideology, literature and philosophy, products as they are of male supremacist culture . . . We regard our feelings as our most important source of political understanding."[5] Many of the women in this group received national attention when they protested the Miss America pageant in September 1968. In the words of Carol Hanisch, one of the originators of the action, the protest

told the nation that a new feminist movement is afoot in the land . . . Yet one of the biggest mistakes of the whole pageant was our antiwomanism. A spirit of every woman 'do her own thing" began to emerge. Sometimes it was because there was an open conflict about an issue. Other times, women . . . just went ahead and did what they wanted to do, even though it was something the group had definitely decided against. Because of this egotistic individualism, a definite strain of antiwomanism was presented to the public to the detriment of the action.[6]

During the 1968 Thanksgiving holidays, a woman's convention was held in Chicago. During the convention the members of the NYRW who were present arbitrarily divided into three small discussion groups. Surprisingly, after the women returned to New York, the three groups retained their constituencies; one, led by Shulamith Firestone and Ellen Willis, eventually became the Redstockings; another formed WITCH (Woman's International Terrorist Conspiracy from Hell),[7] the third dissolved shortly after returning to New York.

The early groups in Chicago and New York struggled to legitimize the idea of an autonomous woman's movement. In their own practice they sought to abolish traditional bureaucratic structures that dominated the male radical movement and to avoid the development of leaders and spokeswomen that could be singled out from other women, especially "leaders" created by the media. "Consciousness raising" in small groups[8] was the preferred means of working out political positions; it

[4] See pp. 24–32 of Cellestine Ware's *Woman Power* (New York: Tower Books, 1970) for detailed description of the early development of the women's movement in New York, in particular, the discussion of NOW, and its radical splinter group, the Feminists, led by Ti-Grace Atkinson. Robin Morgan's *Sisterhood is Powerful* (New York: Vintage, 1970) reprints documents from the Feminists, pp. 536–537.
[5] From Morgan, *op. cit.*, p. 520; the document from which this quote is taken is mistakenly titled "Principles of NYRW." The NYRW never issued a written statement of principles. The excerpt in the Morgan anthology is from the Redstockings Manifesto, issued in July 1969. However, many of the same women who belonged to the NYRW later joined Redstockings (Shulamith Firestone, Rosalyn Baxandall, Pamela Allen, Carol Hanisch, etc.)
[6] "What Can Be Learned (A Critique of the Miss America Pageant)," in Leslie B. Tanner (ed.), *Voices From Women's Liberation* (New York: Signet 1970), pp. 132–133. For a list of the ten points of protest, see "No More Miss America," Morgan, *op. cit.*, 521–524.
[7] For documents from WITCH, see Morgan, *op. cit.*, 538–553.
[8] For a description of the functioning of a small group, see Pamela Allen, *Free Space: A Perspective on the Small Group in Women's Liberation* (New York: Times Change Press, 1970), p. 63.

also allowed each woman to develop her own potential as much as possible. In November 1968 Kathie Sarachild provided what became the model for "Feminist Consciousness Raising and 'Organizing.'"[9]

In December 1968, the Students for a Democratic Society adopted a position paper on women at a National Council meeting. The "National Resolution on Women" states that

women are not oppressed as a class but they are oppressed as women within each class . . . [and] the fact that male supremacy persists in the movement today, raises the issue that although no people's liberation can happen without a socialist revolution in this country, a socialist revolution could take place which maintains the secondary position of women in society. Therefore the liberation of women must become a conscious part of our struggle for people's liberation.[10]

The resolution gives three main material bases of women's oppression: women form a reserve army of labor to bring down wages; they save the economy enormous costs by performing free services such as housekeeping; and they help obscure the class nature of society.[11] "Women in SDS," the resolution continues, "must battle the belief that struggling for their own liberation is not important . . . [and] SDS must battle the belief that the fight for equality of women is solely the business of women, and that only women have the right and responsibility to oppose male domination." Four pragmatic suggestions are given: Launch a campaign to bring the wages of women employees of the university up to the level of men's; struggle for women's equality in educational institutions where working class women are trained and socialized; relate the struggle for women's rights in the schools to the struggle of women generally (women's detention centers, prisons, family court, welfare); and launch fights around curriculum and organize in classrooms to expose how the schools reinforce the male supremacist definitions of 'women's role.'

The SDS resolution was an important document because it set off a debate in the women's movement about the validity of feminists working in mixed organizations:[12] "Why should the organ for revolution be a

[9] Reproduced in Tanner, *op. cit.,* pp. 154–157. The outline is divided into three parts: I. The "bitch session" cell group; II. Consciousness-raising actions; III. Organizing. Part I has five subtitles: A. On-going consciousness-raising expansion, B. Classic forms of resisting consciousness or: How to avoid facing the awful truth, C. "Starting to Stop" —overcoming repressions and delusions, D. Understanding and developing radical feminist theory, E. Consciousness-raiser (organizer) training (every woman in a cell group herself becomes an "organizer" of other groups).
[10] All the quotes are from the pamphlet "The SDS National Resolution on Women," published by the New England Free Press (Boston), 1968. An earlier version of the *Resolution,* "Women's Manifesto," was published in *New Left Notes,* July 10, 1967.
[11] This is explained as follows: "The nature of women's material conditions places them in a relationship which acts as a lightning rod for men's justified frustration, anger, and shame at their inability to control their natural and social environment. This means, for example, that the potentially revolutionary violence of exploited and oppressed people against the original forces of their exploitation and oppression are transformed and diverted into oppressive violence towards those who have even less power than they do (e.g., women)."
[12] Women's caucuses *within* male-run radical organizations appeared after the woman's movement had begun independently, particularly in New York, Boston, and Chicago.

masculine organ within which women's liberation is a function (caucus)?"[13] "The problem at the present time is simply: should a women's liberation movement be a caucus within SDS, or should it be more than that? The radical women's liberationists say the latter."[14] "The females in SDS (at least those who wrote the Manifesto) essentially reject an identification with their own sex and are using the language of female power in an attempt to advance themselves personally in the male power structure they are presently concerned with. . . . For their own salvation and for the good of the movement, women must form their own group and work primarily for female liberation."[15] The document also threw open the whole question of the role of socialist theory in women's liberation.

In an article widely circulated in 1968 and 1969, Beverly Jones and Judith Brown refuted the SDS women's position and called for an independent female liberation movement.[16] They also discussed the role of women under socialism:

In female liberation literature we hear about three groups of women who allegedly "won their freedom" or are winning equality by picking up guns and fighting for the national liberation of one or another country. Cuba, the most often cited case, did use women as troops, much as they are used in SDS. In the war, women had much the same status as the female in SDS, and now that the Cuban revolution has moved into its cultural phase, we know what Castro want them to do: go home, cook, take care of the kids. It is true that many women are becoming doctors (Russia has more female physicians than male; this is the highest rank in the "caring for" professions). Certainly a few are executives in the nationalized Ford Motors to the South. But the largest female group, the Women's Federation, does not crusade for the emancipation of women. Of course, its main function is to implement government work policies ("Cuban Women," by Mary Nelson, *Voice of the Women's Liberation Movement*, June 1968). Mary Nelson, who has just returned, tells us that nothing basic has changed in patterns of dominance between the sexes.[17]

Roxanne Dunbar's 1969 response to the SDS Resolution represents an early attempt to analyze the nuclear family. Answering the SDS publication, she writes, "Marriage or living arrangements, an overwhelming important and absorbing matter in the day to day, and ultimately the whole, lives of the majority of people, were simply not discussed. . . . Upon what basis do New Left Americans and Europeans

---

[13] Roxanne Dunbar, "Female Liberation as the Basis for Social Revolution," written in January 1969 and published in *No More Fun and Games* (Boston), Issue 2, Spring, 1969. A second version of this article, revised in February 1970, appears under the same title in Morgan, *op. cit.*, pp. 477–492.

[14] Kathy McAfee and Myrna Wood, "Bread and Roses," *Leviathan* (June 1969).

[15] Beverly Jones and Judith Brown, "Toward a Female Liberation Movement," reproduced in Tanner, *op. cit.*, pp. 362–415.

[16] In Part II of the "Toward a Female Liberation Movement," written by Judith Brown, the subtle and not-so-subtle sexism of most radical male activists is discussed. For a more lengthy and excellent analysis of this subject, see Marge Piercy, "The Grand Coolie Dam" originally published in *Leviathan* (May 1970) and reproduced in Morgan, *op. cit.*, pp. 421–438.

[17] Jones and Brown, *op. cit.*, in Tanner, *op. cit.*, pp. 409–410.

analyze (or refuse to analyze) the family? Surely not Marx and Engels."[18] In the second version (January, 1970) of her article, Dunbar develops her theory that all women are oppressed as a caste:

What we find in re-examining history is that women have had a separate historical development from men. Within each society, women experience the particular culture, but on a larger scale of human history, women have developed separately as a caste. The original division of labor in all societies was by sex. The female capacity for reproduction led to this division....

A caste system is a *social system,* which is economically based. It is not a set of attitudes or just some mistaken ideas which must be understood and dispensed with because they are not really in the interest of the higher caste. ...The caste system does not exist just in the mind. Caste is deeply rooted in human history, dates to the division of labor by sex, and is the very basis of the present social system in the United States.[19]

1969–1971: The Movement Comes of Age

In 1969–1971, our movement moved beyond an initial reactive stage and started to consolidate itself into a creative, energetic, and assertive social movement. The New York Redstockings issued a manifesto in July 1969 that rejected the classic Marxist prediction that women will be automatically liberated when capitalism is overthrown. It stated:

Women are an oppressed class. Our oppression is total, affecting every facet of our lives. We are exploited as sex objects, breeders, domestic servants, and cheap labor. We are considered inferior beings, whose only purpose is to enhance men's lives...

Because we have lived so intimately with our oppressors, in isolation from each other, we have been kept from seeing our personal suffering as a political condition....We identify the agents of our oppression as men. Male supremacy is the oldest, most basic form of domination. All other forms of exploitation and oppression (racism, capitalism, imperialism, etc.) are extensions of male supremacy: men dominate women, a few men dominate the rest....Attempts have been made to shift the burden of responsibility from men to institutions or to women themselves. We condemn these arguments as evasions. Institutions alone do not oppress; they are merely tools of the oppressor. To blame institutions implies that men and women are equally victimized, obscures the fact that men benefit from the subordination of women, and gives men the excuse

[18] Dunbar, *op. cit.,* in *No More Fun and Games, op. cit.,* pp. 103–104.
[19] Dunbar, "Female Liberation as the Basis for Social Revolution," in Morgan, *op. cit.,* pp. 479, 486. In "Women: Caste, Class or Oppressed Sex" [first published in *International Socialist Review,* September 1970, and reproduced in *Problems of Women's Liberation* (New York: Pathfinder Press, 1971), Evelyn Reed disagrees with Dunbar (p. 72)]: "I would like clarification from Roxanne Dunbar on the conclusions she draws from her theory. For, if all women belong to an inferior caste, and all men belong to the superior caste, it would consistently follow that the central axis of a struggle for liberation would be a 'caste war' of all women against all men to bring about the liberation of women. This conclusion would seem to be confirmed by her statement that 'we live under an international caste system . . .' If we are to be precise and scientific, women should be defined as an 'oppressed *sex.*' " Reed follows Engels' analysis closely: Male supremacy did not exist in primitive, preclass societies. Women would cease to be oppressed in a modern classless society; thus, women are an oppressed *sex,* not group, class, or caste.

176

hat they are forced to be oppressors. On the contrary, any man is free to enounce his superior position provided that he is willing to be treated like a voman by other men.[20]

Redstockings was important in the development of the women's liberation movement because several of its members developed the language and psychology of sisterhood underlying all of the new feminism—the idea that woman, through knowledge and articulation of her own life experiences, will be led to work for revolutionary changes in her position. It was also an important group in the formation of what is now known as "radical feminism." Redstockings concentrated almost exclusively on consciousness-raising, on ideological and personal self-definition. As a consequence, a new group, New York Radical Feminists (NYRF), devolved, which espoused a more activist approach.

On December 5, 1969, Diane Crowthers, Shulamith Firestone, Ann Koedt,[21] and Cellestine Ware, all of whom had been members of either the Feminists or Redstockings, created the Stanton-Anthony Brigade, the founding unit of the New York Radical Feminists. Their manifesto is similar to Redstockings:

We believe that the purpose of male chauvinism is primarily to obtain psychological ego satisfaction and that only secondarily does this manifest itself in economic relationships ... We do not believe that capitalism, or any other economic system, is the cause of female oppression, nor do we believe that female oppression will disappear as a result of a purely economic revolution. The political oppression of women has its own class dynamic."[22]

However, their organizational structure is more highly evolved than that of Redstockings and action is emphasized:

At that point, it was decided by the original cell to de-centralize the organization into core groups, each of which is to take a six-month formative period in which it will follow the structural procedure set down in the Organizing Principles of the NYRF. Within the formative period, each group can increase its membership up to 15: preferably based on geographical location. There are also to be groups organized around the NYU Law School, the Feminist Repertory Ensemble (a group of actors and actresses staging feminist ideas), and possibly various professions.
NYRF has a three-stage orientation program as the required preliminary before membership as a full Brigade. In Stage I the core group is called a phalanx. . . .
The phalanx is expected to spend its last three months in reading and discussing literature of the current women's movement and feminist history and theory (preferably from direct sources):

(1) to acquaint each person with the broad spectrum of politics already apparent in the Women's Liberation Movement.
(2) to discuss the position of radical feminism within this spectrum and to compare it with other views.

[20] From "The Redstockings Manifesto," in Tanner, op. cit., pp. 109–110.
[21] Authoress of "The Myth of the Vaginal Orgasm," 1969. Printed by the New England Free Press in Tanner, op. cit.
[22] Ware, op. cit., pp. 58–59.

(3) to acquaint each member of the group with her own history and to give her a sense of continuity within the feminist political tradition.

(4) to give the group a good foundation in basic theory on which to build its own later analysis.

(5) to give the group some basis on which to choose its name.

When a phalanx becomes a full Brigade its members must choose their name from the ranks of radical feminists; the Organizing Principles suggest the name of a feminist whose philosophy is in character with the aims of the group. The first group project will be to produce a booklet on the feminist whose name the group is adopting. "The total number of these booklets will form a cheap, easy to distribute, radical feminist library researched by movement women—a first step in erasing the bias and feminine fear of feminism created by the Fifty Year Ridicule."

Upon completion of the six month study period, and when each individual member has signed the NYRF Manifesto, the group is expected to elect their first delegates to the NYRF Coordinating Body. These delegates will be rotated so that each member of the Brigade has served in this office. It is also strongly suggested that the new Brigade "initiate an action from start to finish in which all the other Brigades—and perhaps selected outside groups—will be invited to participate. This includes doing all planning, preparatory work . . . press releases, invitations, etc., required for successful completion of the action."

Afterwards, the Brigade is regarded as an independent unit within NYRF, evolving its own course of winning women's liberation in whatever aspect and by whatever method it shall decide, including effective (as opposed to self-indulgent) action, serious analysis, work with the media, writing and publishing, films, lectures, etc.[23]

On March 21, 1970, San Francisco Redstockings issued a statement, "Our Politics Begin with Our Feelings,"[24] which took a political position similar to the original New York Redstockings Manifesto. To date, however, the most comprehensive analysis of radical feminism is Shulamith Firestone's *The Dialectic of Sex: The Case for Feminist Revolution.*[25] Firestone's book centers upon a revision of orthodox Marxist political anthropology, canonically in Engels' *Origins of the Family, Private Property and the State.* She writes

Throughout history, in all stages and types of culture, women have been oppressed due to their biological functions. . . . The *patriarchal family* was only the most recent in a string of "primary" social organizations, all of which defined woman as a different species due to her unique child-bearing capacity.[26]

This is Firestone's main point. She agrees with the class analysis of history but finds a purely "economist" interpretation limited. For Firestone, "the natural reproductive difference between the sexes led directly to the first division of labor based on sex, which is at the origins of all further division into economic and cultural classes."[27]

[23] *Ibid.*, pp. 61–63.

[24] Reproduced in T. and B. Roszak (eds.), *Masculine/Feminine* (New York: Harper Colophon, 1970).

[25] (New York: William Morrow, 1970). A paperbound edition also exists.

[26] Firestone, *op. cit.*, p. 83.

[27] *Ibid.*, p. 9.

Firestone attempts to develop a view of history based on sexual dialectics:

So that just as to assure elimination of economic classes requires the revolt of the underclass (the proletariat) and, in a temporary dictatorship, their seizure of the means of production, so to assure the elimination of sexual classes requires the revolt of the underclass (women) and the seizure of control of reproduction: the restoration to women of ownership of their own bodies, as well as feminine control of human fertility.[28]

According to Firestone, the psychological, economic, and political oppression generated by the nuclear family invalidates the possibility of love—love being "a situation of total emotional vulnerability" between two equals. She astutely observes that it is a simple phenomenon "unless . . . complicated . . . by an unequal balance of power."[29] Herein lies the catch: the sex class system, which is based on the unequal power distribution within the biological family, prevents equality between men and women. Instead of love, we have an oppressive "culture of romance," fetishized eroticism ("the displacement of other social/affection needs onto sex"[30]) and sexual privatization of women ("the process whereby women are blinded to their generality as a class which renders them invisible as individuals to the male eye"[31]). For example, Firestone attacks the belief, shared by most men, that all women are basically alike—they all like compliments about physical attributes and like to be classified as "blondes, redheads, or brunettes." This sort of regard dupes women into confusing their individuality with their sexuality, and this sexuality, of course, is dependent on men for ultimate realization and evaluation.

In her final chapter Firestone offers four imperatives for feminist revolution:

1. Freeing women from the tyranny of their reproductive biology by every means available (elimination of pregnancy and relegation of reproduction to the test tube), and the diffusion of the child-bearing and child-rearing role to the society as a whole.
2. Full self-determination, including economic independence, of both women and children.
3. Total integration of women and children into all aspects of the larger society.
4. Freedom of all women and children to do whatever they wish sexually.

The feminist revolution would be decisive in establishing "cybernetic socialism," a society that not only distributes wealth equally, but also

[28] *Ibid.*, p. 11.
[29] *Ibid.*, p. 146.
[30] *Ibid.*, p. 166.
[31] *Ibid.*, p. 168.

makes maximum use of technology and industrialization to liberate humanity.

As Anne Sterling has pointed out,

The most striking fact about these four requirements, arrived at by a sex dialectic analysis, is their great similarity with the four structural changes proposed by a socialist feminist, Juliet Mitchell. Mitchell's categories are reproduction, production, socialization and sexuality.

It seems that the major differences between radical feminists and socialist feminists is one of emphasis, the socialists stressing the economic as primary, while the radical feminists tend toward the other three.[32]

Sterling's point about the similarity between the two analyses is correct, but she does not carry her examination far enough. To categorize Mitchell simply as a "socialist feminist" who stresses the "economic as primary" is to obscure the essence of Mitchell's argument, which is that socialist theory, which traditionally classifies economic concerns as primary, is inadequate. Furthermore, as I earlier pointed out, by emphasizing structures that do not arise dialectically from material conditions, Mitchell differs from Marxist analyses (for example, see the following discussion of Margaret Benston).

Firestone and Mitchell both reject aspects of traditional socialist theory and put the fundamental emphasis on sexual oppression: according to Mitchell, the "weakest link in the chain" is marriage and the "dominant sexual ideology"; the first of Firestone's imperatives is the "freeing of women from the tyranny of their reproductive biology." Both women argue that a form of sexual oppression of women maintains itself within the Marxist account of class dynamics and consciousness.

In "The Political Economy of Women's Liberation,"[33] Margaret Benston argues that at the root women's oppression is economically determined, but that women as a group have a special economic relationship to the means of production because of their sex. Women are in charge of household labor, including child care. Although this work is socially necessary,

in a society based on commodity production, it is not usually considered "real work" since it is outside of the trade and market place . . . in a society in which money determines value, women are a group who work outside the money economy. Their work is not worth money, is therefore valueless, is therefore not even real work. And women themselves, who do this valueless work, can hardly be expected to be worth as much as men, who work for money.[34]

A particular type of "work" is thus common to all women (those who earn money outside the home still must find a solution to reproductive and other domestic issues) and is the fundamental source of oppres-

[32] *Women's Caucus Newsletter* of the New University Conference (April 1, 1971), pp. 13–14. Published in Chicago.

[33] This article appeared in *Monthly Review*, vol. 21, no. 4 (September 1969). Margaret Benston teaches chemistry at Simon Fraser University in Canada and is an active member of the Vancouver women's liberation movement.

[34] "The Political Economy of Women's Liberation," in Tanner, *op. cit.*, pp. 281–282.

ion. Benston advocates socialization and industrialization of household work and abolition of the nuclear family:

With socialized production and the removal of the profit motive and its attendant alienated labor, there is no reason why, *in an industrialized society*, industrialization of housework should not result in better production, i.e., better food, more comfortable surroundings, more intelligent and loving child care, etc. than in the present nuclear family . . . [which] is a valuable stabilizing force in capitalist society. Since the production which is done in the home is paid for by the husband-father's earnings, his ability to withhold his labor from the market is much reduced. . . . The woman, denied an active place in the market, has little control over the conditions that govern her life. Her economic dependence is reflected in emotional dependence, passivity, and other "typical" female personality traits.[35]

An aspect of the women's liberation movement which became important in 1970 was the emergence of the radical lesbians. Rita Mae Brown states that, before the development of the women's liberation movement, lesbians frequently joined the Daughters of Bilitis, a national organization that attempts to promote understanding of lesbianism but one that does not have radical politics.[36] In the first years of the movement gay women were discriminated against, and in some cases forced out of the movement. Those who remained were dissatisfied at their treatment by the movement's heterosexual women. In addition, lesbians who had helped found the gay liberation movement were dissatisfied at their treatment by homosexual men. These women came together and tried to define their past lives and to establish what their lives were now becoming through their growth of consciousness. The result of their effort was the paper "The Woman-Identified Woman," which first appeared in *The Ladder*, published in Reno, Nevada. It is one of the most cogent statements on lesbianism to date:

It should first be understood that lesbianism, like male homosexuality, is a category of behavior possible only in a sexist society characterized by rigid sex roles and dominated by male supremacy. These roles dehumanize women by defining us as a supportive/serving caste in relation to the master caste of men, and emotionally cripple men by demanding that they be alienated from their own bodies and emotions in order to perform their economic/political/ military functions effectively. Homosexuality is a by-product of a particular way of setting up roles (or approved patterns of behavior) on the basis of sex; as such, it is an inauthentic category. In a society in which men do not oppress women, sexual expression is allowed to follow feelings, the categories of homosexuality and heterosexuality would disappear.

But lesbianism is also different from male homosexuality and serves a different function in the society. "Dyke" is a different kind of put-down from "faggot," although both imply you are not playing your socially assigned sex role and are not therefore a "real woman" or a "real man." The grudging admiration felt for the tomboy, and the queasiness felt around a sissy boy point to the same thing: the contempt in which women—or those who play a female role—are held. And the investment in keeping in that contemptuous

[35] *Ibid.*, pp. 284–285.
[36] "Living With Other Women," *Women: A Journal of Liberation* (Winter 1971), p. 33.

role is very great. Lesbian is the word, the label, the condition that holds women in line. When a woman hears this word tossed her way, she knows she is stepping out of line. She knows that she has crossed the terrible boundary of sex role. She recoils, she protests, she reshapes her actions to gain approval. Lesbian is a label invented by the Man to throw at any woman who dares to be his equal, who dares to challenge his prerogatives (including that of all women as part of the exchange medium among men), who dares to assert the primacy of her own needs. To have the label applied to people active in women's liberation is just the most recent instance of a long history; older women will recall that not so long ago, any woman who was successful, independent, not orienting her whole life about a man would hear this word. For in this sexist society, for a woman to be independent means she can't be a woman—she must be a dyke. That in itself should tell us where women are at. It says clearly: woman and person are contradictory terms. For a Lesbian is not considered a "real woman." And yet, in popular thinking, there is only one essential difference between a Lesbian and other women: that of sexual orientation, which is to say, when you strip off all the packaging, you must finally realize that the essence of being a "woman" is to get laid by men.

Lesbianism is the negation of the concrete ideology of womanhood. Traditionally, gay women have been considered deviants from the social norm. Because radical lesbians consider the social norm deviant, they transform the personal struggle into a larger social arena. Radical lesbianism challenges the society's accepted value system for females, the whole body of legal, economic, and social duties of women in America (lesbians cannot get married, divorced, claim each other as dependents, etc.). The revolutionary component of radical lesbian thinking is the questioning of the total institutional definition of women. In the sense that they do not articulate lesbianism as the *one* necessary form of woman's consciousness, but as one part of the larger whole, their struggle is parallel to other aspects of the struggle, and a necessary part of it.[37]

In the winter and spring of 1971 the planning and execution of the Canadian Conferences between Indochinese and North American women[38] sharpened the debates about sexism versus capitalism as the primary pragmatic target, and about whether to work in an all-female or mixed organization. Two positions seemed to emerge. The first, that of the "anti-imperialist women," emphasizes that it is urgent for radical women to participate in class and race struggles and in the fight to end the war. The first pages of Marlene Dixon's article (reprinted in Part 2 of this book) contain one articulation of this position.

The Fourth World Manifesto (also reprinted in Part 2 of this book), explains the view of those women who believe that the primary struggle should be against sexism:

[37] In *The Sexual Revolution*, Wilhelm Reich makes the point that Stalin's legislation against homosexuality, even though under "socialist" auspices, inevitably led to a reconstitution of the nuclear family and hence, in general, once again relegated women to an inferior status in society.

[38] In April 1971 women from Vietnam, Laos, and Cambodia met in Toronto and Vancouver with hundreds of women from the United States and Canada, representing, in the main, women's liberation and Women's Strike for Peace. The conferences were requested by the Indochinese women to discuss with American women how to end the war.

We identify with all women of all races, classes and countries all over the world. The female culture is the Fourth World . . . Because the male culture is dominant and in control in every nation the "national" culture becomes synonymous with, and in fact is, the male culture. The female culture exists "invisibly" in subjection to the male defined "national" culture.

Conclusion

It seems apparent that as women we are oppressed *both* economically and biologically. Within the general contours of Marxist analysis, specific attention must be given to woman's role in reproduction. Clearly one is defined by the work one does, and in our economy, the "best" work is reserved for males and the "worst"—that is, the labor that receives no wages—is for women. Under the aegis of the nuclear family, a woman performs domestic labor for one man, and bears and rears his children. And her biological constitution has served to "naturally" reinforce this role.

Although I am sure every woman, regardless of race or class, has been stifled and repressed by some man in her life, economic differences separate women, and white women have a "racial edge" on third world women, and as a consequence, generally an economic one too. Females, then, are an oppressed sex within each of the larger class and race divisions. This does not mean that because we may have been born into white middle class conditions we are irreversibly locked into them and thus somehow "inherently" less revolutionary than poor white or third world women. It does mean, however, that the majority of us who are white and middle class must make it explicit by our actions and programs that women's liberation is serious about fighting racism and capitalism and is not just concerned with "liberating" white middle-class women. That task is yet to be done.

The frequently expressed statement that a small circle of white males oppresses the rest of us in this country is true. However, it is possible to be oppressed and to be an oppressor too—for example, almost every man, third world as well as white, oppresses a woman in his daily life, no matter what his politics are. That happens because he is concerned with "larger and more important things" than the implementation of the eradication of sexism, even if his *theory* is "correct" on the subject. In order not to be an oppressor, the average man must deal with the day-to-day practical ramifications of abolishing sexism on many levels and in all classes of society.

In the process of struggling for a more just distribution of wealth for everyone, many of us (and by "us" I mean white women with a certain degree of economic security) have the means and technology to urge the abolition of marriage and pregnancy. As women committed to creating a socialist America (and to uniting with some men, under certain conditions, in that struggle) we can negate the nuclear family, the institution that ultimately oppresses all women. In an effort to do away with a distorted obsession with the sexual side of life, part and parcel of capitalism's commodity fetishism, we can insist on "non-institutionalized" monogamy: reciprocal fidelity without "legal" ties that can be humiliating. We can also demand not only the right to abortion but the right to artificial reproduction, which is the key to real control of our own bodies and autonomy to determine our own lives.

White radical women can become the link to "Third Worlders" interested in radical change—a link that the white male left has been unable to create—by seeking to understand the position of black, Asian and Latin women and to then work with them. Due to the consequences of living in and being products of a racist society white women who are seriously concerned with black women, for example, cannot sleep with black men and expect to be trusted by the women.

A theory and practice that involves a long-term rejection of men as a class is unworkable because men comprise nearly 50 percent of the population. If we are ever to redistribute the power in this country, we cannot ignore one-half of the population. We need a class analysis that is bisexual, not unisexual.

It is our task to be aware of the subtle manifestations of sexism on all levels of society—those that speak to us and those that speak to many other women. We should not tolerate their existence in any person we consider a comrade or friend; that is the beginning of the fight against institutional oppression. If we want a society where there is no ruling class and no ruling sex, we must struggle for both goals simultaneously, with equal priority and energy assigned to each.

WHY WOMEN'S LIBERATION—2?

Marlene Dixon

Marlene Dixon was one of the leaders in the early days of the women's movement in Chicago. She taught sociology at the University of Chicago until she was dismissed for radical and for feminist activities in 1968. Currently she teaches at McGill University in Canada and continues working in the women's liberation movement there.

The following article is a sequel to the widely circulated "Why Women's Liberation?" which appeared in *Ramparts* magazine in December 1969. It is a comprehensive overview of the issues and forces that are the key to the women's movement in 1968–69. The revisions, written in April 1971, and evident particularly in the conclusion and epilogue, are a strong and lucid criticism of what Dixon sees as the shortcomings in the development of the women's liberation movement since 1969. She attacks "the mysticism of sisterhood": the overly easy analysis that emphasizes a commonality in all women's psychological oppression and considers economic and racial differences secondary to the oppression that all women share as a sex. Dixon makes an eloquent plea to transform a "self-serving middle class ideology" into a perspective not based on "female chauvinism," "racism" and "liberal guilt."

Rise of Women's Liberation

The old women's movement burned itself out in the frantic decade of the 1920s. After a hundred years of struggle, women won a battle, only to lose the campaign: the vote was obtained, but the new millennium did not arrive. Women got the vote and achieved a measure of legal emancipation, but the real social and cultural barriers to full equality for women remained untouched.

For over thirty years the movement remained buried in its own ashes. Women were born and grew to maturity virtually ignorant of their own history of rebellion, aware only of a caricature of blue stockings and suffragettes. Even as increasing numbers of women were being driven into the labor force by the brutal conditions of the 1930s and by the massive drain of men into the military in the 1940s, the old ideal remained: a woman's place was in the home and behind her man. As the war ended and men returned to resume their jobs in factories and offices, women were forced back to the kitchen and nursery with a vengeance. This story has been repeated after each war and the reason is clear: women form a flexible, cheap labor pool that is essential to a capitalist system. When labor is scarce, they are forced onto the labor market. When labor is plentiful, they are forced out. Women and blacks have provided a reserve army of unemployed workers, benefiting capitalists and the stable male white working class alike. Yet the system imposes untold suffering on the victims—blacks and women—through low wages and chronic unemployment.

With the end of the war, the average age at marriage declined; the average size of families went up; and the suburban migration began in earnest. The political conservatism of the fifties was echoed in a social conservatism that stressed a Victorian ideal of the woman's life: a full womb and selfless devotion to husband and children.

As the bleak decade played itself out, however, three important social developments emerged that were to make a rebirth of the women's struggle inevitable. First, women came to make up more than a third of the labor force, the number of working women being twice the prewar figure. Yet the marked increase in female employment did nothing to better the position of women, who were more occupationally disadvantaged in the 1960s than they had been twenty-five years earlier. Rather than moving equally into all sectors of the occupational structure, they were being forced into the low-paying service, clerical and semiskilled categories. In 1940, women had held 45 percent of all professional and technical positions; in 1967, they held only 37 percent. The proportion of women in service jobs meanwhile rose from 50 to 55 percent.

Second, the intoxicating wine of marriage and suburban life was turning sour; a generation of women woke up to find their children grown and a life (roughly thirty more productive years) of housework and bridge parties stretching out before them like a wasteland. For many younger women, the empty drudgery they saw in the suburban life was a sobering contradiction to adolescent dreams of romantic love and the fulfilling role of woman as wife and mother.

Third, a growing civil rights movement was sweeping thousands of young men and women into a moral crusade—a crusade that harsh political experience was to transmute into the New Left. The American Dream was riven and tattered in Mississippi and finally napalmed in Vietnam. Young Americans were drawn not to Levittown, but to Berkeley, Haight-Ashbury, and the East Village. Traditional political ideologies and cultural myths, sexual mores and sex roles with them, began to disintegrate in an explosion of rebellion and protest.

The three major groups that make up the new women's movement—working women, middle-class married women, and students—bring very different kinds of interests and objectives to women's liberation. Working women are most concerned with the economic issues of guaranteed employment, fair wages, job discrimination, and child care. Their most immediate oppression is rooted in industrial capitalism and felt directly through the vicissitudes of an exploitative labor market.

Middle-class women, oppressed by the psychological mutilation and injustice of institutionalized segregation, discrimination, and imposed inferiority, are most sensitive to the dehumanizing consequences of severely limited lives. Usually well educated and capable, these women are rebelling against being forced to trivialize their lives, to live vicariously through husbands and children.

Students, as unmarried, middle-class girls, have been most sensitized to the sexual exploitation of women. They have experienced the frustration of one-way relationships in which the girl is forced into a "wife" and companion role with none of the supposed benefits of marriage. Young women have increasingly rebelled not only against passivity and dependency in their relationships, but also against the notion that they must function as sexual objects, being defined in purely sexual rather than human terms, and being forced to package and sell themselves as commodities on the sex market.

Each group represents an independent aspect of the total institutionalized oppression of women. Yet, in varying degrees all women suffer from economic exploitation, from psychological deprivation, and from exploitive sexuality. Within women's liberation there is a growing understanding that the common oppression of women provides the basis for uniting to form a powerful and radical movement.

Racism and Male Supremacy

Clearly, for the liberation of women to become a reality, it is necessary to destroy the ideology of male supremacy that asserts the biological and social inferiority of women in order to justify massive institutionalized oppression.

The ideology of male chauvinism can only be understood when it is perceived as a form of racism, based on stereotypes drawn from a deep belief in the biological inferiority of women. The very stereotypes that express the society's belief in the biological inferiority of women are images used to justify oppression. The nature of women is depicted as dependent, incapable of reasoned thought, childlike in its simplicity and warmth, martyred in the role of mother, and mystical in the role of sexual partner.

It has taken over fifty years to discredit the scientific and social "proof" that once gave legitimacy to the myths of black racial inferiority. Today most people can see that the theory of the genetic inferiority of blacks is absurd. Yet few are shocked by the fact that scientists are still busy "proving" the biological inferiority of women.

Yet one of the obstacles to organizing women remains women's belief in their own inferiority. This dilemma is not a fortuitous one, for the entire society is geared to socialize women to believe in and adopt as immutable necessity their traditional and inferior role. From earliest training to the grave, women are constrained and propagandized. Spend an evening at the movies or watching television and you will see a grotesque figure called woman presented in a hundred variations upon the themes of "children, church, kitchen" or "the chick sex-pot." Such contradictions as these show how pervasive and deep-rooted is the cultural contempt for women, how difficult it is to imagine a woman as a serious human being, or conversely, how empty and degrading is the image of woman that floods the culture.

Countless studies have shown that black acceptance of white stereotypes leads to mutilated identity, to alienation, to rage and self-hatred. Human beings cannot bear in their own hearts the contradictions of those who hold them in contempt. The ideology of male supremacy creates self-contempt and psychic mutilation in women; it creates trained incapacities that put women at a disadvantage in all social relationships.

It is customary to shame those who would draw the parallel between women and blacks by a great show of concern over the suffering of black people. Yet this response itself reveals a refined combination of white middle-class guilt and male chauvinism, for it overlooks several essential facts. For example, the most oppressed group within the feminine population is made up of black women, many of whom take a dim view of the black male intellectual's adoption of white male attitudes of sexual superiority. Neither are those who make this pious objection to the racial parallel addressing themselves very adequately to the millions of white working-class women living at the poverty level, who are not likely to be moved by this middle-class, guilt-ridden one-upmanship while having to deal with the boss, the factory, or the welfare worker day after day. They are already dangerously resentful of the gains made by blacks, and much of their "racist blacklash" stems from the fact that they have been forgotten in the push for social change. Emphasis on the real mechanisms of oppression—on the commonality of the process—is essential lest groups such as these, which should work in alliance, become divided against one another.

White middle-class males already struggling with the acknowledgment of their own racism do not relish an added burden of recognition: that to white guilt must soon be added "male." It is therefore understandable that they should refuse to see the harshness of the lives of most women —to face honestly the facts of massive institutionalized discrimination against women.

We must never forget that the root of the ideology of male superiority, female inferiority, and white racism is a system of white male supremacy. White male supremacy is part of the ideology of imperialism, first European, then American. The European powers stripped India, China, Africa, and the New World of their wealth in raw materials— in gold, slaves, in cheap labor. Such brutal forms of exploitation required justification, and that justification was found in the doctrines of white racial superiority and the supremacy of European and American "civilization" over the "heathen" civilizations of Africa, Asia, and Latin America. Even more, we must never forget that the doctrine of white supremacy included the *supremacy of white women* as well as of white men.

The rise of capitalism in the West was based upon the wealth looted from other civilizations at the point of a gun: imperialism was the root and branch of racism and genocide then as it is now. It is at the root of mass prostitution in Saigon, of the torture and murder of innocent Vietnamese and Indochinese women and children, of all the sufferings of war inflicted upon the innocent at home and in Indochina. White American women must understand their oppression in its true context, and that context *is* a brutal, antihuman system of total exploitation having its corporate headquarters in New York and its political headquarters in Washington, D.C. And white women must understand that they are part of the system, benefiting from the loot secured through genocide.

This is why we must clearly understand that male chauvinism and racism *are not the same thing*. They are alike in that they oppress people and justify systems of exploitation, but in no way does a white woman suffer the exploitation and brutalization of women who are marked by both stigmata: being female *and* nonwhite. It is only the racism of privileged white women, self-serving in their petty, personal interests, who can claim that they must serve their own interests first, that they suffer *as much* as black women or Indochinese women or any women who experience the cruelty of white racism or the ruthless genocide of American militarism.

188

The contradiction of racism distorts and contaminates every sector of American life, creeps into every white insurgent movement. Understanding their own oppression can and must help white women to confront and to repudiate their own racism, for otherwise there will be no freedom, there will be no liberation.

Marriage: Genesis of Women's Rebellion

The institution of marriage is the chief vehicle for the perpetuation of the oppression of women; it is through the role of wife that the subjugation of women is maintained. In a very real way the role of wife has been the genesis of women's rebellion throughout history.

Looking at marriage from a detached point of view, one may well ask why anyone gets married, much less women. One answer lies in the economics of women's position, for women are so occupationally limited that drudgery in the home is considered to be infinitely superior to drudgery in the factory. Secondly, women themselves have no independent social status. Indeed, there is no clearer index of the social worth of a woman in this society than the fact that she has none in her own right. A woman is first defined by the man to whom she is attached, but more particularly by the man she marries, and secondly by the children she bears and rears—hence the anxiety over sexual attractiveness, the frantic scramble for boyfriends and husbands. Having obtained and married a man, the race is then on to have children, in order that their attractiveness and accomplishments may add more social worth. In a woman, not having children is seen as an incapacity somewhat akin to impotence in a man.

Beneath all of the pressures of the sexual marketplace and the marital status game, however, there is a far more sinister organization of economic exploitation and psychological mutilation. The housewife role, usually defined in terms of the biological duty of a woman to reproduce and her "innate" suitability for a nurturant and companionship role, is actually crucial to industrial capitalism in an advanced state of technological development. In fact, the housewife (some 44 million women of all classes, ethnic groups, and races) provides, unpaid, absolutely essential services and labor. In turn, her assumption of all household duties makes it possible for the man to spend the majority of his time at his work place.

It is important to understand the social and economic exploitation of the married woman, since the real productivity of her labor is denied by the commonly held assumption that she is dependent on her husband, exchanging her keep for emotional and nurturant services. Household labor, including child care, constitutes a huge amount of socially necessary labor. Nevertheless, in a society based on commodity production, it is not usually considered even as 'real work' since it is outside of trade and the marketplace. In a society in which money determines value, women are a group who work outside the money economy. Their work is not worth money, is therefore valueless, is therefore not even real work. And women themselves, who do this valueless work, can hardly be expected to be worth as much as men, who work for money.

Women are essential to the economy not only as free labor, but also as consumers. The American system of capitalism depends for its survival on the consumption of vast amounts of socially wasteful goods, and a prime target for the unloading of this waste is the housewife. She is the purchasing agent for the family, but beyond that she is eager to buy because her own identity depends on her accomplishments as a consumer and her ability to satisfy the wants of her husband and children. This is not, of course, to say that she has any power in the economy. Although she spends the wealth, she does not own or control it—it simply passes through her hands.

In addition to their role as housewives and consumers, increasing numbers of women are taking outside employment. These women leave the home to join an exploited labor force, only to return at night to assume the double burden of housework on top of wage work—that is, they are forced to work at two full-time jobs. No man is required or expected to take on such a burden. The result: two workers from one household in the labor force with no cutback in essential female functions—three for the price of two, quite a bargain. Regardless of her status in the larger society, within the context of the family, the woman's relationship to the man is one of proletariat to bourgeoisie. One consequence of this class division in the family is to weaken the capacity of oppressed men and women to struggle together against it.

For third-world people within the United States, the oppressive nature of marriage is reflected negatively—for example, motherhood out of wedlock is punished, either through discriminatory welfare legislation or through thinly disguised and genocidal programs of enforced sterilization. This society punishes unmarried women even more than it punishes married women. As a result, many third-world and poor white women want help with their families and need a husband in the home. The destruction of families among poor people, as a result of economic exploitation and social oppression, results in the deprivation of every facet of life for poor women and children. White middle-class women, bound up with the psychological oppression of marriage, have often been blind to the extent of suffering—and the extent of the needs—that the deliberate destruction of the families of the poor has created. Unemployment and pauperization through welfare programs creates very different problems than does the experience of boredom in the suburbs.

In all classes and groups, the institution of marriage nonetheless functions to a greater or lesser degree to oppress women; the unity of women of different classes hinges upon our understanding of that common oppression. The nineteenth-century women's movement refused to deal with marriage and sexuality and chose instead to fight for the vote and to elevate the feminine mystique to a political ideology. That decision retarded the movement for decades. But 1969 is not 1889. For one thing, there now exist alternatives to marriage. The cultural revolu-

tion—experimentation with life-styles, communal living, collective child rearing—have all come from the rebellion against dehumanized sexual relationships, against the notion of women as sexual commodities, against the hardship, alienation, and loneliness of American life.

Lessons must be learned from the failures of the earlier movement. The feminine mystique must not be mistaken for politics or legislative reform for winning human rights. Women are now at the bottom of their respective worlds and the basis exists for a common focus of struggle for women in American society. It remains for the movement to understand this, to avoid the mistakes of the past, to respond creatively to the possibilities of the present.

Economic Exploitation

Women's oppression, although rooted in the institution of marriage, does not stop at the kitchen or the bedroom door. Indeed, the economic exploitation of women in the work place is the most commonly recognized aspect of the oppression of women.

The rise of new agitation for the occupational equality of women also coincided with the reentry of the "lost generation"—the housewives of the 1950s—into the job market. Women from middle-class backgrounds, faced with an "empty nest" (children grown or in school) and a widowed or divorced rate of one-fourth to one-third of all marriages, returned to the work place in large numbers. But once there, they discovered that women, middle class or otherwise, are the last hired, the lowest paid, the least often promoted, and the first fired. Furthermore, women are more likely to suffer job discrimination on the basis of age, so the widowed and divorced suffer particularly, even though their economic need to work is often urgent. Age discrimination also means that the option of work after child rearing is limited. Even highly qualified older women find themselves forced into low-paid, unskilled, or semiskilled work—if they are lucky enough to find a job in the first place.

Most women who enter the labor force do not work for "pin money" or "self-fulfillment." Sixty-two percent of all women working in 1967 were doing so out of economic need (that is, were either alone or with

191

husbands earning less than $5,000 a year). In 1963, 36 percent of American families had an income of less than $5,000 a year. Women from these families work because they must; they contribute 35 to 40 percent of the family's total income when working full time and 15 to 20 percent when working part time.

Despite their need, however, women have always represented the most exploited sector of the industrial labor force. Child and female labor were introduced during the early stages of industrial capitalism, at a time when most men were gainfully employed in crafts. As industrialization developed and craft jobs were eliminated, men entered the industrial labor force, driving women and children into the lowest categories of work and pay. Indeed, the position of women and children industrial workers was so pitiful and their wages were so small that the craft unions refused to organize them. Even when women organized themselves and engaged in militant strikes and labor agitation—from the shoemakers of Lynn, Massachusetts, to the International Ladies' Garment Workers and their great strike of 1909—male unionists continued to ignore their needs. As a result of this male supremacy in the unions, women remain essentially unorganized, despite the fact that they are becoming an ever larger part of the labor force.

The trend is clearly toward increasing numbers of women entering the work force: women represented 55 percent of the growth of the total labor force in 1962, and the number of working women rose from 16.9 million in 1957 to 24 million in 1962. There is every indication that the number of women in the labor force will continue to grow as rapidly in the future.

Job discrimination against women exists in all sectors of work, even in occupations that are predominantly made up of women. This discrimination is reinforced in the field of education, where women are being short-changed at a time when the job market demands higher educational levels. In 1962, for example, while women constituted 53 percent of the graduating high school class, only 42 percent of the entering college class were women. Only one in three people who received a B.A. or M.A. in that year was a woman, and only one in ten who received a Ph.D. was a woman. These figures represent a decline in educational achievement for women since the 1930s, when women received two out of five of the B.A. and M.A. degrees given, and one out of seven of the Ph.Ds. While there has been a dramatic increase in the number of people, including women, who go to college, women have not kept pace with men in terms of educational achievement. Furthermore, women have lost ground in professional employment. In 1960 only 22 percent of the faculty and other professional staff at colleges and universities were women—down from 28 percent in 1949, 27 percent in 1930, 26 percent in 1920. 1960 does beat the 20 percent of 1919: "you've come a long way, baby"—right back to where you started! In other professional categories, 10 percent of all scientists are women, 7 percent of all physicians, 3 percent of all lawyers, and 1 percent of all engineers.

Even when women do obtain an education, in many cases it does them little good. Women, whatever their educational levels, are concentrated in the lower-paying occupations. The figures tell a story that most women know and few men will admit: most women are forced to work at clerical jobs, for which they are paid, on the average, $1,600 less per year than men doing the same work. Working-class women in the service and operative (semiskilled) categories, making up 30 percent of working women, are paid $1,900 less per year on the average than are men. Of all working women, only 13 percent are professionals (including low-pay and low-status work such as teaching, nursing, and social work), and they earn $2,600 less per year than do professional men. Household workers, the lowest category of all, are predominantly women (over 2 million) and predominantly black and third world, earning for their labor barely over $1,000 per year.

Not only are women forced onto the lowest rungs of the occupational ladder, they are in the lowest income levels as well. The most constant and bitter injustice experienced by all women is the income differential. While women might passively accept low-status jobs, limited opportunities for advancement, and discrimination in the factory, office, and university, they choke finally on the daily fact that the male worker next to them earns more and usually does less. In 1965, the median wage or salary income of year-round, full-time women workers was only 60 percent that of men, a 4 percent loss since 1955. Twenty-nine percent of working women earned less than $3,000 a year as compared with 11 percent of the men; 43 percent of the women earned from $3,000 to $5,000 a year as compared with 19 percent of the men; and 9 percent of the women earned $7,000 or more as compared with 43 percent of the men.

What most people do not know is that in certain respects all women suffer more than do nonwhite men and that black and third-world women suffer most of all.

Women, regardless of race, are more disadvantaged than are men, including nonwhite men. White women earn $2,600 less than white men and $1,500 less than nonwhite men. The brunt of the inequality is carried by 2.5 million nonwhite women, 94 percent of whom are black. They earn $3,800 less than white men, $1,900 less than nonwhite men, and $1,200 less than white women.

There is no more bitter paradox in the racism of this country than that the white man, articulating the male supremacy of the white male middle class, should provide the rationale for the oppression of black women by black men. Black women constitute the largest minority in the United States, and they are the most disadvantaged group in the labor force. The further oppression of black women will not liberate black men, for black women were never the oppressors of their men—that is a myth of the liberal white man. The oppression of black men comes from institutionalized racism and economic exploitation, from the world of the white man.

Consider the following facts and figures. The percentage of black working women has always been proportionately greater than that of white women. In 1900, 41 percent of black women were employed, as compared to 17 percent for white women. In 1963, the proportion of black women employed was still a fourth greater than that of whites. In 1960, 44 percent of black married women with children under six years were in the labor force, in contrast to 29 percent for white women. While job competition requires ever higher levels of education, the bulk of illiterate women are black. On the whole, black women—who often have the greatest need for employment—are the most discriminated against in terms of opportunity. Forced by an oppressive and racist society to carry unbelievably heavy economic and social burdens, black women stand at the bottom of that society, doubly marked by the caste signs of color and sex.

Faced with discrimination on the job—after being forced into the lower levels of the occupational structure—millions of women are inescapably presented with the fundamental contradictions in their unequal treatment and their massive exploitation. The rapid growth of women's liberation as a movement is related in part to the exploitation of working women in all occupational categories.

Conclusion

Male supremacy, marriage, and the structure of wage labor—each of these aspects of women's oppression and exploitation has been crucial to the resurgence of the women's struggle. It must be abundantly clear that revolutionary social change must occur before there can be significant improvement in the social position of *all* women.

The heart of the movement, as in all freedom movements, rests in women's knowledge, whether articulated or still only an illness without a name, that they are not inferior—not chicks or bunnies or quail or cows or bitches or ass or meat. Women hear the litany of their own dehumanization each day. Yet all the same, women know that they are not animals or sexual objects or commodities. They know their lives are mutilated, because they see within themselves a promise of creativity and personal integration. Feeling the contradiction between the essentially creative and self-actualizing human being within her and the cruel and degrading less-than-human role she is compelled to play, a woman begins to experience the internal violence that liberates the human spirit, to experience the justice of her own rebellion. This is the rage that impels women into a total commitment to women's liberation, a ferocity that stems from a denial of mutilation. It is a cry for life, a cry for the liberation of the spirit.

Yet, we must never forget that we women are not unique in our oppression, in our exploitation. Understanding ourselves should help us understand all others like us and not divide us from them. We must also remember that in one way white American women are unique, for they suffer least of all: their experience cannot approach the abysmal suffering of the third-world women or of third-world men, subject to

American racism and imperialism. How does one understand rape; forced prostitution; torture; and mutilation; twisted, crippled children; deformed babies; a homeland laid waste; memories of perpetual war; perpetual oppression? It is not a question of guilt; it is a question of revolutionary struggle.

Epilogue
1969–1971

1969 was a year of explosive growth and measureless optimism for women's liberation. It was the year of sisterhood: "sisterhood is powerful!" "sisterhood is beautiful!" "sisterhood is unity!" The turning point for the women's struggle was 1969, the year in which the movement came up from underground by gaining recognition and legitimacy—recognition from the male-dominated white left and legitimacy as a protest "issue" in the larger society. The slogans of sisterhood reflected a joyful optimism, an overwhelming intuitive belief that *all* women could identify with each other, all women could struggle together—even lead—a vast movement or social transformation.

By 1971, the joyful optimism was increasingly being replaced by a sense of dismay and conflict in many women: "women's liberation is a nonstruggle movement"; "women's liberation is a racist movement"; "women's liberation is an apolitical movement"; "women's liberation is a class chauvinist movement"; "women's liberation is a liberal, middle-class movement." What did all of this mean? What had happened to the women's movement?

The United States of America had "happened" to women's liberation: all of the contradictions of a society torn by class and racial conflict, all of the contradictions of a society that is in fact based upon militarized state capitalism and institutionalized racism and class exploitation began to tear the women's movement apart. The apolitical simplicity of "sisterhood is unity" and "understand your own psychological oppression" was powerless to contend with or understand the internal, disruptive forces of the most exploitative, brutal, and complex oppressor nation in the history of Western imperialism—the United States of America.

The women's movement is no longer a struggling, tender shoot; it has become a mass movement; and women remain, often despite the movement, potentially a powerful, radical force. In the beginning, women were attacked from every quarter, most destructively from the left, for left politics became identified with male chauvinism. Originally, the attack from the left was corrupt, a ploy by radical men to keep women down. Now, however, the criticism does not come from the men, but from women within women's liberation. A movement that cannot learn from its past, that is too insecure and fearful to engage in self-criticism, that is too self-interested to be able to change its direction, too blind to see that all women are *not* sisters—that class exploitation and racism are fundamental to American society and exist *within* the

women's movement—becomes a trap, not a means to liberation. In the brief critique that follows, I am correcting some of my own mistakes, for I too believed in sisterhood, I too believed that "common oppression provides the basis for uniting across class and race lines." In that belief I was wrong; this is what I have learned from the past year of the movement. There are many women and many groups within the women's struggle to which the following criticism does not apply, but there are still more who were, and still are, wrong.

Class Conflict

The mysticism of *sisterhood* disguised the reality that most women in women's liberation were white, young, and middle class, so that under all the radical rhetoric the movement's goals were reformist and its ideology was almost exclusively of middle-class female psychological oppression. The women's movement did not talk about *exploitation*, but about *oppression*—always in subjective terms. The women's movement did not talk about class struggle, nationalization of medicine, abolition of welfare, or the ultimate destruction of American imperialism. The needs of poor women, of working women, of black women were nowhere central to the demands or the rhetoric of women's liberation. The middle-class, reformist nature of the movement was not clearly and objectively revealed until the struggle over the equal rights amendment —an amendment that would have made *discrimination* unconstitutional but would not have included a single reference to exploitation, an amendment that would have benefited professional women at the expense of working-class women.

Fighting against *discrimination* is a middle-class, reformist goal—it says: let us *in* so that the privileges of our middle-class men can be extended to us middle-class women. Fighting against *exploitation* is revolutionary. To end exploitation, it is necessary to end "militarized state capitalism." To end class exploitation, it is necessary to abolish classes. To end racism, it is necessary to abolish white male supremacy, to abolish imperialism. White middle-class America, male and female, enjoys an affluence that is looted from half the world, that is stolen by means of poor white and black soldiers, that is turned into new cars and washing machines by workers, black and white, male and female. White middle-class America, *male and female,* enjoys incomes protected from inflation by means of the deliberate unemployment of workers, black and white, male and female, who suffer enforced pauperization so that the young girls of the middle class can go to the university and struggle for a women's center to give them a better education, the better to enjoy their class privileges, the better to explore the meaning of life and the adventures of a new, untrammeled sexuality. Genocide is committed against the people of Vietnam; war spreads to all the peoples of Indochina. So who cares? It's only a "penis war." It is of no concern to the young women of the middle class, who will never be soldiers, never be workers, never be on welfare, never suffer racism. The problem is *discrimination.* Women can only earn $10,000 a year teaching college while men earn $15,000 a year—that is the problem! "Sisterhood is unity! Don't criticize the movement! Don't make us feel guilty! Don't show us the blood on *our* hands—after all, we are oppressed too!"

Racism

The "black analogy" was originally used in women's liberation to help women through their understanding of their own oppression, to understand the oppression of others. By 1971 the "black analogy" has become a tool of white racism. The cries "we are oppressed too" and even more terrible "we are equally oppressed" permitted white middle-class women to dismiss the black struggle, to dismiss their complicity in a racist system, to dismiss criticisms of the movement from black women as motivated by the influence "the male chauvinism of black men" has upon them—ultimately to complete the cycle of white middle-class racism by reducing black and third-world people within the United States to invisibility. White middle-class women, bloated with their own pious claims to oppression, blind within their own racism, refused to see that black women were trying to teach them something when they spoke at conferences, saying: "I am black and a woman, but am I first black or first a woman? First I am black." Or "we fear the abortion program, it may be used against us." Or "we must destroy exploitation and racism *before* black women can be liberated—for what does it mean to us, black women, if you white women end discrimination? We are still black; we are still exploited; we are still destroyed and our children with us." All the white women could answer with was "black male chauvinism!" They remained completely blind to the fact that third-world people are a colony and a minority within the heart of the monster, that their survival depends upon a resolution to the contradiction of male chauvinism and male supremacy that *does not* divide black women and black men into antagonistic factions.

Female Chauvinism

The purest expression of self-serving middle-class ideology is reflected in the blind hatred of men that makes no distinction between the system of white male supremacy and male chauvinism. Only very privileged women can in the security of their class status and class earning power create a little "manless Utopia" for themselves. They need only withdraw from the psychological discomfort of male chauvinism to create a new and different life for themselves—they are not faced, as a class, with the necessity to struggle against another class; they are not driven by exploitation and repression to understand that male chauvinism is reactionary but that it can also be defeated, so that men and women can resolve the contradiction between them, emerge stronger, and unite in mutual opposition to their real enemies—the generals, the corporate bosses, the corrupt politicians.

Liberal Guilt

Liberal guilt is worthless. Appealing to women who are completely devoted to their own self-serving class interests is equally useless. There is no mass movement in the United States that can avoid the contradictions of racism and class conflict, thus moralistic pleas are a waste of time. Nonetheless, women in the United States—and everywhere outside of the revolutionary world—are oppressed and exploited, suffer and die in silence. For the thousands and thousands of women who are poor, who are working class, who were born into the middle class but have turned away from it in disgust and revulsion, the women's movement, as a revolutionary struggle, remains their chief commitment and their only hope. Our challenge is to correct past mistakes, to learn what we must know to avoid future mistakes, to teach and to learn from each other. We *must* learn how to build, within the very heart of the monster, a revolutionary movement devoted to the liberation of all people *in practice.* Such a movement will not be self-serving, cannot be merely reformist. It must be political, must know history and economics, must understand that all revolutionary movements in the world today are interdependent. We can no longer be an island of affluence, blind to the lesson that what happens to women in Vietnam happens to us, that what happens to a black woman happens to us. The United States is not an empire that will stand for a thousand years, but is an oppressive monster that the peoples of the world will dismember and destroy before the world is all finished. We must choose which side we will be on—the path of revolution or the path of exploitation and genocide.

The women's movement is turning and twisting within its contradictions. Some women speed off into mysticism, claiming, but not explaining, how women by rejecting "male" politics and finding "female" politics effect world revolution—a world revolution in which the people's war in Vietnam plays no part, in which all previous world revolutions—Russian, Chinese, North Vietnamese, North Korean, Cuban—play no part. Still others seek escape in "sexual liberation," hoping to find, as does the youth movement, a personalized, individual salvation in a "life-style revolution" in which racism is dismissed as a problem of "black male chauvinism" and Vietnam is dismissed as a "penis war" of no concern to women. To be in the "vanguard," it is only necessary to love a woman sexually. Still others cling to the worn-out slogans of the early days, continuing with "consciousness raising" as weekly therapy and engaging in endless discussions of anti-elitism (an elite being anyone who does anything at all threatening to any woman in a small group) and "anti-elitist structure" in the organization of the women's center.

These tendencies reflect the other face of women's oppression, not anger or strength, but fearfulness, turning inward to avoid challenge, to avoid thinking, to avoid struggle, to avoid the large and frightening world of conflict and revolution, which cannot be contained within a small group or understood through the subjective oppression of a privileged woman. Women *are* mutilated, especially passive, nurturant middle-class women. They are made manipulative, dishonest, fearful, conservative, hypocritical, and self-serving. Celebrating women's weakness—elevating mutilation to a holy state of female grace—corrupts the movement into a reactionary and self-serving force.

Women are seen as absurd, and they blame the media. Women are criticized for being reactionary and racist. They howl "male defined," "male identified." Women are isolated from the liberation struggles of other people, and they scream that those movements are *male-dominated*! How many more excuses will be found until women have the strength to confront their mistakes and their failures? How many revolutions are we going to be called upon to make to assure rich and comforting interpersonal relationships and unhampered fucking for the people whose privilege is so great that they can afford to worry about their spirits instead of their bellies? How many more people are we going to help die in Indochina by howling that fighting against imperialism is "antiwoman" or a "penis war" or "dominated by men"? How long are we going to remain absurd because, in the eyes of the vast majority of peoples in the world, *we are absurd, self-seeking, blind,* and *ignorant*!

It is time, past time, to get our heads together, to listen to and learn from women who have made and are making revolutions, to study to fight, to fight to win, with strength and dignity and a proper respect for the suffering of others and a complete devotion to ending all oppression practiced against the majority of the peoples of the world, male and female, in the colonies of the monster and in the heart of the monster. Then, and only then, shall we know something of liberation.

THE TRIP

Roxanne Dunbar

Roxanne Dunbar is an important figure in the woman's movement. She has made theoretical contributions ("Female Liberation as the Basis for Social Revolution"[1]), produced numerous literary works, and is an active organizer.

Born in 1939 in Oklahoma, "on the wrong side of the tracks," as she puts it, she married, had a child, and attended college in southern California. She was one of the founders of Cell 16, Female Liberation, in Boston, and one of the frequent contributors and editors of *No More Fun and Games: A Journal of Female Liberation*. Her writings about women's oppression include poetry, autobiography, fiction, and essays. "The Trip" first appeared in the October 1968 issue of *No More Fun and Games* and is part of a longer, as yet unpublished, autobiographical essay.

"The Trip" is a powerful statement on the hopelessness and desperation that paralyze many women before we realize that the problem is not inside of us, that it is not our fault. It is also a moving testament of the pain a woman goes through in the process of struggling to liberate herself.

In 1970 Roxanne Dunbar went to New Orleans to found the Southern Female Rights Union, an organization for and of poor white and black southern women. The organization is constituted on the following principles:

1. We demand free, non-compulsory public childcare . . . 24 hours every day of the year, regardless of parents' income. All meals, medical and dental care, clothing, and equipment must be available . . . in the schools, so no child is deprived by parents' inadequate support . . . staffed by equal number of females and males.
2. We demand an adequate guaranteed annual income (minimum $2400) for every individual (not family) in this country.
3. We demand an end to sexual (and racial) discrimination in hiring, firing, wages, and job-training.

[1] Reproduced in Robin Morgan, *Sisterhood Is Powerful* (New York: Vintage, 1970).

4. We demand free self-defense instruction for females of all ages in the public schools.
5. We demand that the present hormonal birth control pills be withdrawn from the market as deadly. Women who have been harmed . . . must be compensated.
6. We demand that the television, radio, and newspaper industries . . . remove all discriminatory allusions to females.

When she woke, it was 10:30. She had wanted to get up earlier. Already the room was steaming with heat. Now she could not walk around the city without sweating until late afternoon. They had planned to wake at 7:00. She vaguely remembered a knock at the door, but had gone back to sleep. Now she got up slowly telling herself that the limpness in her body was due to the heat, but she knew better. She knew the lethargy well by now. Depression. She walked to the window—really a narrow glass door opening onto a tiny balcony overlooking the streetcar terminal. The streetcars had awakened her several times, stopping at 4:00. She squinted at the dull, blinding whiteness of the broad street, and could see the ocean a little—the Gulf, really—grey and murky.

He was sleeping so soundly, but as usual she went to him and whispered that he had promised to go walking with her. He groaned, tried to pull her into bed, mumbled a request for coffee—to get rid of her. If ever just once he would get up before her . . . but there was something to do—get coffee. She dressed quickly in a long-sleeved dress. It would be hot, but preferable to the cat-calls which she would receive anyway, but not as many.

She left the little room, down the humid, poster-paint blue stairway, past some grotesque Indian cleaning ladies, past the sleazy cashier, onto the hot street. Around the corner, there was another world. It really was there. There was the center of Vera Cruz—a square surrounded by outdoor cafes with their cool, marimba music—inside another world still, for men only. Now she got excited—a strange exotic place, a foreign land, and it was lovely. She sat down at one of the tiny tables, and ordered fresh pineapple juice, and tried to feel excited. A man asked to sit with her, and then another.

So she walked—down to the wharf, past some fisherman bringing in an enormous net of squirming fish. Then she found herself in a residential area of ugly, squat stucco houses, swarming with family members doing their daily chores. It was hot and very boring. She knew it ought not be boring—just as she used to feel walking around San Francisco alone during the day. Somehow, nothing was very exciting without someone to share it and John, like her husband, had no interest in exploring.

Suddenly she was downtown—a sort of imitation of a medium-sized mid-western American city. But on closer view, it was decidedly Mexican with its dirty little eating places. It was dreary. She did not like picturesque poverty. Back where she started, in the square, she ordered the coffee, and walked slowly back to the hotel. She had a headache; perspiration was trickling from behind her ears. Her head itched.

Back up the blue stairway, now rancid from the dirty cleaning water, and into the room. He was still asleep; she hated him. She began making noises to wake him, and finally his eyes opened—full of guilt, which made her hate him even more. He sat up in the bed, smiling, asking the usual questions of what time, where did you go, and sweet baby. Yes, he wanted to go shopping because they were leaving for Mexico City in the afternoon, and he wanted to buy a present for his mother. She began crying, as usual, and as usual, he could not understand why.

ON THE TEMPTATION TO BE A BEAUTIFUL OBJECT
November, 1968

Dana Densmore

We are programmed to crave sex. It sells consumer goods. It gives you a lift and promises a spark of individual self-assertion in a dull and routinized world. It is a means to power (the only means they have) for women.

D. Densmore, "On Celibacy"

Most of what passes for sex need is need for attention, affection, ego gratification, security, self-expression, to win a man or conquer a woman, to prove something to somebody. Sex is very rarely about sex.
Assuming that the "natural" attraction is heterosexual, I think that homosexuality arises because of the unnaturalness of the roles forced on men and women.
Women can't face the degradation imposed by men, so they turn to women. Men can't respect women so they turn to men they can respect. Or they can't identify with the he-man image so they turn to men not to have to play out the role. The false male-female dichotomy is then responsible for homosexuality.

D. Densmore, "Sexuality"

Dana Densmore, along with Roxanne Dunbar, Jayne West, Jeanne Lafferty, Betsy Warrior, and Lisa Leghorn, was one of the major contributors to the first issues of *No More Fun and Games: A Journal of Female Liberation,* and was active in the early organizational efforts of the women's liberation move-

Dana Densmore, "On the Temptation to Be a Beautiful Object," *No More Fun and Games: A Journal of Female Liberation,* 16 Lexington Ave., Cambridge, Mass. November, 1968. Reprinted by permission.

ment in Boston. Her articles include an incisive denunciation of *Cosmopolitan* magazine ("Women's Magazines and Womanhood"), "Chivalry—The Iron Hand in the Velvet Glove," "On Celibacy," and "Sexuality," all published in *No More Fun and Games.*

We are constantly bombarded in this society by the images of feminine beauty. There is almost an obsession with it.

It is used extensively in advertising, particularly in advertising directed at women: be like this, they are saying, use our product.

The image sells everything, not just beauty products, but the beauty products reap the benefits of the image having sunk so well into everyone's consciousness.

And oh! those beauty products. Shimmering, magical, just waiting to turn the plainest girl into a heartbreakingly beautiful, transfixing graven image.

Or so they claim and imply, over and over, with extravagant hypnotizing advertising copy and photograph after photograph of dewy-fresh perfect faces.

Inevitably it penetrates the subconscious in an insidious and permanent way.

We may be sophisticated enough (or bitter enough) to reject specific advertising claims, but we cannot purge the image from us: if only we *could* get that look with a few sweeps of a lambsdown buffer dusting on translucent powder making our faces glow like satin, accented with shimmery slicked-on lip glow, a brush of glittery transparent blusher, eyes soft-fringed and luminous, lash-shaded and mysteriously shadowed ...suppose we *could* get the look they promise from their products and the look they all sell in their advertising? Ah, how few could resist!

Many of us are scarred by attempts as teenagers to win the promised glamor from cosmetics. Somehow it always just looked painted, harsh, worse than ever, and yet real life fell so far short of the ideals already burned into our consciousness that the defeat was bitter too and neither the plain nor the painted solution was satisfactory.

How often the date sat impatiently below while the girl in anguish and despair tinged with self-loathing applied and wiped away the magical products that despite their magic were helpless against her horrifying plainness. She would never be a woman, mysteriously beautiful.

Then, as we grow older and better looking, our faces more mature and our handling of cosmetics more expert, there are times when nature and artifice combine to make us unquestionably beautiful, for a moment, an hour, or an evening.

The incredible elation of looking in a mirror (the lighting just right ...) and seeing, not the familiar, plain, troublesome self, but a beautiful object, not ourselves, but a thing outside, a beautiful thing, worthy of worship ... no one could resist falling in love with such a face.

The lighting changes, or the evening wears on, and the face slips imperceptibly back into plainness, harshness. Happy gaiety becomes

forced gaiety, we laugh louder because we must make up for the ugliness we suddenly found, must distract attention from it.

Or we crawl back into ourselves in an agony of humiliated self-consciousness. We had thought ourselves beautiful, and carried on, attracting attention to what we thought was irresistible beauty but had somehow shifted into plainness again. How they must be laughing at us.

We do succeed, we make ourselves objects, outside ourselves, something we expect others to admire because we admire, and which we admire through others' admiration.

But it's not us really. Narcissism is not really love of the self, because self is the soul, the personality, and that is always something quite different, something complex and complicated, something strange and human and very familiar and of this earth.

That beautiful object we stand in awe before has nothing to do with the person we know so well; it is altogether outside, separate, object, a beautiful image, not a person at all. A feast for the eyes.

A feast for the eyes, and not for the mind. That beautiful object is just an object, a work of art, to look at, not to know, total appearance, bearing no personality or will. To the extent that one is caught up in the beauty of it, one perceives object and not person.

This goes for others as well as for ourselves. The more beautiful we are, the more admired our appearance, the closer we approach the dream of the incredible beauty, the less reality our personality or intellect or will have.

It is unthinkable that this work of art has a will, especially one which is not as totally soft and agreeable as the face it presents. You cannot be taken seriously, people will not even hear what you say. (If they did they would be shocked and displeased—but since they do not take it seriously they say "You are too pretty to be so smart"—by which they mean, you are an object, do not presume to complicate the image with an intellect, for intellect is complex and not always pleasing and beautiful. Do not dare to spoil my pleasure in your beauty by showing it to be only the facade of a real person; I will not believe that, you will only succeed in marring your beauty.)

How can anyone take a manikin seriously? How, even, can one take a heartbreakingly beautiful face seriously? One is far too caught up in admiration of the object presented. It is merely beautiful, but it becomes an object when it is presented to the world.

This only goes for women, of course; men's character and personality and will always shine through their appearance, both men and women look at them that way, But one is taught in society by the emphasis on the images of feminine beauty to view women differently. The important thing is not the mind, the will, but the appearance. You ARE your appearance.

And if your appearance is pleasing, you are sunk, for no one will ever look beyond. You have fulfilled all that is expected of you and you may rest (this all assumes you have the feminine womanly virtues of non-character such as kindness, gentleness, and the "pleasing personality").

In fact, if you are beautiful, or if you have made yourself beautiful, you had BETTER leave it at that, because you have no chance of compelling people to look beyond. They are so enchanted with what they see.

They adore you for your appearance. If you are "brainy," it will be taken as quaint, a charming affectation. If you are disagreeable it is offensive, a particularly stinging affront, disrespect for your beauty, the sacrilege of a work of art. (This does not detract from the mystique of the beautiful bitch. That is just another form of flirtation, tantalizing the man by simultaneously alluring with the beauty and playing hard to get by putting up a verbal fence—a fence, by the way, which the man sees himself ultimately surmounting in triumph.)

It is true that this is part of the burden of being a woman. We are expected to be beautiful and not being beautiful does not make us automatically accepted as people. To some extent and for some people we are never more than our appearance.

If we are ugly and plain men demand angrily (at least in their own minds) why we don't DO something with ourselves; surely a more becoming hairdo, better make-up, or even (if the situation is bad enough) a new nose.

Women react the same way to women. All are victimized by the image of woman as object, appearance. "Why doesn't she DO something with herself?"

A man who is neat and clean may get away with being ugly; if he is intelligent and personable he may even be immensely popular, but for a woman being neat and clean is never enough if she is still plain, if she doesn't at least TRY to improve on nature with the most flattering hairdo (however limp or unruly her hair is, however many hours of effort and frustration she must put into the endeavor), the newest make-ups artfully and painstakingly applied, every new exercise and diet fad, the newest and choicest clothes. The ugly woman who does her best in this way will still be a "dog" but she won't be a threat and may even be popular if she has the other qualifications, popular as a "sister."

If you are truly ugly it is always an offense against your role as woman. You can never be truly feminine, womanly. Always an affront to men and women both, trapped as they are in the myth of feminine beauty.

How dare you be ugly? You are a woman, an object, you exist to please the eye, and yet you fail so utterly. They will still be obsessed with your appearance, only this time they are affronted rather than admiring.

They will still have difficulty listening to what you are saying, this time because they are so busy wondering why on earth you don't get a nose job or something.

Still, being ugly has its advantages. At least they will not be lulled into hypnotic admiration with you as a beautiful object.

You will be a constant gadfly, shattering their preconceived notions. At least they cannot say "you're too pretty to be so smart." They will have to say "You had better be smart because you're certainly not pretty." This is certainly a healthier situation for an individual who wishes to be more than a passive object.

The most fortuitous situation for a woman might be to be inoffensively plain, thoroughly nondescript. It would be very difficult for her to win initial attention, for with a woman one notices only the beautiful (admirable) and the ugly (repulsive); one does not offer a woman a chance to show by words or actions what her personality or character is in the way one automatically does to a man.

But when one does command attention there would be least distraction from the person by the appearance, least temptation for the woman to be made an object in the minds of the beholders.

And yet this thoroughly nondescript looking woman is the one cosmetics advertisements aim at. They want to take the mouses and with their magic powders and creams transform them into princesses.

And for many mice they can succeed. Even men, as we have seen in the case of drag queens, can often make themselves into beautiful women with enough of the magic powders and creams.

But to the extent that we keep our self-image as persons as we manipulate our appearance in this way, it will seem artificial and unnatural, and look strange and perhaps even frightening.

Only as we slip into the schizophrenic world of play-acting and narcissism will we be able to enjoy the beauty we create. And then we will be imprisoned within the walls of the object we created in the minds of others and in our own minds—we will no longer be able to function as persons, or only fitfully, self-consciously, and puzzling others by our strange behavior.

DOUBLE JEOPARDY: TO BE BLACK AND FEMALE

Frances Beal

Racism and chauvinism are anti-people. And a man cannot be politically correct and a chauvinist too . . . Invariably I hear from some dude that Black women must be supportive and patient so that Black men can regain their manhood. The notion of womanhood, they argue—and only if pressed to address themselves to the notion do they think of it or argue—is dependent on his defining his manhood. So the shit goes on.

—Toni Cade, "On the Issue of Roles," in *The Black Woman*

Where the white woman is the wife, the Black woman is the mother on welfare and the bearer of future workers for the state; where the white woman is the call girl or mistress, the Black woman is the street prostitute; where the white woman is married to a man who can afford it, a Black woman takes over the care of the home and children for her. In short, to be a Black woman is to operate almost totally as a physical body without the inducements offered her white counterpart.

—Kay Lindsey, "The Black Woman as Woman," in *The Black Woman*

In the United States black women have traditionally been viewed as "Aunt Jemimas" (a saccharine version of the old house slave), as some super-exotic sex object (largely by white men) or, in Pat Robinson's words, "We Black women are considered 'animals' by North American Black and white men."[1] Black women have been charged with being dominating and castrating. They are condemned as the creators of a "matriarchy" that keeps black men in their

[1] Pat Robinson and Group, "A Historical and Critical Essay for Black Women in the Cities, June 1969," in Toni Cade (ed.), *The Black Woman* (New York: Signet Books, 1970), p. 198.

place. Our society has consistently denied black men access to economic and social dignity. Menial jobs (e.g., as domestics), are more available for black women than parallel "unskilled labor" for black males in the United States, so the percentage of females as primary wage earners is much higher in black families than in white ones. As a consequence, black women have been made to assume a disproportionate responsibility for family life and children. One can hardly call that a matriarchy; rather, it is a question of human beings learning how to survive. The primary injustice is, of course, the position all black people have been forced into.

The relationship between black and white women's liberation is still tenuous for the same reasons that divide and separate women from men and black women from white women in a society fraught with racism and sexism. "Double Jeopardy: To Be Black and Female" gives an overall view of the situation of black women in America, and discusses their relationship to black men ("Those who are exerting their 'manhood' by telling Black women to step back into a domestic, submissive role are assuming a counter-revolutionary position.") and to white women's liberation ("A major differentiation is that the white women's liberation movement is basically middle-class. Very few of these women suffer the extreme economic exploitation that most Black women are subjected to day by day.")

Frances Beal lives in New York, and has been active in SNCC's Black Women's Liberation Committee, the National Council of Negro Women, and several other black women's study groups.

In attempting to analyze the situation of the Black woman in America, one crashes abruptly into a solid wall of grave misconceptions, outright distortions of fact, and defensive attitudes on the part of many. The system of capitalism (and its afterbirth—racism) under which we all live has attempted by many devious ways and means to destroy the humanity of all people, and particularly the humanity of Black people. This has meant an outrageous assault on every Black man, woman, and child who reside in the United States.

In keeping with its goal of destroying the Black race's will to resist its subjugation, capitalism found it necessary to create a situation where the Black man found it impossible to find meaningful or productive employment. More often than not, he couldn't find work of any kind. And the Black woman likewise was manipulated by the system, economically exploited and physically assaulted. She could often find work in the white man's kitchen, however, and sometimes became the sole breadwinner of the family. This predicament has led to many psychological problems on the part of both man and woman and has contributed to the turmoil that we find in the Black family structure.

Unfortunately, neither the Black man nor the Black woman understood the true nature of the forces working upon them. Many Black women tended to accept the capitalist evaluation of manhood and womanhood and believed, in fact, that Black men were shiftless and lazy, otherwise they would get a job and support their families as they ought to. Personal relationships between Black men and women were thus torn asunder and one result has been the separation of man from wife, mother from child, etc.

America has defined the roles to which each individual should subscribe. It has defined "manhood" in terms of its own interests and "femininity" likewise. Therefore, an individual who has a good job, makes a lot of money, and drives a Cadillac is a real "man," and conversely, an individual who is lacking in these "qualities" is less of a man. The advertising media in this country continuously inform the American male of his need for indispensable signs of his virility—the brand of cigarettes that cowboys prefer, the whiskey that has a masculine tang, or the label of the jock strap that athletes wear.

The ideal model that is projected for a woman is to be surrounded by hypocritical homage and estranged from all real work, spending idle hours primping and preening, obsessed with conspicuous consumption, and limiting life's functions to simply a sex role. We unqualitatively reject these respective models. A woman who stays at home caring for children and the house often leads an extremely sterile existence. She must lead her entire life as a satellite to her mate. He goes out into society and brings back a little piece of the world for her. His interests and his understanding of the world become her own and she cannot develop herself as an individual having been reduced to only a biological function. This kind of woman leads a parasitic existence that can aptly be described as legalized prostitution.

Furthermore it is idle dreaming to think of Black women simply caring for their homes and children like the middle-class white model. Most Black women have to work to help house, feed, and clothe their families. Black women make up a substantial percentage of the Black working force, and this is true for the poorest Black family as well as the so-called "middle-class" family.

Black women were never afforded any such phony luxuries. Though we have been browbeaten with this white image, the reality of the degrading and dehumanizing jobs that were relegated to us quickly dissipated this mirage of womanhood. The following excerpts from a speech that Sojourner Truth made at a Women's Rights Convention in the nineteenth century show us how misleading and incomplete a life this model represents for us:

. . . Well, chilern, whar dar is so much racket dar must be something out o' kilter. I tink dat 'twixt de niggers of de Souf and de women at de Norf all a talkin' 'bout rights, de white men will be in a fix pretty soon. But what's all dis here talkin' 'bout? Dat man ober dar say dat women needs to be helped into carriages, and lifted ober ditches, and to have de best place every whar. Nobody ever help me into carriages, or ober mud puddles, or gives me any best places, . . . and ar'nt I a woman? Look at me! Look at my arm! . . . I have plowed, and planted, and gathered into barns, and no man could head me—and ar'nt I a woman? I could work as much as a man (when I could get it), and bear de lash as well—and ar'nt I a woman? I have borne five chilern and I seen 'em mos' all sold off into slavery, and when I cried out with a mother's grief, none but Jesus heard—and ar'nt I a woman?

Unfortunately, there seems to be some confusion in the Movement today as to who has been oppressing whom. Since the advent of Black power, the Black male has exerted a more prominent leadership role in our struggle for justice in this country. He sees the system for what it really is for the most part, but where he rejects its values and mores on many issues, when it comes to women, he seems to take his guidelines from the pages of the *Ladies' Home Journal.* Certain Black men are maintaining that they have been castrated by society but that Black women somehow escaped this persecution and even contributed to this emasculation.

Let me state here and now that the Black woman in America can justly be described as a "slave of a slave." By reducing the Black man in America to such abject oppression, the Black woman had no protector and was used, and is still being used in some cases, as the scapegoat for the evils that this horrendous system has perpetrated on Black men. Her physical image has been maliciously maligned; she has been sexually molested and abused by the white colonizer; she has suffered the worse kind of economic exploitation, having been forced to serve as the white woman's maid and wet nurse for white offspring while her own children were more often than not starving and neglected. It is the depth of degradation to be socially manipulated, physically raped, used to undermine your own household, and to be powerless to reverse this syndrome.

It is true that our husbands, fathers, brothers, and sons have been emasculated, lynched, and brutalized. They have suffered from the cruelest assault on mankind that the world has ever known. However, it is a gross distortion of fact to state that Black women have oppressed Black men. The capitalist system found it expedient to enslave and oppress them and proceeded to do so without consultation or the signing of any agreements with Black women.

It must also be pointed out at this time that Black women are not resentful of the rise to power of Black men. We welcome it. We see in it the eventual liberation of all Black people from this corrupt system of capitalism. Nevertheless, this does not mean that you have to negate one for the other. This kind of thinking is a product of miseducation; that it's either X or it's Y. It is fallacious reasoning that in order for the Black man to be strong, the Black woman has to be weak.

Those who are exerting their "manhood" by telling Black women to step back into a domestic, submissive role are assuming a counterrevolutionary position. Black women likewise have been abused by the system and we must begin talking about the elimination of all kinds of oppression. If we are talking about building a strong nation, capable of throwing off the yoke of capitalist oppression, then we are talking about the total involvement of every man, woman, and child, each with a highly developed political consciousness. We need our whole army out there dealing with the enemy and not half an army.

There are also some Black women who feel that there is no more productive role in life than having and raising children. This attitude often reflects the conditioning of the society in which we live and is adopted from a bourgeois white model. Some young sisters who have never had to maintain a household and accept the confining role which this entails tend to romanticize (along with the help of a few brothers) this role of housewife and mother. Black women who have had to endure this kind of function are less apt to have these utopian visions.

Those who project in an intellectual manner how great and rewarding this role will be and who feel that the most important thing that they can contribute to the Black nation is children are doing themselves a great injustice. This line of reasoning completely negates the contributions that Black women have historically made to our struggle for liberation. These Black women include Sojourner Truth, Harriet Tubman, Mary McLeod Bethune, and Fannie Lou Hamer, to name but a few.

We live in a highly industrialized society and every member of the Black nation must be as academically and technologically developed as possible. To wage a revolution, we need competent teachers, doctors, nurses, electronics experts, chemists, biologists, physicists, political scientists, and so on and so forth. Black women sitting at home reading bedtime stories to their children are just not going to make it.

Economic Exploitation of Black Women

The economic system of capitalism finds it expedient to reduce women to a state of enslavement. They oftentimes serve as a scapegoat for the evils of this system. Much in the same way that the poor white cracker of the South, who is equally victimized, looks down upon Blacks and contributes to the oppression of Blacks, so, by giving to men a false feeling of superiority (at least in their own home or in their relationships with women), the oppression of women acts as an escape valve for capitalism. Men may be cruelly exploited and subjected to all sorts of dehumanizing tactics on the part of the ruling class, but they have someone who is below them—at least they're not women.

Women also represent a surplus labor supply, the control of which is absolutely necessary to the profitable functioning of capitalism. Women are systematically exploited by the system. They are paid less for the same work that men do, and jobs that are specifically relegated to women are low-paying and without the possibility of advancement. Statistics from the Women's Bureau of the Department of Labor show that in 1967 the wage scale for white women was even below that of Black men; and the wage scale for non-white women was the lowest of all:

White Males $6704
Non-White Males $4277
White Females $3991
Non-White Females $2861

Those industries which employ mainly Black women are the most exploitive in the country. Domestic and hospital workers are good examples of this oppression; the garment workers in New York City provide us with another view of this economic slavery. The International Ladies Garment Workers Union (ILGWU), whose overwhelming membership consists of Black and Puerto Rican women, has a leadership that is nearly all lily-white and male. This leadership has been working in collusion with the ruling class and has completely sold its soul to the corporate structure.

To add insult to injury, the ILGWU has invested heavily in business enterprises in racist, apartheid South Africa—with union funds. Not only does this bought-off leadership contribute to our continued exploitation in this country by not truly representing the best interests of its membership, but it audaciously uses funds that Black and Puerto Rican women have provided to support the economy of a vicious government that is engaged in the economic rape and murder of our Black brothers and sisters in our Motherland, Africa.

The entire labor movement in the United States has suffered as a result of the super-exploitation of Black workers and women. The unions have historically been racist and chauvinistic. They have upheld racism in this country and have failed to fight the white skin privileges of white workers. They have failed to fight or even make an issue against the inequities in the hiring and pay of women workers. There has been virtually no struggle against either the racism of the white worker or the economic exploitation of the working woman, two factors which have consistently impeded the advancement of the real struggle against the ruling class.

This racist, chauvinistic, and manipulative use of Black workers and women, especially Black women, has been a severe cancer on the American labor scene. It therefore becomes essential for those who understand the workings of capitalism and imperialism to realize that the exploitation of Black people and women works to everyone's disadvantage and that the liberation of these two groups is a steppingstone to the liberation of all oppressed people in this country and around the world.

Bedroom Politics

I have briefly discussed the economic and psychological manipulation of Black women, but perhaps the most outlandish act of oppression in modern times is the current campaign to promote sterilization of non-white women in an attempt to maintain the population and power imbalance between the white haves and the non-white have-nots.

These tactics are but another example of the many devious schemes that the ruling-class elite attempt to perpetrate on the Black population in order to keep itself in control. It has recently come to our attention that a massive campaign for so-called "birth control" is presently being promoted not only in the underdeveloped non-white areas of the world,

but also in Black communities here in the United States. However, what the authorities in charge of these programs refer to as "birth control" is in fact nothing but a method of outright surgical genocide.

The United States has been sponsoring sterilization clinics in non-white countries, especially in India, where already some three million young men and boys in and around New Delhi have been sterilized in makeshift operating rooms set up by the American Peace Corps workers. Under these circumstances, it is understandable why certain countries view the Peace Corps not as a benevolent project, not as evidence of America's concern for underdeveloped areas, but rather as a threat to their very existence. This program could more aptly be named the Death Corps.

Vasectomy, which is performed on males and takes only six or seven minutes, is a relatively simple operation. The sterilization of a woman, on the other hand, is admittedly major surgery. This operation (salpingectomy)[1] must be performed in a hospital under general anesthesia. This method of "birth control" is a common procedure in Puerto Rico. Puerto Rico has long been used by the colonialist exploiter, the United States, as a huge experimental laboratory for medical research before allowing certain practices to be imported and used here. When the birth-control pill was first being perfected, it was tried out on Puerto Rican women and selected Black women (poor), using them as guinea pigs, to evaluate its effect and its efficiency.

Salpingectomy has now become the commonest operation in Puerto Rico, commoner than an appendectomy or a tonsillectomy. It is so widespread that it is referred to simply as *la operación. On the island, 10 percent of the women between the ages of 15 and 45 have already been sterilized.*

And now, as previously occurred with the pill, this method has been imported into the United States. These sterilization clinics are cropping up around the country in the Black and Puerto Rican communities. These so-called "maternity clinics" specifically outfitted to purge Black women or men of their reproductive possibilities are appearing more and more in hospitals and clinics across the country.

A number of organizations have been formed to popularize the idea of sterilization, such as the Association for Voluntary Sterilization and the Human Betterment (! ! ! ?) Association for Voluntary Sterilization, Inc., which has its headquarters in New York City.

Threatened with the cut-off of relief funds, some Black welfare women have been forced to accept this sterilization procedure in exchange for a continuation of welfare benefits. Black women are often afraid to permit any kind of necessary surgery because they know from bitter experience that they are more likely than not to come out of the hospital without their insides. (Both salpingectomies and hysterectomies are performed.)

---

[1] Salpingectomy: Through an abdominal incision, the surgeon cuts both fallopian tubes and ties off the separated ends, after which act there is no way for the egg to pass from the ovary to the womb.

We condemn this use of the Black woman as a medical testing ground for the white middle class. Reports of the ill effects, including deaths, from the use of the birth control pill only started to come to light when the white privileged class began to be affected. These outrageous Nazi-like procedures on the part of medical researchers are but another manifestation of the totally amoral and dehumanizing brutality that the capitalist system perpetrates on Black women. The sterilization experiments carried on in concentration camps some twenty-five years ago have been denounced the world over, but no one seems to get upset by the repetition of these same racist tactics today in the United States of America—land of the free and home of the brave. This campaign is as nefarious a program as Germany's gas chambers, and in a long-term sense, as effective and with the same objective.

The rigid laws concerning abortions in this country are another vicious means of subjugation and, indirectly, of outright murder. Rich white women somehow manage to obtain these operations with little or no difficulty. It is the poor Black and Puerto Rican woman who is at the mercy of the local butcher. Statistics show us that the non-white death rate at the hands of the unqualified abortionist is substantially higher than for white women. Nearly half of the childbearing deaths in New York City are attributed to abortion alone and out of these, 79 percent are among non-whites and Puerto Rican women.

We are not saying that Black women should not practice birth control. *Black women have the right and the responsibility to determine when it is in the interest of the struggle to have children or not to have them, and this right must not be relinquished to anyone.* It is also her right and responsibility to determine when it is in her own best interests to have children, how many she will have, and how far apart. The lack of the availability of safe birth-control methods, the forced sterilization practices, and the inability to obtain legal abortions are all symptoms of a decadent society that jeopardizes the health of Black women (and thereby the entire Black race) in its attempts to control the very life processes of human beings. This is a symptom of a society that believes it has the right to bring political factors into the privacy of the bedchamber. The elimination of these horrendous conditions will free Black women for full participation in the revolution, and thereafter, in the building of the new society.

Relationship to White Movement

Much has been written recently about the white women's liberation movement in the United States, and the question arises whether there are any parallels between this struggle and the movement on the part of Black women for total emancipation. While there are certain comparisons that one can make, simply because we both live under the same exploitative system, there are certain differences, some of which are quite basic.

The white women's movement is far from being monolithic. Any white group that does not have an anti-imperialist and anti-racist ideology has absolutely nothing in common with the Black woman's struggle. In fact, some groups come to the incorrect conclusion that their oppression is due simply to male chauvinism. They therefore have an extremely anti-male tone to their dissertations. Black people are engaged in a life-and-death struggle and the main emphasis of Black women must be to combat the capitalist, racist exploitation of Black people. While it is true that male chauvinism has become institutionalized in American society, one must always look for the main enemy—the fundamental cause of the female condition.

Another major differentiation is that the white women's liberation movement is basically middle-class. Very few of these women suffer the extreme economic exploitation that most Black women are subjected to day by day. This is the factor that is most crucial for us. It is not an intellectual persecution alone; it is not an intellectual outburst for us; it is quite real. We as Black women have got to deal with the problems that the Black masses deal with, for our problems in reality are one and the same.

If the white groups do not realize that they are in fact fighting capitalism and racism, we do not have common bonds. If they do not realize that the reasons for their condition lie in the system and not simply that men get a vicarious pleasure out of "consuming their bodies for exploitative reasons" (this kind of reasoning seems to be quite prevalent in certain white women's groups), then we cannot unite with them around common grievances or even discuss these groups in a serious manner because they're completely irrelevant to the Black struggle.

The New World

The Black community and Black women especially must begin raising questions about the kind of society we wish to see established. We must note the ways in which capitalism oppresses us and then move to create institutions that will eliminate these destructive influences.

The new world that we are attempting to create must destroy oppression of any type. The value of this new system will be determined by the status of the person who was low man on the totem pole. Unless women in any enslaved nation are completely liberated, the change cannot really be called a revolution. If the Black woman has to retreat to the position she occupied before the armed struggle, the whole movement and the whole struggle will have retreated in terms of truly freeing the colonized population.

A people's revolution that engages the participation of every member of the community, including man, woman, and child, brings about a certain transformation in the participants as a result of this participation. Once you have caught a glimpse of freedom or experienced a bit of self-determination, you can't go back to old routines that were established under a racist, capitalist regime. We must begin to understand that a revolution entails not only the willingness to lay our lives on the firing line and get killed. In some ways, this is an easy commitment to make. To die for the revolution is a one-shot deal; to live for the revolution means taking on the more difficult commitment of changing our day-to-day life patterns.

This will mean changing the traditional routines that we have established as a result of living in a totally corrupting society. It means changing how you relate to your wife, your husband, your parents, and your co-workers. If we are going to liberate ourselves as a people, it must be recognized that Black women have very specific problems that have to be spoken to. We must be liberated along with the rest of the population. We cannot wait to start working on those problems until that great day in the future when the revolution somehow miraculously is accomplished.

To assign women the role of housekeeper and mother while men go forth into battle is a highly questionable doctrine for a revolutionary to maintain. Each individual must develop a high political consciousness in order to understand how this system enslaves us all and what actions we must take to bring about its total destruction. Those who consider themselves to be revolutionary must begin to deal with other revolutionaries as equals. And so far as I know, revolutionaries are not determined by sex.

Old people, young people, men and women, must take part in the struggle. To relegate women to purely supportive roles or to purely cultural considerations is dangerous doctrine to project. Unless Black men who are preparing themselves for armed struggle understand that the society which we are trying to create is one in which the oppression of *all members* of that society is eliminated, then the revolution will have failed in its avowed purpose.

Given the mutual commitment of Black men and Black women alike to the liberation of our people and other oppressed peoples around the world, the total involvement of each individual is necessary. A revolutionary has the responsibility not only of toppling those that are now in a position of power, but of creating new institutions that will eliminate all forms of oppression. We must begin to rewrite our understanding of traditional personal relationships between man and woman.

All the resources that the Black community can muster up must be channeled into the struggle. Black women must take an active part in bringing about the kind of society where our children, our loved ones, and each citizen can grow up and live as decent human beings, free from the pressures of racism and capitalist exploitation.

POLITICS OF DAY CARE

New Families for Old (straight title)
Family Structure and Revolution (not so straight title)
or think of your own

Kate Ellis

Child care is a central concern of the women's liberation movement and a great deal has been written about the politics and practice of day care.[1] In the following article, Kate Ellis gives an historical survey of the development of female domesticity, women, and the nuclear family, and states the need for child care as a basis for changing woman's role. "But," she asserts, "there could be day care centers all over the country and no improvement in the social position of women." The remainder of the article describes dangers that must be avoided in establishing day care.

Kate Ellis became active in the struggle for day care as a graduate student trying to bring up a child in New York City. She is coauthor of "I Am Furious: Female,"[2] a pamphlet dealing with the political basis of the oppression of women, is a member of the New University Conference, and currently teaches English at Livingston College (Rutgers University) in New Jersey.

In our efforts to transform the anger of women, first into revolutionary consciousness and then into action, the women's movement is faced with a whole range of forces that are setting women against each other as never before. The growth of technology has brought with it the promise of immense leisure. Once only the rich could conspicuously consume. Now (so the myth goes) this "privilege" is within the reach of all. The reality behind this myth is that to maintain a stable capitalist economy, continuous growth is necessary, and this means that increased leisure and increased consumption must go hand in hand, as cause and effect. Veblen had observed that conspicuous consumption has traditionally been seen as good because it denoted membership in the class that had all the power. But since Veblen, technology has made it possible to turn that cause and effect relationship around and to promote consumption on the grounds that it actually creates leisure.

This article was written especially for this book. Printed by permission of the author, Kate Ellis.

[1] Other important articles are "On Day Care," by Louise Gross and Phyllis MacEwan in *Women: A Journal of Liberation* (Winter 1970), reproduced in Leslie B. Tanner (ed.), *Voices From Women's Liberation* (New York: Signet Books, 1970), and Rosalyn Baxandall, "Cooperative Nurseries," *Women: A Journal of Liberation* (Spring 1970), reproduced in Sookie Stambler (ed.), *Women's Liberation: Blueprint for the Future* (New York: Ace Books, 1970).
[2] Available from the New England Free Press, and reproduced in Michele Hoffnung Garskof (ed.), *Roles Women Play: Readings Toward Women's Liberation* (California: Brooks/Cole, 1971).

The emphasis on consumption is part of a more general transformation from a rural, agricultural economy to an urban, industrial one, though the lure of "the big city" still lies in the things you can buy there that are not available at your local store. It is in the city, then, that we find a new kind of division of labor, a new family structure geared to the needs of an economy based on mass production. Lewis Mumford sees the beginnings of this new social unit in the cities of England and Europe toward the end of the eighteenth century:

The change in the constitution of the household manifested itself in various ways. First, by the gradual divorce of the home, henceforth a place for eating, for entertaining, and in a secondary way for rearing children, from the work-place. The three functions of producing, selling and consuming were now separated into three different institutions, three different sets of buildings, three distinct parts of the city.

As a result of the household's becoming exclusively a consumer's organiza-tion, the housewife lost her touch with the affairs of the outside world: she became either a specialist in domesticity or a specialist in sex, something of a drudge, something of a courtesan, more often, perhaps, a little of both. There-with the "private house" comes into existence: private from business and spatially separated from any visible means of support. Every part of life came increasingly to share this privacy.[1]

This new household came into being as masses of people were be-ginning to exchange a rural for an urban way of life. Where "wide open spaces" are accessible, the exaltation of the private world, the world untouched by social pressures and limitations, has little relevance to anyone who is not a member of the leisure class. But with the emer-gence of an industrial proletariat, we begin to notice a saccharine element in popular culture that was not there before.[2] From the eighteen fifties on, the notions of female purity and domestic bliss that we know from Dickens and Tennyson and Thackeray had trickled down to the penny broadsides, displacing a fairly candid sexuality with a thoroughly middle class ideal. Here is Tennyson's version of it:

One walked between his wife and child,
With measured footfall firm and mild,
And now and then he gravely smiled.

The prudent partner of his blood,
Lean'd on him, faithful, gentle, good,
Wearing the rose of womanhood.

And in their double love secure,
The little maiden walk'd demure,
Pacing with downward eyelids pure.[3]

[1] Lewis Mumford, The City in History (London: Penguin Books, 1969), p. 437.
[2] The progressive dilution and sweetening of the content of working class literature is traced by Richard Hoggart in The Uses of Literacy (Boston: Beacon Press, 1961).
[3] Alfred, Lord Tennyson, "The Two Voices," in Jerome Buckley (ed.), The Poems of Tennyson (New York: The Riverside Press, 1958), p. 82.

This middle class woman is clearly more of a specialist in domesticity than a specialist in sex; the opposite of a courtesan yet less of a drudge than her poorer sisters. There are, in other words, class differences in the ways in which women are affected by the cult of domesticity. But whether women are upper class courtesans or lower class courtesans, whether they work for money or specialize in domesticity full time, they share a common job and a common workplace: the home.

This job is probably the single most essential factor that keeps our economy going and growing, not only because it insures increasing levels of consumption but also because the function of the home itself, at every level of society, is to obscure the hard realities of the power structure in an industrial state, to soften the blow in such a way that it does not lead to class consciousness and solidarity with one's fellows, much less to action that could challenge those hard realities.

In their article, "Bread and Roses," Myrna Wood and Kathy McAfee show very clearly the way in which the woman's role in the working class family acts to undermine not only her own class consciousness but that of her entire family:

. . . it is a woman's responsibility to make up for the failures of the system. In countless working class families, it is mother's job that bridges the gap between week-to-week subsistence and relative security. It is her wages that enable her family to eat better food, to escape their oppressive surroundings through a trip, an occasional movie, or new clothes. It is her responsibility to keep the family healthy despite the cost of decent medical care; to make a comfortable home in an unsafe neighbourhood; to provide a refuge from the alienation of work and to keep the male ego in good repair. It is she who must struggle daily to make ends meet despite inflation. She must make up for the fact that her children do not receive a good education, and she must salvage their damaged personalities.[4]

What is interesting, when we look at the unwritten history of working class women, is that in the eighteen fifties, when the cult of domesticity first began to be incorporated into working class culture, we also have the beginnings of an organized labor movement in England. In her study of British working class poetry, Martha Vicinus comments on the consequences of this conjunction:

. . . working class literature functioned both as a reminder of a traditional heritage and as a socializing force within the new industrial society. In this latter capacity, literary works are valuable evidence as to why and how the English worker, thought to be close to revolution through the 1840's, came to accept industrial life as inevitable and to emulate many of the values and characteristics of the dominant middle class.[5]

All these values and characteristics converge upon, and radiate out from, the nuclear family portrayed by Tennyson. This means that working class—and now black—emulation of the nuclear family pattern is

---

[4] Kathy McAfee and Myrna Wood, "Bread and Roses," *Leviathan*, Vol. 1, No. 3, June 1969.
[5] Martha Vicinus, "The Study of British Working Class Poetry," in *An Anti-Text in Literature*, Paul Lauter and Louis Kampf (eds.) (New York: Pantheon Books, 1970).

essential to the diffusion of a whole range of ideals and controls. When the family is exalted as a refuge from the harshness of life in the ghetto or on the assembly line, the effect of this is to undermine the sense of solidarity that a shared workplace or neighbourhood could provide. It thus turns potential militants away from one another and toward a private solution in a private context, a context in which they can turn their anger against those wth less power than they have, against one another and against their *own* women and children, rather than against those who own them, that is, their employers—or unemployers.

It is no coincidence, then, that the sentimental notions about women and children that are embodied in the bourgeois family, notions whose essence is sexual repression, became widespread at a time when a desperate urban proletariat was recovering from the "hungry forties" and beginning to organize.[6] In *The Mass Psychology of Fascism*, Reich argues that there is a connection between the repressive character of the nuclear family and its social function:

Sexual repression aids political reaction not only through a process which makes the mass individual passive and unpolitical, but also by creating in his structure an interest in supporting the authoritarian order.
    The important point is that sexual inhibition is a means of producing a fixation to the authoritarian family, that it turns an original biological tie of the child to its mother—and of the mother to the child—into an indissoluble sexual fixation, and this creates the inability to establish new relationships. The core of the family tie is the mother fixation. The subjective, emotional core of the ideas of homeland and of nation are the ideas of mother and family. The mother is the homeland of the child, as the family is its "nation" in miniature.[7]

Though Reich is primarily concerned with the effects of this tie on the child and on the mass individual (male), his ideas have enormous implications for a militant movement that is taking up the cause of the mother as well as the child. Things will fall apart once the "center" is freed from her role as a natural lightning rod for male frustration and anger. But the nuclear family deprives her of her most natural allies in her struggle to be free. It directs her energy toward a world from which the only escapes are through daydreams, competition and small scale exploitation. It damages women by setting up one male, for whose affection there is rivalry not only among the children but between the mother and the children.

But it also divides women into those who have only one "job," and work full time in the home, and those who have a second job in the labor force: a division reminiscent of the division of slaves into "field niggers," whose work had no "prestige" at all, and the "house niggers" whose place was in their master's home and who were supposed to be

[6] August Meir and Elliot Rudwick, *From Plantation to Ghetto* (New York: Hill and Wang, 1966), pp. 60–71.
[7] Wilhelm Reich, *The Mass Psychology of Fascism* (New York: Basic Books, 1940), pp. 26, 47–48.

grateful to him for putting and keeping them there. We know from accounts of slave rebellions that this division was one aspect of a strategy on the part of slave owners to keep their blacks pacified.[8] The field niggers could see that the house niggers had more privileges. They also saw that within the master-slave system, "good behavior" was the only way to get these privileges.

This is precisely the position that women are in now in the "developed" countries of the world. The black "house nigger" might have been more privileged than his fellows in the field, but he had no control over his time, most of which was spent at the beck and call of his master. And there was always the threat of the field if he backslid. Similarly, cleaning your own house may be less alienated labor than cleaning someone else's, but it takes, according to one survey, an average of seventy hours a week,[9] and the only way to be free of it is to marry into the middle class where you can hire a woman who does not have the option of staying at home, and pay her to take care of your house and kids.

As long as property is privately owned (he paying for it, she taking care of it for him) and as long as children are the private responsibility

[8] E. J. Hobsbawm, *Industry and Empire* (Baltimore: Penguin Books, 1968), pp. 109–124.
[9] "Women During the War and After," Bryn Mawr College, 1945.

of their parents (the mother taking care of them, the father legally obligated to foot the bills), women will remain niggers whether they are in the house or in the field. Within this system, women can only reinforce existing class and race divisions in the name of a whole network of myths which deny the harmful effects of these divisions. Specifically, as long as there are no day care centers, women will remain part of the surplus labor force on the grounds that they already have a full time "job." That is, she is either a mother, a potential mother or an old maid: any of these counts is grounds for exploitation. Women have therefore a choice as to how they will serve their masters. They can increase their profits by taking "women's" jobs at "women's" wages, or they can increase their husbands' productivity by staying home.

But there could be day care centers all over the country and no improvement in the social position of women. Many industries are getting interested in day care, while others are themselves becoming day care industries, setting up corporations with fay names like Pied Piper Inc. to sell franchises for day care centers run along the lines of Mac-Donald's hamburger stands, with costs cut by marketing a uniform "product" at every center, bulk buying and so forth.[10]

The criteria for success in these day care centers are not difficult to determine. For the franchisers, the primacy of the profit motive is not even concealed, while in the work-related projects the consideration of profit is obscured under a cloud of company paternalism. In a proposal put out by the KLH Company in Cambridge, it is argued that everybody benefits: the families, the company and the Federal government, whose Department of Health, Education and Welfare provided a grant for the project. So under "Potential Benefits to Government," the proposal states that

in times of manpower shortages, it is valuable to government that employment be offered to a wider group of workers, *including some mothers on welfare.* This could help prevent competition for workers which pushes up wage rates, promotes inflation and causes production bottlenecks.[11]

By freeing the surplus labor pool, or however large a part of it would be needed to prevent competition for workers, a day care center becomes a useful tool for keeping wages down. "Government" benefits from this

[10] Other franchisers are: MiniPearl Chicken, Romper Room, Kinder Care, Mary Moppet, Child Minders and We Sit Better. On May 3, an ad appeared on the *New York Times* financial page for a conference on the subject, "Profit Possibilities for the '70s in Early Learning and Day Care," run by Knowledge Industry Publications, Inc., publishers of the *Educational Marketer*. The ad said, "You are invited for a fee of $225 to join investment analysts, educational marketers, franchisers, publishers, toy manufacturers, and others at the first business conference of its kind on this fast-growing field. Hear industry leaders discuss the markets, the materials, the plans, the potential profits and problems. Among the topics to be covered—Which markets offer the greatest potential: public education, private, at home? How does Wall Street evaluate the field? How do you control franchisers? What the government's policies? At what age do you teach what?"
[11] "A Proposal to Establish a Work-Related Child Development Center" submitted by KLH Child Development Center, Inc., Cambridge, Mass. Copies of this proposal are available by writing to the company.

service only to the extent that what is good for KLH is good for the country.

The potential advantages to industry of a project like the KLH center include reduction of employee turnover, with a potential saving of $2,000 per employee,[12] increased efficiency due to a lessening of "family-related anxiety," and the practicality of day care as a fringe benefit.

But the most subtle piece of manipulation comes in the discussion of benefits to the families who use the center:

Many urban people have little sense of social identification within their neighbourhoods. They seldom belong to organizations, with the exception of churches. . . . In a sense, a factory is a community. Workers spontaneously form committees for various activities related and unrelated to their jobs, become involved in group activities initiated at work, such as sports and parties. They attend one another's weddings and funerals, and celebrate birthdays constantly. The gifts they exchange are elaborate, and indicate the importance to them of their relationships to their fellow workers. They identify with the work situation in a way that some of them are not likely to do in their urban neighbourhoods. This project aims to make use of this sense of group identification, along with the sense of responsibility engendered by a cooperative ownership of the school, to bring about participation in the education offered.[13]

Many companies have found ways to make use of their employees' sense of group identification without offering them day care, as Elinor Langer's articles on the telephone company have shown.[14] But the actual "participation" of the worker in one of the benefits offered him by his employer will certainly bind the employee to his boss with hoops of steel. Nor will this effect be limited to the workers.

The child will have as a model a working parent, rather than welfare support. Moreover, he will gain a familiarity with the world of work, and feel at home there, through the school's association with an industry. Fatherless children will have an association with men who work. The relation of the school to the adult world can give a context to the education offered.[15]

Worker control of their day care center is no substitute for worker control of the company itself, but if the workers accept the former gratefully, it is unlikely that they will ask for too much more.

But the greatest danger in such a center is that it will duplicate, through the built-in paternalism implicit in the proposal, the environment and psychological climate of the nuclear family. For, as Reich points out:

the interlacing of the socioeconomic with the sexual structure, as well as the structural reproduction of society, takes place in the first four or five years of life, and in the authoritarian family. In this way the authoritarian state develops its enormous interest in the authoritarian family: the family is the factory of its structure and ideology.[16]

[12] *Ibid.*, p. 10.
[13] *Ibid.*, p. 6, 4.
[14] Elinor Langer, "Working for the Telephone Company," *New York Review of Books*, Vol. XIV, Nos. 5 and 6 (March 12 and March 20, 1970).
[15] KLH, p. 4.
[16] Reich, *op. cit.*, p. 24.

He concludes: "The main weapons in the arsenal of freedom, therefore, are the gigantic vital forces in each new generation."[17]

Reich's observations about the state are as true for this country today as they were for the Germany of the twenties and thirties that he was writing about. A high level of tolerance for fascism on the part of its workers is an advantage to any state. It must be built up slowly though, and the classroom is an important part of this process.

It is therefore of the greatest urgency for people with a program for revolutionary change in this country that children be raised, especially during those crucial first four or five years, in an environment that is not designed to make him passive and unpolitical, nor to create in his structure· an interest in supporting the authoritarian order. We have seen tendencies in this direction in the centers set up by the "private sector" of the economy, and it might be interesting to examine the much-discussed "failure" of the Federal Government's Head Start and Upward Bound programs in this light.

It is clear, not only from our analysis of the identification of women with their primary "job" in the home but from the experience of people working on day care programs whose aim is to free women and children, that an anti-authoritarian (as opposed to a non-authoritarian) day care center must be community based and community controlled, so that the "participation" of the parents is not mediated by, or made possible by, some all-powerful third party like an employer or the state. Child care must be seen as a right open to all, not a benefit conditional upon meeting state eligibility requirements, or upon behaving on the job in such a way that the "advantages to industry" cited by KLH are apparent to your employer.

It also seems clear, from what we have said, that a dependence upon authority generally, and upon male authority in particular, is reinforced when day care is created by "experts" and then handed down from above, as a service to another group who will use the center. Even when control of the center is later handed over to its clients, as the KLH center was, the participation of those parent-employees will be different from that of a group of parents who come together simply out of a shared need for day care rather than because they have a common employer, or a common social stigma known as being on welfare, or a common level of "cultural deprivation."

Moreover, the guidelines that must be followed if the center is to be licenced under state and city regulations are such that a hierarchical structure is unavoidable. They require the workers in the center to be divided into at least half a dozen job categories, each with different educational requirements, salaries, and areas of "turf." Finally, there is the dubious effect upon children of travelling long distances, usually in rush hour conditions, to accompany his or her parent to the parent's workplace.

The struggle to set up and maintain community-based and non-hier-

[17] *Ibid.*, p. 301.

archical day care centers is therefore an important part of a strategy for a prolonged revolutionary battle. It may be argued that the negative features of work-related day care are the outcome of capitalist social relations, and that their proximity to workplaces makes them valuable as revolutionary bases. I would argue against this on the grounds that the ability of management to coopt and bureaucratize the leadership of struggles around the workplace is, as technology advances, increasing rather than decreasing. It is my contention that the authoritarian features of modern industries extend into work-related day care centers, and that this makes them less useful as revolutionary bases than those organized in the workers' home territory.

People become committed to revolutionary change not solely, or even primarily, because they are oppressed. It is, rather, because they discover, through action with others, an alternative to the way they thought things had to be, an alternative that is presently realizable but denied them by the class organization of society. The most formidable obstacle to this discovery is the nuclear family. If this kind of family is, as Reich says, "the factory of the structure and ideology" of the authoritarian state, it follows that as long as the structure of the family is perceived to be fixed and unchangeable, the structure of the state will be seen in the same light. The same can be said, as Juliet Mitchell points out, of the role of women:

Like woman herself, the family appears as a natural object, but it is actually a cultural creation. There is nothing inevitable about the form or role of the family any more than there is about the character or role of women. It is the function of ideology to present these given social types as aspects of nature herself.[18]

This is why the revolutionary potential of the women's movement is so enormous and so crucial to the success of any struggle for profound social change. But to fulfill that potential, we need to create new institutions in the (if you will pardon the expression) belly of the old, institutions that make clear the ways in which the old ones serve the needs of our masters and thus deny us the genuinely human life that would otherwise be ours.

[18] Juliet Mitchell, "Women: The Longest Revolution," *New Left Notes*, November-December 1966, p. 11.

227

WOMAN AND HER MIND: THE STORY OF DAILY LIFE

Meredith Tax

Meredith Tax studies "woman's alienation from herself, through the lenses of experience [Part I] . . . of existential psychology [Part II] . . . through a Marxist analysis by examining woman's work and her place in the modern capitalist economy" [Part IV]. (For lack of space, only Part IV is reprinted here.) In examining female schizophrenia, Tax draws on R. D. Laing's view of schizophrenia as a social process *(The Politics of Experience, The Divided Self).* "Woman and Her Mind" is an important study because it combines an acute perception of the uniqueness of female oppression in our society to an analysis of the economic and political factors that created and perpetuate it.

Meredith Tax lives in Boston where she was active in "Bread and Roses," one of the important women's liberation groups. Currently she is writing an historical study of women's role in the American Left between 1890 and World War I, with particular emphasis on the labor movements. She also composes feminist songs ("There Was a Young Woman Who Swallowed a Lie"), several of which Pete Seeger recorded in 1971.

Production of the Self: the Most Alienated Work of All

So far this paper has examined the problem of women's alienation from herself, through the lenses of experience and of existential psychology. We can also view it through a Marxist analysis, by examining woman's work and her place in the modern capitalist economy. (Note: a similar analysis could be made of woman's place in earlier economic stages, or in a socialist society.) To begin with, let's take a look at the general terrain: what is work?

Work is a relationship that takes place between you and nature, involving some material interchange. You take a chunk of raw material and do something to it; both you and the raw material are changed as a result. You put some of your mental and physical energy into the material, thus losing this energy, and the material becomes a product, a thing to be consumed by others.

In capitalist society, the chunk of raw material belongs to the capitalist; so does your energy, which you rent out at some fixed rate. So the capitalist takes the product that you have made. You have been making whatever-it-is, not for yourself, but for someone else, as his agent or tool. This is alienated labor—when your work is done on material you don't own, towards ends that are mysterious to you, and from which you get nothing but money. You lose part of yourself and get nothing back but the ability to buy the products of other people's labor.

Labor takes place when the same interchange between you and nature (raw material) goes on, but without an intermediary between you (the producer) and the consumer. There is no very good example of this in capitalist society. Even work done for yourself becomes alienated before it reaches the consumer; the fine art market is an example of this alienation in its crassest form. The only comprehensible example in capitalist society would be selling something you've made to a friend. Say you carve a statue from wood. The wood is changed in the process; it becomes a statue. You are changed as well; you are exhilarated and exhausted. You are not *made less* as you are under capitalist conditions of production; you have had an experience you can understand, it has given you pleasure, and you have something that you made out of yourself and wood. Unalienated labor is similar to play, but in play the producer and the consumer are one.

Leisure is the span of time that is free from alienated labor.

In your labor, you build up certain abilities. Take muscular ones as an example: by toting that barge and lifting that bale, you become physically strong. This strength, your productive power, is what the capitalist buys. When you go home, you must recoup this productive power that has been used up, by eating, sleeping, watching TV, etc. This is *recuperation.*

On the brute levels of existence, where survival is at stake, recuperation cannot be elevated to an art form as it is on higher economic levels. The important thing is for the worker to recoup himself physically and mentally; the quality of the means by which he does it (hamburger or filet mignon, comic books or Shakespeare) isn't important.

All work in this society is alienating. Jobs which prohibit friendly contact between workers, which are highly regimented, repetitive, physically exhausting, and degrading, are brutalising as well. The greater the degree of brutalization, the less possible it is for the worker to recover his humanity. He is likely to use his leisure time expressing his despair: getting drunk, or beating his wife and children, are such expressions. Where labor is less exhausting (professional jobs, for instance), artistic means of recuperation become possible; a man may use yoga, for example, to recover the use of a body which has been sacrificed to a sedentary form of labor.

Some jobs do not use up all a man's labor power (strength of various kinds); he has some left over, or can build up a little extra over the weekend. In such cases, he can use what energy he has left for himself. This is *play,* the consumption of one's labor power by oneself for one's own ends. It can mean exercise, sex, going to the movies or on an excursion. It can involve an interchange with nature, or the kind that characterizes unalienated work, but in this case the work will be for oneself alone. One will paint a picture or practise an instrument for the sake of doing it, not for the public utility or pleasure in the result, and not for money.

Many people cannot play; they never recoup themselves to that point. Others have developed labor skills, or powers, that are so specialised that they cannot use them off the job, and they are unable to ease the extreme character of their alienation. Computer programmers or skilled machinists are examples of this problem. They will attempt to play on the job—by making up joke programs or stamping out jewelry—but this is fake play, a reaction against the extremity of their alienation rather than a completed game, for the joke programmes are never carried out, and the programmers cannot make up real ones of their own (play as *invention*) under capitalist conditions.

If the categories describing man's use of his labor-power are work, labor, recuperation, and play, what categories describe woman's use of her labor-power? Women are not only exploited as workers in the same ways as men; women are also exploited as housewives and as sex-objects, both at the workplace and at home.

What men produce on the job are labor-products for someone else's consumption. What do women produce at home for other people's consumption?

Laundry. Cleaning. Taking care of children. Sewing and mending. Washing clothes and dishes. Shopping. Cooking.

In our stage of society, where most necessary production work has been taken out of the home (like baking bread, raising chickens, weaving cloth), the job of housewife is to produce the labor-power of others. The housewife feeds, clothes, cares for, and does psychological repair work on her husband and children, so that they can be resold in the capitalist marketplace each morning. She is not paid in any way that is defined as remuneration for this work, because it is not defined as a job. Her husband supports her as an appendage of himself, but no employer pays her for her labor. Apart from this central fact, the jobs of cooking, cleaning, and child-care are not intrinsically more alienating, or as alienating, as work in an office or a factory.

But there are two crucial differences between a housewife's work and work in the public sphere, and in these lie the peculiar alienation of the job.

The housewife does not produce anything tangible, anything that lasts, or that has market value. Her job is to maintain the *status quo*. Her labor never ends, because it is involved in maintaining a process, rather than making products.

The other difference is that, unlike other lowgrade maintenance work, the work of the housewife is done in solitude. Its reality and value are not acknowledged either by payment, or by the presence of others engaged in the same work. The housewife's work is treated by society simply as though it did not exist as work! It takes place in some limbo of private time and space. Even its standards are subjective; there are certain obvious things the housewife must do (like cook dinner), but she does them according to standards set by her own or someone else's personal preferences, and not by some necessary standard inherent in the work. Mostly no one else even notices her work or considers it as such. It is as if the 60 to 80 hour work week she puts in (according to the Chase Manhattan Bank) were imaginary, and all she really did, as far as others were concerned, was to sit on the sofa, munch chocolates, and read *True Romances*, as she does in cartoons.

There is one other thing that woman produces for the consumption of others: *herself*. This is obvious on the material level. She interacts with material objects (makeup, curlers, diet soda, pretty clothes) and both come out changed. She had made the *material* part of herself a more appealing article of consumption, but what has happened to the *producer* part of herself? What more severe alienation can there be than in this case? A split between mind and body is inevitable; the kind of fear, or disgust, or wonder, or ignorance, that most women feel about their bodies is a by-product.

But yet another kind of labor is involved, for women must be desirable objects of consumption not only in body, but also in behavior. This necessitates a kind of *immaterial production* difficult to define, which consists of one part of a woman's mind directing her behavior (to be appealing, sexy, comforting, etc.) to be attractive. Her behavior is an object of consumption not only as a sex-object, but also as a 'wife,' in which role she must be comforting, undemanding, restful, without needs of her own, a buffer zone between a man and his rage at being alienated from himself. The split in a woman's mind which this process necessitates is more severe and detrimental than the split between mind and body, and can be called *female schizophrenia*.

When producing your own mind and body is your work, there's no such thing as leisure—no time when you can really recuperate. The hour or two of privacy which are free from housework are insufficient to relieve the strain. And so the housewife's production process, nervous and physical, frequently breaks down.

In the ideal form of male-dominated society, *sex* is *labor* for *women* and *play* for *men*. For men, sex is the consumption of their labor-power for their own ends. For women, sex is the consumption of their labor-power by another (the consumer), and the use of their labor-product (which is their material and behavioral selves) by another. It is therefore alienated.

In this ideal pattern, sex appears to men as a means of transcending their everyday experience, that is, it is something special and extraordinary, the subject of fantasy. In sex, men make use of their labor-power, the productive ability they have built up at work and use on the job. They experience sex as play because it is 1) using this ability for themselves, not for others, and 2) using it in a qualitatively different way from labor. It is a transcendence of their role as worker.

In fact, in our society, many men cannot experience sex as transcendent. The patterns that they bring to relationships with women are those they have been taught are 'masculine' in other situations: the same anxiety about not measuring up; the same competitiveness; the same tendency to regard everything as a threat to their masculinity; and the same achievement-orientation, which concentrates on results rather than process, prevail. These attitudes which are socialized into men, are tremendously destructive of any possibility of meaningful personal relationships. But these patterns, while oppressive to the men involved, also cause these men to oppress women. Men may suffer from the fragmentation, the anxiety, the false consciousness, and the sense of undefined loss common to oppressors in other situations. But messed up as they may be, they still have the power in most sexual relationships.

For it is material power in society, not psychological givens, that determines the structure of sexual relationships in general. Men are consumers of women because they hold most of the power in our society. Some men have more power than other men. And a few women, like the Queen of the Netherlands, have more power than most men. But almost every man has power over some woman; and men as a sex control almost all social institutions, including those that only women use (like pregnancy wards), dictate public policy, earn most of the national income, and control almost all jobs. The marriage relation is a business deal; the man hires the woman, in both her aspects of producer and product, for an unspecified length of time. Either one of them can get out of the contract, these days, if they wish; but the woman will have to end up being 'hired' by someone else (unless she gets lots of 'severance pay') if they do. Getting doors opened for you isn't power.

Sex is not transcendent to women, because it is a continuation of their work role. Even in their housework, in their shopping, they are trained to relate to everything, to all the world, as a latent sexual object. Sex is no enrichment of their work experience, or change from it; it is no alternative mode of being; it is merely the fulfillment of an everyday expectation. It is a relief (they have been successful on their job) but not an escape. It is just another way of giving service. Women are taught to think that they are sexual failures if they don't take pleasure in even the most perfunctory or brutalized sex (cf. *Cosmopolitan*), and so they will act the part of mistress, even when they feel nothing but exhaustion or despair. They fake their own experience so that their man will not be denied the illusion that he has pleased them, so that they will not feel failures as women, so that they will not have to answer a string of questions beginning with 'Did you come?' This falsification of the emotional content of sex adds another dimension of alienation to the problem. But at least their product has been consumed. Most women's lives are so limited that their only outlet is fantasy. And even their fantasy life is all too often merely a glorification of the objectified sex roles they are cast in every day.

In the socialist society one imagines, all labor will be unalienated. The worker will understand the whole process, know what it is for, know how he fits in and feels so much a part of the community that consumes his product that it will be as if he were producing for his friends and himself. There will be time for play, on the job, with the same raw materials. Women will work alongside of men, at the same jobs. Power relationships between people will vanish, and institutions which are based on inequities in power, like the bourgeois family, will vanish or be transformed.

How does this projection relate to sex? What will sexual relationships be like in a truly socialist society? Will women free themselves from being both objects of consumption and the products of their own labor? Is it possible that they will cease to need to be 'attractive' or 'comforting' as these are now defined?—that men will cease to demand it of them, or that equal material opportunities will change the relation between men and women so drastically as this? If work were not so decimating, 'comfort' would be unnecessary. 'Attractiveness' would become a personal quality in each of us, rather than a market ideal. Will we live to see such changes in society as a whole?

One thing is certain: women will never be able to experience sex as play—for ourselves—until each of us has a self—that is, not three or four conflicting selves, but one integrated self. Out of the conflict between our pain and the way we were socialized has been born a new creation: the women's liberation movement. Out of the conflict between the women's liberation movement and society will be born a creature who does not yet exist: a liberated woman.

FOURTH WORLD MANIFESTO

Barbara Burris, in agreement with Kathy Barry, Terry Moon, Joann DeLor, Joann Parent, Cate Stadelman

The *Fourth World Manifesto* was published in Detroit on January 13, 1971.[1] Reproduced here are the sections entitled "Spectre of feminism," "Imperialism," and "Fourth World."

The first section of the *Manifesto* takes issue with the way in which the planning and selection of delegates to go to the April, 1971 Canadian conferences with Indochinese women[2] took place, and disagrees with the part of the women's liberation movement that is "trying to get women to work on 'anti-imperialist' issues in a certain way as defined by the male Left . . . It's one thing to be against the Vietnam War and all wars and quite another for a group of women to try to draw women working in their own Movement away from it into the male dominated very narrowly defined anti-war and anti-imperialist Movements . . . Women, who have nothing to say about running the country or fighting in the war will never end war except by attacking and ending male domination and the sex roles where men learn their war-mentality."[3]

Barbara Burris, *et al.,* "The Fourth World Manifesto," Parts 1 and 4. (Detroit: Women–Fourth World, 1971). Reprinted by permission.

[1] Women-Fourth World, 741 Bethune, Detroit, Michigan 48202.
[2] See "The Development of the American Women's Liberation Movement," p. 169.
[3] *Fourth World Manifesto,* p. 4.

Other sections of the *Manifesto* persuasively argue that women should not limit feminist activities to "women's caucuses" or "collectives" within the male dominated Left: "Women must face facts. Men will never, until forced by circumstances, place first, or even urgent, priority upon a struggle against the oppression of women . . . Indeed the idea is so repugnant to many men that they cannot tolerate a woman who refuses male leadership in order to address her energies primarily to the liberation of her sisters."[4] And finally the point is made that feminine oppression is the primary one:

One should compare the stereotypes of blacks and other minority groups . . . to the female stereotypes . . .

Woman was the first group oppressed and subordinated as a caste to another group—men. Without going into all the reasons for this subordination we can still discuss the psychological and cultural results . . . Men are seen as positive, forceful, aggressive, dominant, objective, strong, intellective, etc. While women have been defined for thousands of years as weak, . . . passive, emotional, intuitive, mysterious, unresponsible, quarrelsome, childish, dependent, evil, submissive . . ."[5]

Spectre of Feminism

The only real threat to male supremacy is the independent Women's Movement. Therefore the male Left has done a great deal to impede the development of independent Women's Liberation and tried in numerous ways to co-opt the energies of women away from working independently with other women on women's issues. There have been numerous devices used by the Left to this end depending on the situation and the consciousness of the women involved.

The first tactic in reaction to Women's Liberation was laughter. But that didn't stop some women—in fact it made some of them so furious they left and began "organizing" other women. The next tactic was anger. "You castrating bitches," "What do you women want anyway?" And that didn't work either—even more women left to join the newly emerging independent Women's Movement.

Then the men began to get really nervous—after all, women were leaving the Left in increasing numbers—and the men began to play quilt games. "So what makes you think you're oppressed, you white middle class chick?" (Notice the order of the defining words the male Left uses —"chick" is last.) That tactic made some women even madder but it began to cut deep into many women. And this tactic began to work on some of the less strong women—those who were still full of white male imposed guilt and self-hatred.

The Left males realized that they had struck a tender nerve. And they began to manipulate women's guilt and started becoming very liberal towards the Women's Liberation Movement, that is, when they weren't chuckling about those "frustrated bitches" in male-only company. And

[4] *Ibid.,* p. 4. The quote is from Marlene Dixon in *Radical America,* February 1970.
[5] *Ibid.,* p. 12.

234

they had to be liberal any way because that God-damned Women's Liberation Movement composed only of females was putting the heat on them and they might lose "their" women to it if they didn't play it cool. So they put up with the discomfort of women's caucuses rather than lose all "their" women to the independent Women's Movement. At first it was pretty rough and more than one male Left organization folded under the pressures of the women's caucuses.

But then the Left males began to see that the women's caucuses could have some real value for their organizations. They could be used as important organizing tools for recruiting new members and for working with women associated with the males whose problems the Left organization was concerned with. Such as having the women work with GI wives while the men worked at "organizing" the GI's in the army. Women in the caucuses express best the male attitudes of the organization towards "women's issues" and women's struggle for liberation. We give only two examples out of many. One is a leaflet passed out by PAR (People Against Racism) women at a Women's Liberation Conference in Detroit in 1968. They list as one of their concerns something which reveals the manipulative way in which the Women's Movement is viewed. They wish to use "Women's Liberation as an organizing tactic for broader political movement." Bernadine Dohrn's equally blatant statement in the *New Left Notes* special issue on women is every bit as revealing. She says, "Everywhere around us there are concentrations of women: dorms, women's schools, education and home economics departments, high schools, jobs—women can be mobilized to fight against imperialism and racism." Maybe women's caucuses were really a boon to the male Left and not the threat they had expected them to be and which they were—at first.

So a pattern was generally established throughout the male Left that women could stay in the caucuses and organize other women into the Left male dominated Movement as long as they concentrated on:
1) Raising women's issues mainly as they related to the structure of the male dominated organization whom the women remained working for
2) Raising women's issues on the periphery of the male defined "important" issues of the organization
3) Relating to the Women's Liberation Movement as caucus members only of the primary male organization to "raise" the issues of the male organization in the Women's Movement, and, if possible, get its focus off independent women's struggle and onto how women can relate to male defined Left issues.

Women's collectives, unless they are truly autonomous women's collectives working from their own analysis on women's issues, can be and are used in much the same manner as the Left women's caucuses. Because they too relate primarily to the male Left Movement and only secondarily as females to female liberation issues. They are one step ahead of the women's caucuses if only because they know they can no longer work with the males in the organizations—but they still remain working for them even though now working in women's collectives. Also "women's collectives" is now being used by a number of women as synonymous with caucus group—but a more "hip" term than caucus.

Imperialism

There are two definitions of imperialism. The Webster dictionary states that imperialism is "the policy and practises of forming and maintaining an empire; in modern times, it is characterized by a struggle for the control of raw materials and world markets, the subjugation and control of territories, the establishment of colonies, etc."

The imperialist is defined by Webster's as a person favoring imperialism.

Fanon and the whole black liberation struggle have recently extended the dictionary definition of imperialism or colonialism to mean a group which is prevented from self-determination by another group—whether it has a national territory or not. The psychological and cultural mutilation is particularly intense and the colonialism more brutal when the group that colonizes and the group colonized have different defining physical characteristics that set them clearly apart.

All of the above definitions apply to the subjection of women, as a sex.

The dictionary definition of imperialism included "the subjection and control of territories . . ." Women, set apart by physical differences between them and men, were the first colonized group. And the territory colonized was and remains our women's bodies.

Our bodies were first turned into property of the males. Men considered female bodies as territory over which they fought for absolute ownership and control. Consider the imperialist implications of the language. He related his sexual conquests, she surrendered to him, he took her, etc. Marriage (exclusive property rights) and the patriarchal family system are colonial institutions created and controlled by males for the subjugation of females.

Our bodies are free territory to other male colonizers when not "protected" by an individual male colonist. What is rape but an imperialist act upon the territory of our bodies.

There are two forms of the colonization of our bodies (territories) by males. Most males have an individual colonial relationship to an individual female and most males identify with and act on the group colonization of women. For instance, rape is an individual male imperialist act against an individual woman while the abortion laws are male group control over their collective female territories. (We realize that we are generalizing here about males and that some of them do not perceive women simply as open territory for conquest. But unfortunately, there are too few males who perceive females as equal human beings to change the generalization much at this point.)

Another example of group colonization of women is the way our bodies are defined as open territory for exploitation (compare the exploitation for sexual satisfaction for the male colonizer to exploitation for raw materials—female bodies are the raw materials). In all forms of the dominant male culture—advertising, pornography, the underground press, literature, art, etc.—female bodies are exploited as territory to demean, subject, control and mock.

The fact that each male petty colonialist has an individual interest in perpetuating the subjection of his individual territory, i.e., woman, makes the colonization of women more complete than that of any other group. The colonial rule is more intense for females as we have no escape into a ghetto and at all times are under the watchful eye of the male colonizers, from father to lover to husband. Therefore our suppression as a group (culture) and as individuals has been more complete as has been our identification with our master's interests (much like the proverbial house nigger).

Fanon shows that it is not enough for the colonizer to control the territory and subject the inhabitants of it to his rule. The colonizer must destroy the culture and self respect of the colonized. And colonialism's condemnation of the colonized's culture over-reaches any national boundaries—for it is the essence of the colonized physical and cultural differences that threaten the colonizer.

Fanon says, in *The Wretched of the Earth,* that "Colonialism . . . turns to the past of the oppressed people, and distorts, disfigures and destroys it." (p. 210) He says the colonized (in his book speaking of blacks) "must demonstrate that a Negro culture exists."

That the great mass of women have been totally ignored in history except where they appear as adjuncts to men is not too difficult to prove to most people. But that the history of Female Liberation Movements has been distorted and almost completely censored is not so obvious. Through the almost complete censorship of the realities of women's condition throughout history, women have been robbed of the means to knowledge about the origins and extent of their subjugation. History (of art, politics, literature, etc.) as related by males has engraved upon women's minds a male image of the world.

Fourth World

Culture is defined by Webster's as the "concepts, habits, skills, art, instruments, institutions etc. of a given people in a given period." We will show that the concepts, habits, skills, art and instruments of women in any period have been different from men's and have been ridiculed and/or suppressed by them. We will show that in all the major institutions of society women receive unequal treatment and the appearance that these institutions are the same for men and women is false.

We also hold that female and male culture began with the definition of females as embodying all those human attributes which males as dominators could not reconcile with their own self-image and therefore projected onto females—thus causing a schizophrenic split of personality into masculine and feminine. That women, defined by these attributes (such as emotional, intuitive, etc.) by males and further limited by their physical position in society as to work and tools, developed a female or "feminine" culture—and a culture of resistance to male domination. Although the concept of the "feminine" was imposed upon women, we have, through the centuries, developed and created within the confines of the feminine, a female culture.

Female and Male Culture

What do most people imagine when they think of differences in culture? They most often think of strange customs and a different language. The traveler to a foreign culture will notice women carrying pails of water on their heads or men riding donkeys, different and strange costumes and white-washed houses. In another culture she will notice people riding bicycles, small towns, sidewalk cafes, small shops, more chic dress, different foods, etc. Especially will the traveler notice the differences in language if there is one.

Although these are just a few of the differences of national culture that distinguish the lives that both women and men lead, and we respect these differences, they are the superficials that cover up the fundamental similarity of all national cultures the world over. This fundamental similarity is the split between male culture and female culture.

Let us go back to some of those superficial differences that the traveler noticed. In the first culture, the women were carrying pails of water on their heads and the men riding donkeys to market. What was seen as one whole is now divided up by sexual work role. The different costumes which were seen as a whole unit are now divided up into male costumes and female costumes. The small shops noticed are owned by men and sometimes staffed by women. A split is now seen between male ownership and female workers. The cafes are served by women, if cheap, and staffed by male waiters if more expensive. A difference in value of work and pay between male and female is perceived. The food production in agriculture is done primarily by males but prepared in each home by females. What was seen as culinary differences now reminds the traveler of the role of women in the home and woman's caste work roles all over the world. The traveler in this second look at the culture begins to notice the basic sameness of the male-female cultural split under the superficial differences that were so striking to her at first.

The problem is that the split is so obvious and taken for granted that practically nobody can see it. Things which are conceived of as "natural" cannot ordinarily be perceived. But the emperor had no clothes in spite of what everybody "saw" and a female culture exists whether or not most people will acknowledge the facts of its existence.

Let us again take up those things (habits, skills, art, concepts and institutions) which distinguish one culture from another according to

238

Webster's definition. Part of the customs of a culture are its habits. Habits here means what people do in their daily lives. It can also include how they go about doing these things. It is clear that women and men have very different daily habits. Women—in most all parts of the world —whether they are working outside the home or not—have responsibility for the cooking, cleaning and child-"raising" chores of the society. This means that most women spend their time with children. This in itself is a cultural split as men go out of the home and mix mainly with other males in the male world outside the home. Generally males do not do any of the work designated as "female work." Women, mainly in the company of other women and children, organize their time and routines and socializing on an entirely different basis than males. Female work— being so completely caste labor—is organized and done by women in ways peculiar to the female view of things (which is very much determined by woman's secluded work place, i.e., the home and its environs). The whole daily routine of a man and a woman is totally different.

The woman develops skills associated with her work role. Her skills are usually different than the male's. She usually knows a lot about cooking, child-care, washing, sewing, colors, decorating, and cleaning while he knows mechanical or carpentry skills and anything he may learn as a skill at his job. The instruments or tools a woman uses are defined by the work and skills she is allowed.

If the woman goes out to "work" she will have all the home chores in addition to her outside "job." But woman's skills outside the home are limited by what the male-run economy will train her for or let her do. She usually fills "service" roles which utilize the "skills" she has learned in her role as wife and mother. She is allowed limited acquisition of physical skills in such things as typing and small tedious work. She fills completely different job roles than males in the male dominated economy and is segregated into "female jobs" almost completely. Males do almost all the specialized skillful work—for higher pay.

At one time in the process of the cultures women did almost everything and men did nothing but hunt and make weapons and war. As men had free time due to women's performing all the drudge work for them (as slave labor really) they began to develop skills in certain things. As a skill developed women were no longer allowed to perform the task and it was passed on from father to son. As specialization increased, women had more of the skills and trades taken away from them and were left only with the drudge chores of cleaning, washing, cooking, "raising" children, etc. This culminated in Europe in the all-male guilds in feudal times.

When the feudal guild system broke down with the onset of industrialism, cheap unskilled labor was needed and women were used again— sewing, mining metal, etc., factories. It was on the backs of cheap "unskilled" female labor (and child labor) that the grotesque edifice of western industrialism was built. Female slave labor in the cotton mills and black slave labor in the cotton fields produced industrialism for the white male western world.

And when industrialism was achieved, hordes of women were sent back home and men replaced them in the factories. So that now we have a small body of lowest paid female labor in the factories but almost totally female personnel in sales and service roles (typing, nursing)—which were once male "skills" but are now just very low paying drudge work with no advancement.

The final three parts of Webster's definition of culture are the art, concepts, and institutions of a people.

Women have been excluded from contributing to the art, philosophy and science of all national cultures. These things are in tight male control. The male culture, which is the dominant culture in every nation (i.e., is synonymous with the national culture) cannot accept a female view of things as expressed by female writers, artists and philosophers. When some women break through male prejudice to create truly great art, which is often very sensitive to the female culture and values, they are not given the recognition they deserve. Because males—looking through their own culturally distorted view of the world—cannot give any credence to an art that expresses the female view. In fact, most males cannot understand what is going on in female culture—art. The worth of female art is thoroughly suppressed in a male dominated society.

The female soul, suppressed and most often stereotyped in male art, is defined by negative comparisons to the male. The eternal feminine is seen as a passive, earth-to-be-molded-and-formed, mysterious, unthinking, emotional, subjective, intuitive, practical, unimaginative, unspiritual, worldly, evil, lustful, super-sexual, virginal, forever-waiting, pain-enduring, self-sacrificing, calculating, narcissistic, contradictory, helpless, quivering mass of flesh.

The fact that women live under the power of belief in these characterizations causes a certain outlook which molds the female culture. Woman's position in society, her economic and psychological dependence, reinforce the female stereotypes. Because of the belief in these attributes and women's position in society, not because of our inherent "female nature," women's concepts of the world are much different from men's.

Almost everything that has been defined as a male view of the world has its opposite in a female view. Because of the child-raising role and the emphasis on personal relationships, women have a more personal subjective view of things. Because of our subjection, women have a more fatalistic, passive view of the world. We are more in touch with our emotions and often find it necessary to use emotions in manipulating men. **Through the imposition of a servant status on women the female culture has elaborated a whole servile ethic of "self-sacrifice." Self-sacrifice—as the major ethic of the female culture—has been one of the most effective psychological blocks to women's open rebellion and demand for self-determination. It has also been a major tool of male manipulation of females.**

The institutions of a people are an essential part of their culture. The major institutions of every culture are the same—the family, religion, government, army and economy. Men and women have a completely different relationship to the institutions of "their" culture. In fact there are two cultures being hidden by the appearance of one culture under one set of institutions.

Women are excluded, except sometimes in token numbers and in the lowest working ranks, from participation in government, the army and religion. These are basically two economic institutions of a society—the sub-structure or family and the super-structure or outside world of work. Women are limited to an economic dependence in "their" caste work in the family. In work outside the family, women are caste laborers in the lowest paid drudge work. Women are kept from management or decision making in work outside the home.

Though it appears that both men and women live together within the institutions of a society, men really define and control the institutions while women live under their rule. The government, army, religion, economy and family are institutions of the male culture's colonial rule of the female.

A female culture exists. It is a culture that is subordinated and under male culture's colonial, imperialist rule all over the world. Underneath the surface of every national, ethnic, or racial culture is the split between the two primary cultures of the world—the female culture and the male culture.

National cultures vary greatly according to the degree of the suppression of the female culture. The veil and seclusion of women and their almost total segregation in Arab culture make for differences between them and, for example, Sweden. A Swedish woman may not be able to tolerate the suppressed life of Arab women but she also, if she is sensitive, may not be able to tolerate her suppression as a female in Sweden. Crossing national boundaries often awakens a woman's understanding of her position in society. We cannot, like James Baldwin, even temporarily escape to Paris or another country from our caste role. It is everywhere—there is no place to escape.

The repression of female culture is only a question of degree all over the world—the underlying reality is basically the same—the denial of self-determination for women. Women traveling to a foreign country can readily communicate and understand other women in that country because female work and roles (culture) are basically the same all over the world. But it too often happens that women falsely identify with "their" country's dominant male culture and so cannot communicate with their sisters in subjection in other lands or in other races. This female identification with male cultural supremacy must be overcome if the Women's Movement is to be a truly liberating force.

Most males all over the world perceive and compare females as a caste group all over the world. A male of any culture perceives a woman as a woman first and only secondly as "representing" a national or

ethnic culture. And he treats every woman as females as a caste is treated. The "Miss World" and "Miss Universe" etc. female flesh auctions—comparing various nationalities of female flesh—are only one example of many. The best way for any woman to find out the truth of this statement is to do some traveling to different countries.

Bibliography

In the last year (1970) the women's liberation movement has effected all corners of the publishing world. Past history is being rediscovered with new editions of works long out of print—works like those of John Stuart Mill, Mary Wollstonecraft, Emma Goldman. Present history is being recorded in the anthologies now being collected. Also, serious research is being undertaken about the history and social role of women in the United States, drawing upon the wealth of largely unexamined journals, letters, organizational records, newspapers, and books dealing with women. Most of this material is in the collections of the Library of Congress, New York Public Library, Sophia Smith Collection at Smith College, the Women's Archives at Radcliffe College, and the State Historical Society of Wisconsin at the University in Madison.

Anyone interested in reading or writing about women should begin by examining Lucinda Cisler's sixteen-page bibliography (*Women: a Bibliography*, available at $.50 a copy at 102 West 80 Street, New York City, 10024), which is organized by discipline—historical studies, sociology, law, medicine, psychology, and so on. Robin Morgan's anthology, *Sisterhood is Powerful*, also contains a good bibliography. It is organized by topics and includes more current material than Cisler's. I also recommend the model course syllabi for women's studies included in Female Studies I (1969) and II (1970) (available from KNOW, Inc., P.O. Box 10197, Pittsburgh, Pa. 15232). These course models offer varied and original approaches to the study of women and also include valuable bibliographies.

In a book like *Female Liberation*, considerations of limited space require that a bibliography be focused, rather than all-encompassing. The following bibliography thus concentrates on writings of and about today's movement.

ANTHOLOGIES

Adams, Elsie, and Mary Louise Briscoe (eds.). *Up Against the Wall Mother . . . On Women's Liberation.* Beverly Hills, Cal.: Glencoe Press, 1971.

Belkin, Madeline. *Liberation Now!* New York: Dell, 1971.

Cade, Toni (ed.). *The Black Woman.* New York: Signet, 1970.

Come Out! Selections from the Radical Gay Liberation Newspaper. New York: Times Change Press, 1971.

Cooke, Joanne, Charlotte Bunch-Weeks, and Robin Morgan (eds.). *The New Women.* New York: Fawcett, 1971.

Fuchs, Cynthia, and William J. Goode (ed.). *The Other Half: Roads to Women's Equality.* Englewood Cliffs, N.J.: Prentice-Hall, Spectrum Books, 1971.

Garskof, Michele Hoffnung (ed.). *Roles Women Play: Readings Toward Women's Liberation.* Belmont, Cal.: Brooks/Cole, 1971.

Gornick, Vivian, and Barbara Moran (eds.). *Woman in Sexist Society: Studies in Power and Powerlessness.* New York: Basic Books, 1971.

Kraditor, Aileen (ed.). *Up From the Pedestal: Selected Documents from the History of American Feminism.* Chicago: Quadrangle, 1968.

Morgan, Robin (ed.). *Sisterhood is Powerful: An Anthology of Writings from the Women's Liberation Movement.* New York: Vintage, 1970.

O'Neill, William L. (ed.). *The Woman's Movement: Feminism in the United States and England.* New York: Barnes and Noble, 1969.

Robins, Joan (ed.). *Handbook of Women's Liberation.* Cal.: Now Library Press, 1971.

Rossi, Alice (ed.). *John Stuart Mill and Harriet Taylor Mill, Essays on Sex*

Equality (with long introductory essay by Rossi). Chicago: University of Chicago Press, 1971.

Roszak, Betty and Theodore (eds.). *Masculine/Feminine*. New York: Harper Colophon, 1970.

Scott, Anne Firor (ed.). *The American Woman: Who Was She?* Englewood Cliffs, N.J.: Prentice-Hall, Spectrum Books, 1971.

Shulman, Alix (ed.). *The Traffic in Women and Other Essays on Feminism by Emma Goldman*. New York: Times Change Press, 1971.

Stambler, Sookie (ed.). *Women's Liberation: Blueprint for the Future*. New York: Ace Books, 1970.

Tanner, Leslie B. (ed.). *Voices from Women's Liberation*. New York: Signet Books, 1970.

Thompson, Mary Lou (ed.). *Voices of the New Feminism*. Boston: Beacon Press, 1970.

OTHER BOOKS

Allen, Pamela. *Free Space: A Perspective on the Small Group in Women's Liberation*. New York: Times Change Press, 1971.

Bardwick, Judith M. *Psychology of Women: A Study of Bio-Cultural Conflicts*. New York: Harper & Row, 1971.

Bird, Caroline. *Born Female: The High Cost of Keeping Women Down*. New York: McKay, 1968.

Colon, Clara. *Enter Fighting: Today's Woman: A Marxist-Leninist View*. New York: New Outlook Publishers, 1970.

Cudlipp, Edythe. *Understanding Women's Liberation*. New York: Paperback, 1971. (This is written from the point of view of the mass media and shows precisely that Cudlipp does not understand Women's Liberation.)

Discrimination Against Women. 2 vols. Hearings held in June and July 1970 before House Committee on Education and Labor (subcommittee on education). Available from congressmen or women.

Ellis, Julie. *Revolt of the Second Sex*. New York: Lancer Books, 1971.

Epstein, Cynthia Fuchs. *Woman's Place: Options and Limits in Professional Careers*. Berkeley: University of California Press, 1970.

Figes, Eva. *Patriarchal Attitudes: The Case for Women in Revolt*. New York: Fawcett, 1971.

Firestone, Shulamith. *The Dialectic of Sex: The Case for a Feminist Revolution*. New York: Morrow, 1970.

Flexner, Eleanor. *A Century of Struggle*. Cambridge, Mass.: Harvard University Press, 1959.

Gallion, Jane. *Woman as Nigger*. Canoga Park, Cal.: Weiss, Day and Lord, 1970.

Jensen, Oliver. *The Revolt of American Women: A Pictorial History*. New York: Harcourt Brace Jovanovich, 1971.

Komisar, Lucy. *The New Feminism*. New York: Franklin Watts, 1971.

Kraditor, Aileen. *Ideas of the Woman Suffrage Movement, 1890–1920*. New York: Columbia University Press, 1965.

Lerner, Gerda. *The Woman in American History*. New York: Addison-Wesley, 1971.

Millett, Kate. *Sexual Politics*. New York: Doubleday, 1970.

Moody, Anne. *Coming of Age in Mississippi*. New York: Dell, 1970.

Negrin, Su. *A Graphic Notebook on Feminism*. New York: Times Change Press, 1971.

O'Neill, William L. *Divorce in the Progressive Era*. New Haven: Yale University Press, 1967.

―――――. *Everyone Was Brave: The Rise and Fall of Feminism in America*. Chicago: Quadrangle, 1969.

244

Reed, Evelyn. *Problems of Women's Liberation*. New York: Pathfinder Press, 1971.

Reeves, Nancy. *Womankind—Beyond the Stereotypes*. New York, 1971.

Schulder, Diane, and Florynce Kennedy. *Abortion Rap*. New York: McGraw-Hill, 1971.

Scott, Anne. *The Southern Lady: From Pedestal to Politics*. Chicago: University of Chicago Press, 1971.

Showalter, Elaine. *Women's Liberation: A Sourcebook of Feminism and Literature*. New York: Harcourt Brace Jovanovich, 1971.

Sinclair, Andrew. *The Emancipation of the American Woman*. New York: Harper Colophon, 1965.

Solanis, Valerie. *SCUM Manifesto*. New York: Olympia Press, 1969.

Suelzle, Marijean. *What Every Woman Should Know About the Women's Liberation Movement*. Cal.: Amazon Graphics, 1971.

Ware, Cellestine. *Woman Power: The Movement for Women's Liberation*. New York: Tower Books, 1970.

WOMEN'S LIBERATION PERIODICALS

Tooth and Nail, c/o Wesley Foundation, 2398 Bancroft Way, Berkeley, Cal. 94704.

Off the Pedestal, 376 Addison Street, Palo Alto, Cal. 94301.

Off Our Backs, 2318 Ashmead Place N.W., Washington, D.C. 20009.

Women's Monthly, c/o Media Women, P.O. Box 1592, New York, N.Y. 10001.

It Ain't Me Babe, c/o Women's Liberation Office, 2398 Bancroft Way, Berkeley, Cal. 94704.

Rat, 241 E. 14 St., New York, N.Y. 10003.

Up From Under, 339 Lafayette Street, New York, N.Y. 10012.

No More Fun and Games: A Journal of Female Liberation, 371 Somerville Ave., Somerville, Mass. 02143 (Last number under original editors published in 1970.)

Pedestal, c/o Vancouver WL, 307 Broadway, Vancouver, British Columbia, Canada.

Aphra, P.O. Box 355, Springtown, Pa. 18081.

Lilith, c/o Women's Majority Union, P.O. Box 1895, Seattle, Wash. 98111.

Everywoman, 6516 W. 83 Street, Los Angeles, Cal. 90045.

Southern Journal of Female Liberation, c/o Southern Female Rights Union, P.O. Box 30087, Lafayette Square Station, New Orleans, La. 70130.

Women: A Journal of Liberation, 3028 Greenmount Ave., Baltimore, Md. 21218.

The Ladder, P.O. Box 5025, Washington Station, Reno, Nev. 89503.

The Spokeswoman, 5464 South Shore Drive, Chicago, Ill. 60615.

Hysteria, Box 116, Cambridge, Mass. 02138.

Awake and Move, 928 Chestnut St., Philadelphia, Pa. 19107.

Lavender Vision (for gay women's community), c/o Media Collective, 2 Brookline St., Cambridge, Mass.

Goodbye to All That, P.O. Box 3092, San Diego, Cal. 92103.

Common Woman, P.O. Box 2267, Station A, Berkeley, Cal.

The Woman's Page, 1227 37 Ave., San Francisco, Cal. 94122.

Feminist Studies, 294 Riverside Drive, New York, N.Y. 10025.

Woman's World, P.O. Box 949, Radio City Station, New York, N.Y. 10019.

The Second Wave: A Magazine of the New Feminism, P.O. Box 303, Kenmore Square Station, Boston, Mass. 02215.

ALSO

How Harvard Rules Women, New University Conference, 622 West Diversey, Chicago 60614.

Transaction Magazine, Rutgers University, New Brunswick, N.J. Special issue on women, November/December 1970.

Radical Education Project, P.O. Box 561A, Detroit, Mich. 48232; publishes over fifteen articles on women, available for purchase.

New England Free Press, 791 Tremont Street, Boston, Mass. 02118; has published over thirty articles on women, available for purchase.

The Red Papers, #3, "Women Fight for Liberation." Bay Area Revolutionary Union, San Francisco, Cal. (Spring 1970).

The Radical Therapist, Issue on Women, August/September 1970, P.O. Box 1215, Minot, N.D. 58701.

International Socialist Review, issue on "Women in Revolt," March 1971.

College English (Wesleyan Univ.), issue on feminist literary criticism, May 1971.

Victorian Studies (Indiana Univ.), special issue on the Victorian woman, September 1970.

Women's Caucus Newsletter, #7 and #8 (April 1971), New University Conference.

Massachusetts Review (Amherst, Mass.), special issue on women, Fall 1971

The Woman's Songbook, Oral Herstory Library, 2325 Oak Street, Berkeley, Cal. 94708.

It Ain't Me Babe Comix, Last Gasp Ecofunnies Publication, 15 Shattuck Square, Berkeley, Cal. 94704.

Woman Physician, Special issue on day care, 1740 Broadway, New York, N.Y. 10019, March 1971.

Female Studies I and II, Anthologies of course syllabi on women's studies, 1969–1971. Available from KNOW, Inc., 726 St. James Street, Pittsburgh, Pa 15232.

Mushroom Effect: A Directory of Women's Liberation, P.O. Box 6024, Albany, Ga. 94706.

FROM EUROPE

Books

Baby, Jean. *Un monde meilleur.* Paris: Maspero, 1964.

Campo de Alange, Maria. *Habla la mujer.* Madrid: Edicusa, 1967.

Capmamy, Maria. *La dona a Catalunya.* Barcelona: Editorial 62, 1966.

Femina Books (write for their catalogue). 1A Montagu Mews North, London, England.

La femme et le communisme: Anthologie des grands textes du Marxisme. Paris: Editions Sociales, 1951.

Sartin, Pierrette. *La promotion des femmes.* Paris: Librairie Hachette, 1966.

Sullerot, Evelyne. *Demain les femmes.* Paris: Robert Laffont, 1965.

————. *La presse féminine.* Paris: Armand Colin, 1963.

————. *La vie des femmes.* Paris: Gonthier, 1965.

Valabrègue, Catherine. *La condition masculine.* Paris: Petite Bibliothèque Payot 1968.

Journals

Socialist Woman, 21 Watcombe Circus, Carrington, Nottingham, England.

Cuadernos para el Diálogo (Special issue dedicated to Women in Spain). Héroes del 10 de agosto, Madrid 1, Spain (December 1965).

Quarto Mondo (Organo del Fronte Italiano di Liberazione Femminile), first issue, March 1971. Piazza SS. Apostoli 49, Rome, Italy.

Partisans, Paris, Winter 1971 (issue dedicated to women).

Espirit, Paris, March 1961 (issue on women).